PRAISE FOR COC

Baseball fans will want to dash right out and buy *Cool of the Evening*, by Jim Thielman. Longtime sports reporter Thielman brings skill, enthusiasm and a bat bag of luscious detail to his account of the 1965 season.

> —*Dave Wood, past vice president of The National Book Critics Circle and former* Star Tribune *book review editor*

There's almost nothing better than kicking back and thumbing through *Cool of the Evening* while listening to the Twins on the radio, except, perhaps, making sure that you get Herb Carneal on the box.

> —*Mudville Magazine*

Thielman's zeal for digging up facts and his unquenchable curiosity show in the book. He tells the story of the 1965 season in a style that takes pleasant divergences from a chronological path, telling anecdotes and painting profiles before returning to that path.

> —*Rochester Post-Bulletin*

This isn't a dry rendition of game recaps, or a series of fun stories about a ball club. The 1965 season serves as the central launching point for a growing metropolitan area, a recently relocated ball club, and plenty of background and foreshadowing of players and coaches careers.

> —*TwinsTerritory.com*

ABOUT THE AUTHOR

Minnesota native Jim Thielman has worked at newspapers in Minnesota, North Dakota and Florida. He covered the Minnesota Twins from 1977 through 1993. An award-winning journalist, he has reported from events such as the National Football Conference Championship, British and U.S. Opens, Rose Bowl, Major League Baseball's All-Star Game, post-season playoffs and World Series.

The internationally published freelance writer has been employed by the Minnesota House of Representatives, University of Minnesota, Cargill, Incorporated, General Mills Incorporated and a Minneapolis law firm.

COOL OF THE EVENING

The 1965 Minnesota Twins

JIM THIELMAN

[signature]

2019

COOL OF THE EVENING
The 1965 Minnesota Twins
By Jim Thielman

Library of Congress Cataloging-in-Publication Data

Thielman, James Carl, 1954-
    p. cm.
    Includes index.
    ISBN 1-886513-72-4 (hardbound)
    ISBN 1-886513-71-6 (perfect bound)

    1.   Baseball players – United States. 2. Baseball – United
         States – History.

GC875.M55 T54 2005
796.357/64/0977659 22
Second edition 2005

ATTENTION: Corporations, Universities, Colleges and Professional Organizations: This book is available at special discounts for educational, gift purposes, or as premiums for increasing magazine subscriptions or renewals. Please contact Kirk House Publishing, P.O. Box 390759, Minneapolis, MN 55439.

Manufactured in the United States of America.
ISBN 1-886513-71-6
Cover design by Tony Mommsen. Interior design by Lance Lewey.
All photos, except author photo, are courtesy of the Minnesota Twins baseball club.

Kirk House Publishers, P.O. Box 390759, Minneapolis, MN 55439
Manufactured in the United States of America

DEDICATION

For my grandfather, George Anderson, and those like him, who sat in the picture window of my Dad's barbershop, the sun soothing their backs as they discussed the day's topic – which was often the Minnesota Twins.

Jim Lemon, Sam Mele and Harmon Killebrew

INTRODUCTION

The players were heroes first. Announcers Herb Carneal, Ray Scott and Halsey Hall painted 50,000-watt portraits of them during WCCO radio broadcasts. Sometimes, the players were wrapped in the gauzy reception of black and white television screens. Newspapers brought most of the baseball coverage, which was plentiful and frank, but rarely strayed into personal lives.

Many fans in the upper Midwest never visited odd little Metropolitan Stadium – carved from a cornfield – to see the sun bounce off the green grass as throws from players in crisp, white, pinstriped uniforms crisscrossed the infield before the first pitch. So it was easy – almost a requirement – for fans of the 1965 Minnesota Twins to fill the gaps and sculpt their heroes atop a pedestal to a height of their choosing.

The players eventually became mere men who faced financial and health problems, aging parents, dissolved marriages, and the other solid realities of life. It was their successes, not them, people knew, so folks continued to line up for autographs decades after these baseball players won the 1965 American League pennant. One man used his turn in an autograph line to tell Harmon Killebrew, who had long-since been inducted into the National Baseball Hall of Fame, "You're the only hero I ever had who never let me down." Killebrew was speechless. When the fan walked away with his freshly autographed, white, red-stitched baseball, he was probably further impressed by Killebrew: his signature might be the classiest of any Hall of Famer.

As a sports writer, I could sit in a dugout at Tinker Field on a sunny Orlando morning and talk with Killebrew, or share a couple innings with Calvin Griffith during the final baseball game played at Metropolitan Stadium. I could loiter behind a batting cage while big leaguers took pre-game hacks at baseballs, spit their tobacco juice and sunflower seeds, and gave each other a bad time.

My memory of standing on the carpet of Minneapolis' Metrodome, enveloped in a hurricane of noise as the Twins celebrated World Series championships in 1987 and '91, is clear as a Minnesota winter night in Grand Marais, but I was in grade school when the Twins pushed to their first American League pennant. Memories of the 1965 team were flecked with holes. Was that team mostly Killebrew, Tony Oliva, Bob Allison, Jim Kaat and Camilo Pascual? Did Zoilo Versalles deserve the Most Valuable Player award? Were these heroes worth having? What was the world like then, and could a baseball team make a difference in adults' lives?

People around the country were no different than today, hungry for diversion from the nightly news. Mom and Dad could watch one of the three nightly network newscasts in color on an RCA Victor TV – if they had $400 – or trade in their old black-and-white set and pay less. It was not as disposable a society then, but, as always, a troubled one.

Secretary of Defense Robert McNamara told parents the United States was "stepping up" the war in Vietnam in 1965. A sick, estranged husband in New York dressed his children in Easter finery and abandoned them. A note on their coats explained he couldn't care for them anymore. There were some intriguing, O.J. Simpson-like murder stories among the rich and famous.

Baseball was the nation's sport, and it gave people a little break from the world. The Minnesota Twins' powerful lineup drew huge crowds in cities such as New York, Boston, and Los Angeles. But in the upper Midwest, this baseball team ultimately soothed a healthy supply of misery for people who lost a son to the wartime draft or a home to the floods and tornadoes that devastated the region in 1965. In a storm-filled year, the Minnesota Twins were the perfect storm.

The team had teased fans with one second-place finish during its first four seasons in Minnesota, but a poor 1964 season brought skepticism. In 1965, the Twins were an endless surprise. Excitement in the state rose like smoke, a little at first, then in huge plumes. A Twin Cities publication printed the "magic number," the combination of wins by the league-leading Twins and losses by contenders that would result in Minnesota's first big-league pennant. It was a tad premature, as there was still about a third of the season left to play.

The scoreboard operator at Metropolitan Stadium was so flustered when the Twins scored six times in the third inning of the first World Series game ever played in Minnesota that it took him three tries to post the correct number of runs. Folks in Minnesota didn't exactly know how to go about this winning thing with James Bond cool.

Some folks did exhibit a bit of James Bond's élan. Eddie Webster's Restaurant was under construction on Interstate 494 near Metropolitan Stadium. On the Fourth of July, a huge sign assured passing motorists: "Will be open for the World Series."

When the World Series between the Twins and Dodgers arrived – the first Series between two franchises that ran away from home and relocated west – Nicollet Avenue, soon to become the retail and restaurant mall in the heart of downtown Minneapolis, was vibrant with red, white and blue bunting. Store windows featured images of Twins' players, images three times larger than life. A hotel converted its lobby into an attraction for local college students by decorating it to resemble the Twins' clubhouse.

The pace of life in 1965 seems quaintly slow now, as it always does in retrospect. A player such as Frank Kostro might begin his drive from Denver to spring training in Florida, stop to visit friends and relatives along the way, only to arrive in Orlando with no contract. It was mailed to his home after he left, and never caught up. There was no cell phone to track Kostro and no elaborate database to track his career. The apocryphal story goes that Twins' owner Calvin Griffith had really wanted Andy Kosco on his team, but a miscommunication resulted in the Twins' acquiring Kostro. Griffith eventually got Kosco as well. (Fortunately, Andy Pafko was retired, and Corey Koskie hadn't been born.)

The pace did not seem at all slow from the perspective of the era, because people in every era crave progress. Those with hungry fantasies chased and satisfied dreams. Construction of the first covered baseball stadium in Houston was part of the endless quest to change both life and the game of baseball. When the Astrodome was finished, it immediately became a lucrative novelty. The Astros were one of the worst teams in baseball, but their new, air-conditioned stadium translated into more money from baseball's national television package for the Houston franchise than for any other team. The Astros would play to capacity crowds early in the season; in the previous three years they had sold out once.

There was no domed stadium in Minnesota during 1965. The April sun glinted off small, icy mounds of melting snow on the corners of Nicollet Avenue. The sidewalks and streets were always damp, and the gutters echoed with the thin gurgle of trickling snowmelt. Dayton's department store published Sunday newspaper advertisements that boasted "Official Twins' Jackets Make a Hit with the Boys - $6.99." You could buy a navy blue Twins' baseball cap for $1.

Considering the weather, you needed both the jacket and cap as the family drove the Pontiac Tempest down Cedar Avenue to Metropolitan Stadium to watch the Minnesota Twins warm the summer of '65.

COOL OF THE EVENING

Rich Rollins and Jerry Zimmerman

ONE

Where's Versalles? Get him out here.
He can use this, too. – Sam Mele

Hope had gone limp. A dirty crust of snow smothered the grass at Minnesota's Metropolitan Stadium weeks before the 1965 baseball season. The dugouts were filled with two feet of ice. A St. Patrick's Day blizzard had marooned parts of the state in 25-foot snowdrifts, with a promise of more jeweled flakes to come. It would take hours of work and moments of prayer in this reluctant spring to make the field south of Minneapolis and Saint Paul playable for April's baseball season opener against the defending American League champion New York Yankees. The field had been ignored since the Minnesota Vikings and Los Angeles Rams scarred the sod with football cleats during a game five months earlier. Metal folding chairs, orphaned on the field after that final National Football League game, had been wind-blown to the perimeter of the stadium and encased in ice against the chain-link fence.

Billy Robertson, Minnesota Twins' director of stadium operations, stepped off an airplane after vacationing in Jamaica. He drove the short distance to Met Stadium and was astonished. Football yard lines painted on the distressed turf peeked through the snowmelt. Robertson thought the ravages of winter had been unusually severe. How could his Minnesota Twins open on this field in a few weeks?

The weather was fine down in Orlando for the Twins' fifth spring training, but the news from Florida streamed holdouts, trade demands, accusations of favoritism, selfish play, and managerial instability. Poor fielding was costing the team exhibition wins after a shimmering start. The Twins had the most explosive offense in the American League the previous season, but wobbly infield play would certainly mean another losing campaign. Errors, indifference, and a bankrupt bullpen had ushered the Twins to sixth place among 10 teams in 1964. Decent second basemen could not stay healthy, a weakness that had dogged the franchise long before it moved from Washington to Minnesota in 1961. For the first time, Twins' fans were loudly critical, and attendance was falling. Then in early April, days before the season opener, manager Sam Mele pulled All-Star shortstop Zoilo Versalles off the field, mid-game, for lack of effort.

It was an 87-degree April afternoon in St. Petersburg, and the spring's Grapefruit League play was nearly complete. Mele had led his club to second- and third-place finishes before the tumble to sixth place in 1964. The team was to begin working its way north in three days to play a pair of exhibition games in North Carolina and Virginia, then fly to Minnesota to start the season against the Yankees. It was time to look sharp, if not win.

Spring outcomes did not normally consume Mele, but it was late in the schedule and the Mets were on the field that Monday in St. Petersburg. The inept, comical play of the National League's New York team under 75-year-old manager Casey Stengel had oddly endeared the Mets to those New York fans who despised the Yankees and to those who were still fuming over the Dodgers' shift from Brooklyn to Los Angeles in '58.

The Twins were already losing when Mets' outfielder Jim Hickman hit a bounding ball to Versalles, a wiry man who could glide over grass as if gravity gave him scant consideration. The ball bounced a few feet beyond Versalles' left side, his glove hand, and into left-center field. Two Mets scored in New York's eventual 8-1 win.

Mele knew the 24-year-old Versalles didn't always position himself properly in the field against batters, and that his shortstop simply had not developed a focus on his play after four full seasons in the American League. Versalles had handed his sunglasses to an umpire before an inning a few days earlier and then promptly lost a ball in the sun. Mele wondered aloud if he should start dressing his players.

Mele was a man who painted the world with broad strokes and tried to calculate the long-term ramifications of his decisions. He considered Versalles for one more pitch before he uncoiled his lean, six-foot-one frame from the dugout bench.

In what was later widely termed the defining moment of the Twins' 1965 American League championship season, Mele pulled Versalles off the field for "lackadaisical effort." A manager simply did not do this in spring training, but Versalles had contributed to Mele's recent anxieties. Versalles had complained of arm problems – part of an annual aches-and-pains ritual – and had not played as much or as hard as Mele preferred. The resulting dugout clash between Mele and Versalles dissolved into a bizarre bidding scene regarding the size of Versalles' fine, with Versalles taunting Mele to up the ante.

Mele's more typical player was someone like Johnny Klippstein, a veteran player who left his cold-weather career and arrived at spring training to drop a couple pounds, shake off 20 weeks of inactivity and recalibrate mental gears. Few veterans engaged in off-season conditioning programs. They were expected to play themselves into shape, and then shine during the second half of the two-dozen spring games.

Baseball wasn't even necessarily a player's most lucrative employment option. Some players would wonder why they continued. Klippstein was a 37-year-old relief pitcher, originally signed at age 16 during a tryout camp in Appleton, Wisconsin. He was also a salesman for a box manufacturer and found himself engaged in debate with his boss, who wanted Klippstein to abandon more than 20 years of professional baseball travels to work in sales year-round.

Mele was one of the younger managers in the league. He was a sincere, 43-year-old Italian from Long Island with wiry, graying hair, a grin that revealed straight, white teeth and "Mother" scripted beneath a rose tattooed on his right bicep. He starred in basketball at New York University, but a close relationship with his uncles – major league baseball players Al and Tony Cuccinello – steered him toward the diamond. The former Marine began his playing career with the Boston Red Sox, who regarded the Yankees unkindly. Mele always enjoyed beating the Yankees, even in the spring when it didn't really count. He thought it "established a little superiority" if his players could snatch a win from the team that was often the best in baseball. Other than that, Mele knew spring training was when men played themselves into shape.

An outwardly calm, fair, unaffected man who lost sleep easily, Mele was weary from a month of controversy and five weeks of play that began with the team winning seven of its first 10 games; the Twins won just four times during their last three weeks in Florida. There was winter-long media speculation that Billy Martin, the combative former New York Yankee who was hired to coach third base, was really there to take Mele's job. This grew into spring-long speculation, which irritated Martin more than it did Mele. On the field, Mele was clearly in control, walking about the diamond with his ubiquitous fungo bat, gently needling players.

If Mele greatly disliked what he saw, though, he tightened his grip. He was unhappy with the team's fielding early in the spring and called for an extra drill. Martin had excused Versalles, who then left Tinker Field for the clubhouse. Mele simmered. "Where's Versalles?"

Martin admitted he had excused the player.

"Well, get him out here," Mele demanded. "He can use this, too."

Mele had a longer fuse than Versalles' previous managers, but he finally ignited in St. Petersburg, when he pulled Versalles off the field. Owner Calvin Griffith was happy to hear about it.

Griffith had bristled publicly about what he perceived to be Mele's easy-going approach as the Twins were finishing sixth the previous season. Mele said he treated his players like men, because these weren't the type of people to find trouble off the field. Certainly, Mele admitted, they were no flock of angels, but they would discipline each other, sometimes approaching Mele after the fact to let him know about a situation. So Mele kept his distance.

Griffith had a turnstile count, payroll and media to worry about, and he tore into the players' lifeless approach and shabby play in the middle of the '64 season. The team was all but out of the American

League pennant race in July, so Griffith accused some players of carousing, and he suggested Mele start to fine them. Even a $50 fine was a significant financial hit for most players. Griffith singled out the play of his former Gold Glove and All-Star catcher, Earl Battey, whose poor 1964 summer was eventually attributed to a thyroid problem that had led to Battey being about 30 pounds over ideal playing weight.

Battey was a fun-loving bear of a man from Los Angeles whose extraordinary mental and physical toughness came to national attention during the '65 World Series. He was looking skyward while chasing a foul ball when his exposed throat slammed full force into a metal crossbar near a dugout in Dodger Stadium. As Battey crumpled to the ground a few feet from first baseman Don Mincher, Mincher sagged over the edge of the dugout, weakened by the ugliness of the blow and certain Battey was severely injured. Battey was removed from the game, but he was back behind the plate a day later, unable to speak or turn his head left. He threw out five base runners in the next four games and entered the hospital when the Series ended.

Like most catchers, Battey took a beating behind the plate and was constantly aching. He was sidelined with injuries 14 times in 1965. Yet Battey appeared in almost as many games during the franchise's first five seasons in Minnesota as the team's star, Harmon Killebrew, who played less demanding positions. Battey exemplified the maturity of most veterans on the roster by responding to Griffith's published criticism: "I guess I've got it coming. I've been pretty bad."

Criticism of players was common from most owners and managers, but Griffith's organization was not without tact. Minneapolis and Saint Paul are twin cities that sit on either side of the Mississippi River. Griffith wanted to alienate neither city, so even though no other big-league franchise had been named for a state by 1961, Griffith did just that when he moved his franchise from Washington. The Class AAA Minneapolis Millers were the first tenant of Metropolitan Stadium, but when the Twins replaced them the players did not have an "M" on their baseball caps to represent Minneapolis. What adorned the front were the overlapping letters "TC." It stood for "Twin Cities," but the joke was it meant "Twenty Cubans."

The struggle of Cuban players such as Versalles to adapt to a country quite different from a small, Caribbean island went unnoticed in much of baseball, but within the Griffith organization there was a fairly good understanding of the adjustment process for Latin players. That history stretched a long way back. In 1911, Calvin's adoptive father was managing the Cincinnati Reds. Clark Griffith imported a white, Cuban third baseman named Rafael Almeida for a tryout. Almeida was comfortable financially and smoked $1 cigars. He didn't make the team, but Griffith liked the play of his interpreter, Armando Marsans. Marsans played eight seasons in the big leagues. The club enjoyed wild scouting success in Cuba as Clark Griffith gained financial control of the Washington Senators over a span of years ending in 1920. This effort was largely the work of a rotund scout named "Papa" Joe Cambria.

Born in Messina, Italy, Cambria gained his baseball judgment as a former player and minor league team owner. He spent most of his days in Havana, was the first and most renowned United States scout in the Caribbean, and the man who told Calvin Griffith that a young pitcher the Senators were interested in at the University of Havana lacked a major-league fastball. It was Fidel Castro, or "Fie-dell," as Griffith called him.

No player was ever given more than a couple hundred dollars' bonus to sign with Cambria, but he earned the trust of Latin players because of his success in sending them to the major leagues. He signed about 400 Latin players, in addition to Americans such as 300-game winner Early Wynn. Cambria is credited for paving the way for the Senators to sign Carlos Paula, their first black player.

The Twins' 1965 American League pennant could be termed a posthumous homage to Cambria, who died at age 73 in 1963. Cambria signed Versalles, Camilo Pascual, and Sandy Valdespino, all members of the 1965 Twins, along with Cambria's prize: Tony Oliva. Oliva is the only man to have won American League batting championships in his first two major league seasons. Based on the word of a trusted colleague, Cambria took a flyer on a 19-year-old Oliva in 1960. Cambria saw Oliva in action only once. At the time, the skinny, six-foot-two, left-handed hitting leopard was a very raw talent with unpolished fielding skills. Oliva would later facetiously jest about his early abilities, "If Papa Joe had seen me play more, he wouldn't have signed me."

Opposite of the personable, focused, cheerful Oliva was Versalles, a slight, child-like man who lacked formal education even in his native country. He had a nervous stomach that balked at many American foods and a demeanor that upset the digestion of all his managers. A spring goal for Billy Martin was to guide and focus the mercurial shortstop. Martin as mentor might seem odd, given the former Yankee's reputation as a fiery ballplayer who sometimes forgot his halo at home. He enjoyed hours in saloons and brawls on and off the field, but in uniform there was nobody better. Martin's patience and caring as a coach and manager touched many. The list of players to praise Martin for his role in their development is a long one, and eventual Hall of Famer Rod Carew, who was a 19-year-old second baseman during 1965 spring camp, would put himself near the head of that line.

Versalles believed in Martin long before Mele pulled the shortstop off the field in St. Petersburg. Versalles and Martin had been double-play partners after Cookie Lavagetto, who preceded Mele as Twins' manager, brought his friend Martin to Minnesota in 1961 to end his playing career. Martin graduated from Versalles' teammate to mentor and friend, and coaxed not only the finest season from Versalles' erratic playing career but ensured the words "first Latin American to be named Most Valuable Player" led the obituary of Versalles' brief, rollercoaster life.

Martin announced during spring training that Versalles would win the MVP award. As the '65 season loped on, teammates and opposing players such as New York's Mickey Mantle, Tony Kubek and Bobby Richardson, along with Sabbath Anthony Mele, agreed that Versalles deserved to be called league MVP. The only first-place vote Versalles did not receive in the '65 MVP balloting went to his teammate and countryman, Oliva.

Billy Martin's words of advice and gentle criticism to Versalles from the first day of spring training most certainly helped carve the path to

Versalles' MVP award and the Twins' championship season. The value of this cannot be underestimated. The Twins endured notable injuries at every position in 1965 except the one position for which they had no adequate reserve: shortstop.

Zoilo Versalles played 160 games for the 1965 Minnesota Twins. Without him, their final seven-game lead over the rest of the American League would have scattered like squarely struck bowling pins.

COOL OF THE EVENING

Billy Martin and Sam Mele

TWO

I got into more arguments with Billy Martin
than anyone I've ever met on the face of the earth,
before or since. – Rich Rollins

Billy Martin arrived for his first spring training as a third base coach and busied himself hitting ground balls to infielders. He discussed hitters' tendencies, to help Twins' infielders decide how to position themselves defensively. Martin wore a T-shirt beneath his jersey that read, 'Y.A. Tittle, Comeback Kid,' pitched batting practice, honed the team's bunting skills and built Versalles' ego. Martin instructed the groundskeeper to chalk running routes on the base paths and worked hard on the team's base running. He noticed certain players had the habit of sliding into bases on the same hip. He taught them the value of learning to slide on either side; one benefit was the fielder could not automatically know at which corner of the base to slap a tag.

Martin immediately took to rookie infielder Frank Quilici. Like Martin, Quilici loved to read and discuss the biographies of world and military leaders. Like Martin, Quilici would eventually manage the Minnesota Twins. They were both scrappy Italian infielders who were considered more than a little brash. It was Martin's fiery reputation that had interested Calvin Griffith.

The Twins' press release that announced Martin as third base coach for the 1965 season read he was "signed to battle the umpires and put some life into the Twins on the field." Griffith did not blame Mele for the team's poor showing in 1964. Instead, Griffith took a whiskbroom to his coaching staff. In addition to Martin, Griffith hired former Twins' outfielder Jim Lemon as batting instructor and a highly regarded former pitcher named John Sain as pitching coach. Bullpen coach Hal Naragon was retained.

It was widely reported that Griffith specifically wanted Martin on the staff to provide a convenient replacement for Mele if the Twins struggled early, but it wasn't true. Griffith was a hands-on owner and chose his own coaching staff until 1962, when he let Mele select the staff. Griffith had presented a list of prospective coaches to Mele after the '64 season. Martin was on the list. Mele had liked what he saw of Martin during spring training in 1964, when he asked Martin to work with the infielders. Mele said he wanted Martin as a full-time coach even then.

The playing careers of Martin and Mele shared a dubious similarity: both were traded after scuffles, although Mele's was mere playfulness that turned unfortunate, and the trade was unrelated to the scuffle. Martin's trade was by design.

He was lean, under six-feet tall, and not an offensive power in a formidable Yankee lineup, yet he was the spark of the Yankees – an intense player who preserved one championship with a remarkable catch of a wind-blown pop fly with the bases loaded in the seventh game of the '52 World Series. The next year, Martin clicked off a record 12 hits in the Series – the 12th hit was the game-winner in the last inning of the final game. Martin was in the Army the following year, 1954, the only one of six straight seasons in which the Yankees didn't go to the World Series. He returned from the Army in 1955 to play 20 games; the Yankees won 15 of them and voted Martin a full share of World Series money. This was unheard of for a player with such limited playing time, but he was the most popular man in the clubhouse.

Martin turned 29 in May of 1957. Teammates Whitey Ford and Mickey Mantle insisted on celebrating at Manhattan's Copacabana nightclub after a ball game. Toasts were swallowed, patrons taunted the Yankees, and a fight erupted that resulted in club officials' laying more than $5,000 in fines on the players.

The Yankee front office had pushed manager Casey Stengel to trade Martin for some time. Finally, management had a case. Club officials blamed Martin, Stengel stepped aside, and Martin was traded to Kansas City. He had played in five World Series when he arrived in Minnesota.

Mele had not played in a World Series. He did have a sparring match that many believe cost the Red Sox a pennant.

Mele and the first-place Boston Red Sox headed from Washington to Philadelphia by train in July of 1948 for a game with the second-place A's. Mele was the roommate of Joe DiMaggio's brother, Dom, a close friend of Ted Williams. Mele, Dom DiMaggio and Williams patrolled Fenway Park's outfield together for a time, and Mele showed such promise as a rookie that he was predicted to become a right-handed hitting Ted Williams, a notion Mele later said he found laughable.

Williams loved boxing, and Mele was among the teammates with whom he developed a playful habit of jabbing and sparring. When Williams encountered Mele in the aisle of a coach during the rail trip to Philadelphia, the two playfully took light jabs at each other, and then went separate directions.

Mele was eating breakfast the next morning when Boston batting practice pitcher Paul Schreiber frantically approached the table and stunned him with, "What the hell did you do to Williams?" Williams had injured cartilage in his ribs – badly enough that he was sidelined for a week.

There is fair evidence to suggest Williams suffered the injury when he swung and missed a curve ball during an at-bat the day before. Regardless, the Red Sox lost the pennant to Cleveland in a one-game playoff. It was the closest Mele ever got to a World Series, and it's reasonable to assume Mele and the Sox would have made it to the Series if they hadn't lost the services of the man who was arguably the best hitter in the game's history.

Mele was named to *The Sporting News*' all-rookie team in 1947. He was a fine fielder, thanks in part to Dom DiMaggio's tutoring, and a good enough hitter that he eventually led the league in doubles. Boston manager Joe McCarthy had little use for him in '49, however, and traded

Mele to Washington, where, unlike Martin, he began his long wait for October baseball.

When Mele levied his first fine as a manager, it was Martin who was out $50. Mele had removed him for a pinch hitter in a game toward the end of Martin's playing career. The second baseman reacted by pacing in the dugout while cussing at Mele, who had assessed the game situation and did not think it favored Martin. Mele told him so, but Martin always thought he could do the job. Years earlier in New York, Martin had ripped the starting lineup off a wall and charged into Stengel's office. "What's this, a gag? You've got me batting eighth. That's where the groundskeeper bats."

But Martin's skills were eroding when Mele pulled him from the game.

The evening after Mele fined Martin, the pair got together. Mele realized Martin was frustrated that the end of his career was near, and told him, "Bill, I understand you want to compete, and if you hadn't done that in front of everyone on the bench I'd just overlook the fine. But I'm gonna have to take a little money from you." The fine was going to be $100, but Mele told him he'd take just $50.

When it was clear Martin could no longer play, it was Mele who called him into his office in 1962 to deliver tearfully the news that Minnesota was releasing him. Griffith immediately signed Martin as a scout, but Mele thought Martin belonged on the field. People suggested that putting the bright and ambitious Martin back in uniform would open the door for him to step in as manager, but Mele reasoned if he didn't win he'd be gone, regardless of who was around to pick up the pieces.

"I took the job of a friend, Cookie Lavagetto," Mele said. "That's the way it is in baseball. If you're gone it makes no difference who replaces you. You're still gone."

Mele was a logical man with a subtle sense of humor. He appeared in the clubhouse during a four-game losing streak in July of 1962 and announced it was his birthday. He told the players he would love it if the team could get him a win. The Twins responded with a 9-0 thumping of the Senators, the losing streak was over, and Mele had his birthday present. Sabath Anthony Mele was born on a Sunday, hence the first name, but the Sunday on which he was born happened to be in January, not July.

When there was talk Martin would replace him as manager, Mele managed to joke about that as well. Martin and Mele went fishing with team trainer George "Doc" Lentz one day late during the '65 spring camp. Lentz was in a separate boat when Mele asked if he could try the new fishing rod Lentz had with him. Mele stood, reached for the fishing rod and remained standing as he prepared to cast a line. He saw Martin standing in the way at the other end of the boat and asked him to duck. Martin bent down, the weight of the boat shifted, Mele lost his balance and splashed into the water. Mele emerged from the muck at the bottom of the lake, vegetation draped over his soggy hair, and waved the fishing rod as the trio laughed while Mele congratulated himself for not losing the fishing rod. Then the press heard about it.

"I figured," Martin explained to reporters, "him being an Italian, he was a good fisherman and he knew what he was doing." Someone asked Martin what he did when he saw his manager in the water, but Mele interrupted. "He started rowing away."

Despite the Twins' high-octane offense the club was not fiery, and some thought it was unfocused. So in addition to hiring Martin, club officials mulled the value of naming a captain, although this clearly became more a topic for conjecture among media and fans than it was for the players. On any baseball team, the role of a captain often comes down to approaching the mound when a pitcher is struggling, or discussing disputed plays with umpires. A team's shortstop is the general of the infield and a natural fit for whatever minimal on-field duties a captain is charged with, but Versalles could be moody and reclusive so he didn't have the personality to carry the title. There were really no obvious choices.

Imposing outfielder Bob Allison, a former college football player, stood six-foot-four, weighed 220 pounds, and was not shy about expressing himself. He was the American League Rookie of the Year in 1959 and immediately held out for more money the next spring – something the team's top star, Harmon Killebrew, never did. Allison also had no problem assuming the unpopular chore of being a players' representative, helping to bargain for better benefits from owners. He was the person most likely to call a players-only meeting, and he was a man with an opinion.

Allison was playing first base one night at Chicago in 1961 and didn't think pitcher Camilo Pascual was paying enough attention to White Sox base runner Minnie Minoso. Allison took a few steps toward Pascual to complain, but Pascual waved him off and told Allison he would handle the pitching. Minoso stole second on the next pitch. Allison grabbed Pascual in the dugout after the half inning, pinned him against a steel post and decided to offer his pitching advice anyway. Pascual was a tough man, but at five-foot-eleven, 185 pounds, he disliked the matchup and squirmed away. Allison again corralled Pascual, and the pair were eventually pushed into the dugout runway by teammates and separated.

Allison was mainly an outfielder. A team captain is ideally an infielder or catcher, a position player in the middle of the action and in close proximity to umpires and the pitcher. Killebrew had played mostly in the infield when Lavagetto gave him the title of captain in the spring of '61. The one-season honor carried an additional $500, and Lavagetto hoped it would result in vocal leadership from Killebrew, who was not known in baseball as a "holler guy." Ironically, Killebrew was known as a good listener, which would seem to be a coveted attribute of a leader.

Second baseman Jerry Kindall felt one reason Killebrew disliked the idea of being a captain was because "he did not want to set himself apart. He would consider it an affront to some of the other guys. Why make it formalized anyway? I think we all acknowledged Harmon as the leader, and I don't think we would have responded to Harmon any differently. He was always a gracious guy, and if you started talking he was so attentive."

The strong, quiet Idaho native believed the best way to provide leadership was to set an example through hard work and unselfishness, and this approach was effective as he established himself as one of the premier players in the league. Leadership had been the last thing on

Killebrew's mind earlier in his career. He retired as baseball's career home run leader among right-handed batters and became a Hall of Famer, which suggests the game for him was an effortless stroll. But Killebrew later said about his early years in baseball, "It wasn't easy to reach whatever smidgen of success I've attained. I was too busy surviving to think much about providing leadership to others."

His path to the majors was a broken one, and he was often booed once he reached the big leagues to stay. During those early seasons of his 21-year career, he was criticized for failing to drive in the big run, striking out too much, fielding poorly and running slowly. He worked hard at each category, and former teammates recall him as the best clutch hitter they ever saw. There have been only two other men in the history of baseball to hit more home runs with runners on base: Hank Aaron and Babe Ruth. The only area in which Killebrew never did improve was foot speed.

His nickname, Killer, was a misfire. It was Versalles who would react to inside pitches by threatening to head toward the mound with a bat in his hands during an era in which such displays were rare. Hall of Famer Frank Robinson was notorious for crowding home plate, and he was rewarded with pitches in the ribs often enough that he was hit nearly 200 times in his career. Robinson's reaction was to drop the bat and head to first base. Killebrew did not crowd the plate like Robinson. He said he found pitchers tended to throw a little more at hitters like Robinson and Versalles, players who either crowded home plate or who let pitchers know being thrown at bothered them.

"I found the best way to handle a brush-back pitch," he said after his career ended, "was to just get up and hit a line drive somewhere."

And when that opportunity didn't occur, he still remained calm. In May of '65, 20-year-old Baltimore pitcher Wally Bunker allowed home runs to Earl Battey and Tony Oliva. When Killebrew stepped in, Bunker plunked him in the back with a pitch, even though it was an automatic $50 league fine at the time. When asked about the pitch from Bunker, Killebrew shrugged. "No use making an issue of it. I suppose a fellow has a tendency to remember something like that. It's not easy to forget."

Despite Killebrew's relaxed manner, others in the league saw the team rally around him. California Angels' manager Bill Rigney, who replaced Martin after his one season managing the Twins in 1969, said midway through the '65 season, "I don't know the guy very well, but the player on the Twins who impresses me as a real leader is Harmon Killebrew." Informally, it was always beneficial for a team to have someone they could approach with questions, complaints or to iron out differences. Formally, it probably didn't matter.

During the course of nine months, roughly 40 men with diverse backgrounds, personalities, educations, and nationalities are thrown together only because they share the rare ability to compete in a sport at its highest level. Without baseball, relief pitcher Johnny Klippstein was a box salesman and third baseman Rich Rollins sold bonds. Catcher Jerry Zimmerman thought he would have been a fireman, and Killebrew considered being a horse breeder. Pascual was a fan of space flight and jokingly claimed he wanted to be an astronaut. With baseball as the common denominator, they spent considerable time working and living together in confined areas such as dugouts, clubhouses, buses, and airplanes.

Talented people don't necessarily need to like each other to succeed, and on any team there are always groups. It's obviously better if the groups get along and don't become cliques, but embattled teams have proven they can win despite personality clashes. The Twins, in contrast, took their quiet demeanor from Killebrew.

For fiery inspiration, Martin filled the role.

When he joined the Twins' coaching staff in 1965, Martin was young enough at 36 to smell his playing days. As third-base coach, he had influence with the players and could get friendly with them, if Martin saw that was the best approach. But this was a team of veterans, not wayward novices in need of direction. The average age of the pitching staff was more than 28 years, the oldest in the league. The average age of the position players was about a year younger. Many on the roster had at least some college education, and it seemed that most of them had street smarts.

Years later, Mele said Martin served him well as a liaison with the players, and also ably filled the role of vocal firing pin and instigator, qualities that some teams seek in a captain. A natural extension of Martin's coaching duties was to harp, joke, criticize, or scream, if need be, but he knew at times it was more a ritual than a necessity with this bunch. He would laugh at hearing himself shout trite phrases at the players. He grew weary during his playing days when Yankee coach Frank Crosetti would yell the same words at him. Now here he was, doing it too. Still, Martin could never take things lightly for long. Billy Martin simply loved a good battle.

He saw himself as an underdog and rooted for those such as Quilici: men with more fight than big-league talent. This explained the "Y.A. Tittle, Comeback Kid" T-shirt, which referred to a veteran National Football League quarterback who was traded by the San Francisco 49ers as an aging second-stringer and fought his way back to star status with the New York Giants. No matter how veteran the club or how mature the players, Billy Martin never really shook off his fighting, street-kid mindset from his days in Oakland. Martin also loved being around baseball, and he not only knew how to win after all those years with the Yankees, he expected to.

In 1966, Baltimore had clinched the American League pennant, and the Twins were tied for second place. Mele penciled the lineup card, and Martin saw it wasn't filled with the club's better players. He asked Mele what he was doing. "Let's finish second," Martin said. Mele shrugged. It was the end of the year and the pennant was lost. Martin countered that second place was better than third. Mele looked at Martin, conceded, tore up the lineup card and flew his pencil over a fresh version. The Twins finished second.

Martin similarly tried to wring every ounce of productivity from the '65 Twins, a group of players he viewed as more than capable. In Florida, Martin pressed Rich Rollins to assume informal leadership by taking charge of aligning defenses. The five-foot-ten redhead was in his fourth season as the team's third baseman and a tireless worker who took up racquetball in the off-season in an effort to keep in shape and improve his reactions (and found it distressing when "some 52-year-old guy beat me the other day"). Martin knew Rollins kept scrupulous notes on opposing pitchers and hitters and even cataloged critical remarks about his play. But Rollins was considered to be a "worrisome" player despite having burst upon the major league scene in 1962 by making the All-Star team as a rookie. Martin suggested a wider range of obligations that focused on the team might help Rollins take his mind off his own game and allow the 27-year-old Pennsylvanian to relax.

Rollins was enjoying his best spring in three years after arriving at camp in particularly good shape. He was devoted to baseball and an eager learner. It was easy for Rollins to see Billy Martin knew how to play baseball and knew how to get a player to produce. He could agitate a player just as easily.

Rollins was a rookie during Martin's final season as a player in 1961. Martin rode Rollins mercilessly, told him he didn't belong on the field, that he couldn't go to his left. Rollins said he got so mad he wanted to punch Martin, but instead he set out to prove Martin wrong. Martin later told Rollins' father he always thought Rollins could make the grade, and he needled Rollins only to spur him. Their families grew close, but Rollins said many years later, "I got into more arguments with Billy Martin than anyone I've ever met on the face of the earth, before or since, but the thing about Billy was the next day it was forgotten.

"I remember when Rod Carew was a rookie in 1967. Billy came into the clubhouse after a game and confronted Rod about a throw he had made. I lockered next to Rod, and eventually Billy turned to me and said, 'Tell him, Rich. Tell him he screwed up.' Well, I didn't think Rod had screwed up, and I said that, so then Billy starts in on me. But Billy came in the next day and it was all forgotten. It was always over with Billy. But Billy did have you on your toes all the time. Nobody knew the game better than he did."

Mele admitted he sometimes had to rein in Martin, but he embraced Martin's enthusiasm and baseball knowledge. Martin, in turn, appreciated Mele's approach to the game. While Martin was managing the Yankees in 1977, outfielder Reggie Jackson loafed after a ball during a game on national television. Martin promptly pulled him off the field in the middle of the inning. The parallel to Mele's spring training removal of Versalles in the middle of a game was obvious. Furthermore, the incident between Martin and Jackson occurred in Boston, with Mele, by then a Red Sox employee, sitting in the stands.

Mele and Martin would discuss baseball in the manager's office after home games during their championship season and then straggle to separate homes. Mele's wife was pregnant and back in Quincy, Massachusetts, overseeing construction of a new house. Eventually, Mele's phone might ring: Martin. Mele would hop in his car, pick up some McDonald's or Kentucky Fried Chicken and proceed to Martin's, grab a beer from his fridge, eat, and talk more baseball. Martin liked exciting, aggressive baseball.

Players such as Killebrew, Don Mincher and Rich Rollins were not swift runners, and Earl Battey might have been the slowest man in the league. But as Mele watched the St. Louis Cardinals utilize their speed while beating the Yankees in the 1964 World Series, he decided he wanted to tear up the base paths and get his players swinging to the opposite field, rather than for the fences. He thought about the New York Giants of the mid-1940s, who set home-run records but were lucky to finish in the first division of an eight-team league. Then the Giants picked up Eddie Stanky and Alvin Dark, men who could play defense and put the ball in play. The Giants were soon contenders.

The Twins stranded more than 1,100 base runners in 1964, second in the league to the Chicago White Sox, and left runners on third base with fewer than two out more than 50 times. The team lost 10 of those games by one run and was 28-38 in one-run decisions. Mele saw waiting for the long ball was not working, and on the field it was the third base coach who directed base runners. So Mele instructed Martin to keep the players running, confident that Martin had the savvy to know when to roll the dice.

Opposing defenses had grown accustomed to sitting back on their heels against the Twins, not risking throws because Minnesota players were not known for daring on the base paths. Mele wanted to force the opposition to make mistakes, hurry throws, and be concerned about the hit-and-run, bunting, stealing, and scoring from first on a single. Martin was the man to implement it. The Twins hit 71 fewer home runs in 1965 than in 1964 but stole twice as many bases and grounded into fewer double plays. Most importantly, the Twins scored more runs.

"I remember when we'd go into New York," outfielder Sandy Valdespino recalled, "and Mickey Mantle and Billy Martin were good friends, so Mickey would come up to Billy when we arrived, look at us, laugh and say, 'Oh, no, not these Cubans again,' because Zoilo Versalles had great speed and Tony Oliva could run, and I could run, and the Yankees didn't like it because, really, the whole team was running all the time."

The aggressive approach didn't always work. The screams of fans would cascade over Mele, who was sitting in the dugout, and rain down on Martin in the third-base coaching box after a player was thrown out trying for an extra base. Mele publicly tried to take the heat. He told his players if a reporter questioned any strategy to reply, "Mele ordered it."

More often, however, the new approach worked. An indication of the lengths to which Mele and Martin took this exciting style of play came on the road against the Yankees, whose dynasty was crumbling into a sixth-place finish. The Yankees didn't win the pennant again until Martin managed the club in '76.

It was early August and the Twins had recently lost Killebrew because of a dislocated elbow. Pascual, who was 8-0 to that point in the season, had undergone surgery on his shoulder, and it was uncertain if he would pitch again that season. Meanwhile, the Yankees' Mickey Mantle, aching and contemplating retirement, began to click at the plate and had raised his average to .270. The bigger concern was that the Twins were scheduled to face veteran Whitey Ford and 23-year-old Mel Stottlemyre in consecutive games. Each pitcher already had 13 wins. Stottlemyre won 20 games for a Yankee team that wouldn't win 80. The team would miss Killebrew, who to that point in the season had burned the Yankees with four home runs, 11 runs batted in, and a .365 batting average. This barrage included a two-out, two-run, ninth-inning home run off Pete Mikkelsen that gave Minnesota a dramatic 6-5 win at Metropolitan Stadium the Sunday before the All-Star break. That home run is often considered the hit that sealed the Yankees' tomb and secured the Twins' status as the team to beat in the American League during the summer of 1965.

The Yankees were 15 games out of first place as August began, more distanced from a pennant race at that point in the season than they had been in 35 years. The league still respected their reputation, but it seemed certain the Yankees were not likely to rally and finish first. The Twins' concern was their eight-game lead over Baltimore was hardly secure with 50 games to play – the Philadelphia Phillies had blown a similar lead with only 10 games to play the previous season.

Although the summer had been made longer by the parade of injuries, the Twins were still playing aggressively. On that Tuesday night in early August against New York, Whitey Ford allowed only four base runners and needed just 59 pitches to finish seven innings. The Yankees trailed Minnesota 2-1, so manager Johnny Keane pulled Ford for a pinch hitter. The move worked, and the Yankees tied the score entering the top of the eighth. But a dark cloud hung over Yankee reliever Pete Mikkelsen against Minnesota all season, and he gave up a one-out hit to Versalles in the eighth. It should have been a single, but Versalles was hustling all the way, and he sped into second base when he saw center fielder Tom Tresh make a slow recovery on the ball. Mikkelsen then got Rollins for the second out before Allison hit a check-swing roller back to Mikkelsen for what appeared to be the last out of the eighth inning. Mikkelsen's throw was high and pulled first baseman Joe Pepitone off the bag, Allison was safe at first, and Versalles scored. He would have still been at third base if he had settled for a single on his ball hit to Tresh. The Twins eventually scored five unearned runs in the eighth and won 7-3.

Mikkelsen's high throw was a crucial play, and it's usually a play late in the game that is remembered. The pivot point of the contest is often set earlier, and Martin's aggressiveness in the first inning established the game's direction.

Versalles was on first base when Rollins hit a ball to the left of Mantle, who could no longer cover the vast center field landscape in Yankee

Stadium and spent most of the season in left field. Martin and Mantle were the best of friends, the Copacabana Boys, but that hardly mattered to Martin. Versalles had developed the philosophy, "If you get to one base and you can see the ball on the ground in the outfield, run like hell to the next base," so he streaked toward third base as Rollins' shot forced the right-handed throwing Mantle to range far to his left to field the ball on the hop. Martin knew the aging star's fragile knees would hinder him as Mantle dug the cleats on his left foot into the ground to stop his momentum, shifted his weight and pushed off his right foot to make a decent throw on Versalles. Martin waved Versalles home.

Shortstop Phil Linz was eager to take the relay throw from Mantle and gun the ball home to catcher Elston Howard. Linz knew he had to hurry because of Versalles' speed, and Linz's aim was off, not that it mattered: the ball hadn't reached Howard's mitt when Versalles' left foot slid over home plate. Versalles scored from first on a single for the third time that season, and Rollins eventually scored for the only other run off Ford.

The Yankees would have led 2-0 entering the eighth inning without those crucial first-inning runs, and Keane would not have pinch hit for Ford, who was enjoying an effortless game.

It was the second time during the season that Versalles had scored from first on a ball Rollins hit to Mantle. After the game ended, Versalles dressed in front of his locker in the visiting clubhouse. New York writers approached and asked if he was taking liberties with the aging Mantle.

Versalles didn't bother to look up.

"We're playing in the same league, aren't we?"

COOL OF THE EVENING

Zoilo Versalles and Sam Mele

THREE

I know I have some trouble with the manager last week,
but it's not like Vietnam. – Zoilo Versalles

The music of Zoilo Versalles' life was baseball. At seven he was adept at excuses for avoiding school – torn pants, illness, hunger, no shoes – even though his brother and impoverished schoolmates suffered the same. His father was sporadically employed, life near Havana in Marianao was hard, and there was little concern when a child dropped out of grade school. Versalles quit school after the second grade, taught himself to read his native language, and played baseball on corrugated fields where rocks served as bases. When a businessman provided uniforms to 11-year-old Versalles and his teammates, Versalles slept in his uniform the first night. He focused on emulating Guillermo "Willy" Miranda, a good-field, no-hit countryman whose major-league career ended in Baltimore about the time Versalles was gaining notice as an 18-year-old shortstop in Washington, D.C. The difference was Versalles could hit.

He signed his first contract on the dirt floor of his mother's house after he insisted Cambria pay him the 20-cent bus fare it cost him to attend a tryout earlier in the week. Scouts other than Cambria originally thought Versalles' size – five-foot-ten, 150 pounds after a big meal – meant he would never hit, but he was muscular and swift and showed enough firepower in his first minor league season that Calvin Griffith began to believe Versalles would be a rare blend of power and speed at what had been an offensively destitute position.

There had been a new starting Senator shortstop, on average, every two years after World War II. Those starters supplied fewer than 30 home runs in 15 seasons before Versalles won the job and put nearly that many out of the park in two seasons. He had a powerful arm and rally-killing range in the field. Versalles was positioned close to second base in the opening game of the '65 World Series with switch-hitting Los Angeles Dodger shortstop Maury Wills batting left-handed. Wills hit a foul pop near the third-base dugout, and left fielder Valdespino, third baseman Killebrew, and Versalles all gave chase. Versalles had the longest run but easily reached the ball first.

"Soy-lo Vair-sah-yes" did not slide from the mouth of Americans, so he became Zorro, because broadcast of that popular Walt Disney television program coincided with Versalles' early professional days in the U.S. Zorro was easier to pronounce (and apparently to spell: his rookie baseball card read "Zorro"). Taking the analogy further, it was said that Versalles was "a bandit who stole base hits." He had sad brown eyes, black hair, and an irregular complexion. One look at him made it obvious he had never eaten well. He was 15 years old when he first arrived in the United States to play ball for $2 a game with a barnstorming Cuban team. He was uncomfortable with life in the United States and constantly yearned for home. Versalles was 17 and devastated when his mother died during his first year in the minor leagues. He thought of making a life back in Cuba, but the U.S. was where he could earn a decent living playing baseball.

A gate attraction, he homered twice in his minor league's all-star game in the summer of '59 and had less than two years' experience in the Senators' system – barely 200 games – when he was called to Washington at the end of the season. He arrived in the district early in the morning after a night-long bus ride. He walked to the stadium and sat across the street on a bench for a while, then strolled miles to a park to "listen to the birds wake up. Inside me, I knew I was not going to make it." He later said he was so unsure of himself that he acted cocky to cover his insecurity.

He was 18 that September when, to his surprise, his application for a marriage license appeared in the vital statistics column of a Washington newspaper. He kept quiet about his intended marriage to a 16-year-old Washington girl, but once sports writers learned the news he explained he was old beyond his years: after all, he was sending part of his pay back to Cuba to help his father and brother. He further explained bachelorhood "bores me" and suggested a wife would help him settle down and focus on baseball. He was still a bachelor when he arrived in spring training the following year. He decided the girl was too young.

Versalles soon disappeared during those first days of 1960 Senators' Florida workouts. Manager Cookie Lavagetto gave him permission to handle some personal matters but expected it would mean a one-day absence. Versalles returned days later; the personal matters were in Cuba.

It seemed that to be Zoilo Versalles was like trying to stuff exhaust from a tailpipe into a trouser pocket. He was proud, sensitive and brooding. Some of his health problems stemmed from an impoverished childhood, and some were probably imagined. Tony Oliva recalls it was best to pull Versalles aside to offer even the most constructive criticism. Versalles was not a man who tolerated someone correcting him in public, so it was the ultimate insult when Mele pulled him off the field during spring training in front of teammates and fans. When management publicly criticized him while he was playing for the Senators' Charleston affiliate in 1960, he threatened to return to Cuba.

Each spring was an adventure. He drove to Orlando in '62 and made a mid-trip telephone call to spring headquarters to say he was broke, so the team wired funds. He called later to ask if someone could bail him out after he was jailed for speeding. Club officials wondered what he had done with the money they wired to him, and he explained he used that to pay off a previous speeding ticket. It was later learned he was stopped three times for speeding during the trip. He drove slower the next spring and arrived in camp with $6 in his pocket. Each spring he complained of arm troubles, other aches, and homesickness. He worried about his family back in Cuba, a country in upheaval during Versalles' early years in the U.S. His mercurial behavior reached a zenith in 1961.

Cuba's relations with the U.S. grew increasingly strained in the spring of '61, and the U.S. invasion of the Bay of Pigs was imminent. Incoming Secretary of State Dean Rusk indicated he had no idea what would happen to Cuban players still in that country. The players got out, many through Mexico, but it was clear Versalles' concern for his family was valid. What's more, even though Versalles possessed little in Cuba, he was comfortable there, wanted to be able to visit his homeland, and eventually planned to return there permanently.

Versalles was reported to have married a 17-year-old childhood friend two weeks before leaving Cuba for that first Twins' spring training in Orlando. He still believed marriage would help ease his anxieties. It was uncertain if Cuban President Fidel Castro would allow native players to travel from the country, let alone allow relatives to leave, and Versalles' wife was still in Cuba. Versalles was not known as personable in those days, and separation from Maria Josefa made him more moody and reclusive during camp, coming and going without a word as he fretted over whether he would ever get his loved ones to the United States.

Issues of visas and other immigration matters were a concern to major league owners in previous winters but always more concern to Griffith because his Senators had many Cuban players on the roster. These included star starting pitchers Pedro Ramos and Camilo Pascual. When nationalist and rebel forces clashed near the culmination of Castro's six-year revolution in 1958, Pascual and other players were caught in a crossfire of bullets during a baseball game. They escaped unharmed, but Griffith learned then the stakes could be quite high, which had not always been the case in Cuba.

American teams had played baseball in Cuba since 1891, and players from the two countries frequently tested their skills against each other. Eventually, international visits generated considerable fan and media interest. After World War II, the Brooklyn Dodgers and New York Yankees even conducted a portion of their spring trainings in Cuba, and relations were such that it seemed international major league play was inevitable. In 1948, the Havana Cubans joined the Class B Florida International League, making it the first Cuban squad to play in the U.S. minor leagues.

Similarly, individual American players had long played in the Cuban Winter League, which thrived for decades on the baseball-crazed island before Castro's overthrow of the government in 1959. When Castro assumed power he declared all sports in the country would be amateur. He failed in his anti-American attempt to make soccer, rather than baseball, the national sport, but in 1960 he decreed the game of baseball would have amateur status. This meant Cuban fans would no longer see American players in their stadiums and Cubans who wanted to earn a living playing baseball were without a country.

Versalles reacted with despair when he did not place among the top three American League shortstops in the 1961 All-Star voting, which was done by fellow players. It was important for him to have their respect. The Twins then learned Versalles was trying to raise money after those All-Star results were reported in July, although fund raising wasn't unusual for him. When Charleston fans had voted Versalles their most popular player and gave him a television set in 1960, he promptly sold it to a teammate to get some cash. But Twins' officials thought Versalles' behavior was different in 1961.

He tried to sell his hi-fi record player in the clubhouse after the All-Star voting. He didn't manage money well and always seemed to need more, but a hi-fi was almost a required possession for Latin players, and Versalles, who loved La Traviata, enjoyed sitting by the record player in the clubhouse singing operatic arias. Something was up.

Joe Cambria was traveling with the team to soothe the shortstop while Griffith's lieutenant, Howard Fox, worked to get Maria Josefa out of Cuba. Some people associated with the Twins later thought she was the best thing that ever happened to him. Fox was arranging her exit from Cuba, but Versalles hadn't seen his wife for four months and decided not to wait. He said he was indebted to Griffith, personally and financially, but after the Fourth of July he left the team.

It's hardly surprising a foreigner longed for home. Young American ballplayers were known to grow homesick. Manager Connie Mack couldn't keep 20-year-old Joe Jackson in Philadelphia back in 1908. A rural South Carolinian with little formal education, Jackson couldn't adjust to the big city. *The Sporting News* reported that Connecticut native Steve Blass, a contemporary of Versalles, was homesick and un-happy in Tennessee during his first year of rookie ball with the Pittsburgh Pirates' organization. He mailed his laundry home to his mother before a local family took the 20-year-old under its wing.

A similar situation awaited Versalles, who was such a fan favorite at the team's five-hour welcoming event to Minnesota in 1961 that teammate Jim Lemon said, "Right now, Zoilo Versalles can't even pronounce Minnesota, but by this time next year he may own it." Lemon's notion about Versalles' spot in the heart of the fans surfaced after Cambria convinced Versalles to return to the Twins.

A Minneapolis investment counselor, who had never met the 20-year-old shortstop, telephoned Versalles' hotel room and invited him to come over and make himself comfortable in his family's 30-room house. The Farrell C. Stiehms lived on Irving Avenue in a very comfortable section of Minneapolis – a nearby Victorian mansion became a tourist attraction after exterior shots of it were used in the 1970's Mary Tyler Moore television show. The Stiehms went to Versalles' hotel room to help him pack. "I'm going to mother him," Mrs. Stiehm threatened, and she had the experience – the couple had 11 children, ages 2 to 18.

When he arrived at the Stiehms' neighborhood youngsters besieged the family's front steps, and soon Versalles was happy. "These people are my new father and mother," Versalles said. "They are great company and make me feel at home here." He was soon diagnosed with an ulcer, and then life began to improve.

Griffith modified the announced $500 fine for jumping the team, which would have been a substantial penalty because Versalles was making around $7,000 annually in 1961. Soon after, Versalles was at the Minneapolis airport to welcome Maria Josefa, who would join him at the Stiehms' home. She thought her husband foolish for jumping the team.

Four years later, his older brother thought the same after the clash with Mele in spring training. It was Lazaro Versalles who eventually convinced his brother he needed to approach Mele after their dugout confrontation in St. Petersburg.

During that 1965 spring training game with the Mets, Mele sent reserve Bill Bethea to shortstop one pitch after Jim Hickman's grounder bounded past Versalles. When Versalles reached the dugout, Mele told him to sit down because "he might learn something." Versalles slammed down his glove and screamed that Mele had embarrassed him in front of the fans and teammates. Versalles then looked at Martin and said he would sit on the bench, but "for Beely," not Mele. Mele responded in bold-faced letters.

"That'll cost you $100."

Versalles shouted back, "Why not make it $200?"

"OK, it's $200."

"Why not make it $300?" Versalles blurted.

"That's what it is," Mele said.

Martin grabbed Versalles and told him to get into the clubhouse. In privacy, Martin said, "You let me down. You disgraced yourself, me as your coach, and the whole team."

Neither Mele nor Martin insisted Versalles should have reached the ball, but both agreed he had not made a good effort. Teammates were publicly non-committal when Versalles sought their support. Privately, some veterans thought Versalles' immaturity had been tolerated by management long enough, and they hoped this signaled a new era.

Martin was livid that Versalles had tried to drive a wedge between him and Mele by saying he would sit on the bench out of respect for Martin, not because Mele ordered him to sit. This was particularly outrageous to Martin because the media kept speculating he would soon replace Mele.

Versalles was earning about $25,000 in '65 when a three-bedroom colonial house in the affluent Minneapolis suburb of Minnetonka sold for about $20,000, but club officials suspected the $300 fine for clashing with Mele would never be levied, as was the case earlier that spring. Versalles had adopted a new look on the field when he snipped the narrow stirrups at the bottom of his blue uniform leggings and sewed extra material to the ends. This left a long, thin strip up each side of his ankle that revealed much of the white, sanitary socks players wore beneath leggings, rather than a small, half-moon of white just above the shoe tops. Some players thought this made their legs look sleek. Petty as it seems now, this irritated baseball management. Versalles had not been fined for doing this, because Griffith figured the shortstop already owed him enough money. Versalles enjoyed spending, whether it was purchasing a couple new cars annually or buying most of the interesting trinkets he saw. A fine would just dump Versalles deeper into the financial abyss.

Versalles was the last man off the team bus when it arrived for a game in Cocoa Beach the day after his bidding war with Mele. Versalles carried his equipment bag, spoke to no one, and passed open cubicles in the visiting clubhouse to dress in the men's room. Earl Battey urged him to apologize, but he would not. Mele started rookie Cesar Tovar at shortstop and insisted Griffith would have to fire him if he did not back him.

In Minneapolis, reporters suggested Mele felt pressure to win and was irritated because Griffith completed only one trade all winter: left-handed pitcher Gerry Arrigo, who threw the Twins' first one-hitter in '64, for untested Tovar. Further, sports writers insisted pulling a player off the field for poor play in spring training was untrammeled ground, but Griffith supported Mele and mitigated the event.

"We had flare-ups in spring training before, but they didn't happen on the field and nobody knew about them." Griffith added that when ballplayers don't respect the manager it is time to get new ballplayers, not a new manager, but even with Versalles batting less than .200 for the spring, Griffith knew his value and had no intention of trading him. Griffith had propped up his shortstop through quite a bit by then, and made sure to mention that Versalles' trade value had plummeted since the incident with Mele. This helped quiet outcry that Versalles be traded. Simply put, Versalles was perhaps the best shortstop in all of baseball, and most championship teams have good shortstops.

Martin tried to flatter Versalles all spring, and he didn't turn his back after the April confrontation with Mele. Martin took Versalles out for a meal, some wine and baseball talk. Cambria had long ago called Versalles a hot cup of coffee, and Martin adopted Cambria's suggested approach: don't light a fire under hot coffee; cool it. The Twins broke camp and headed north to play the Mets in Charlotte, home of Minnesota's top minor league team. Versalles hit his team-high fourth home run of the spring to help the Twins win.

The team charter arrived at the Twin Cities airport just 24 hours later on a rainy Saturday night. The team was greeted by about a thousand fans, even though the flight arrived two hours after its scheduled 8 p.m. arrival. As a band played under the lights and Twins' broadcaster Halsey Hall prepared to introduce the team, Versalles walked down the airplane's stairs onto the tarmac with his three-year-old daughter, insisted to reporters the team would win the pennant, then said, "I know I have some trouble with the manager last week, but it's not like Vietnam."

Still, it wasn't until Lazaro Versalles spoke to Mele at a welcoming luncheon, then to his brother, that it was smoothed over. Like his brother, Lazaro grew up as a ballplayer in Cuba. He understood even if Zoilo was right he had to respect his manager – and Lazaro thought his brother was wrong and must apologize. "Often times a person says things he really doesn't mean in a fit of temper," Lazaro said. "I've played a little ball and I'm a little older than Zoilo. I want him to play for the Twins, and I want the Twins to win."

Versalles later shrugged about the fine and mentioned manager Del Wilber fined him in 1960 while Versalles was playing minor league ball in Charleston. "Maybe I had it coming. I get disgusted when I think I'm right. I'm entitled to my opinion, right or wrong. If the manager fines me for lack of effort or flaunting [SIC] his authority, that's his business. He's entitled to his opinion."

Mele would sometimes try to quiet Versalles' mind by telling him, "Zoilo, let me do the worrying." As the season began, Versalles began to ease Mele's worries by doing things he had never done before, things that would never appear in a box score. In early May the Twins were leading the White Sox 4-3 when Mele brought in left-handed relief pitcher Mel Nelson with two on and none out. Nelson induced a ground out and a short fly out before Smokey Burgess, one of the game's better pinch hitters, came to the plate. Just before Nelson threw a pitch, Versalles moved back three steps and then took a couple steps to his left. Burgess stung Nelson's pitch to the exact spot where Versalles stood. The game was over.

"I saw him change position out of the corner of my eye as the pitch was coming in," Burgess said. "He'd never have made that play from where he was originally."

Versalles said he realized he was out of position and made the adjustment. Billy Martin had taught Versalles well.

The lineup card was constantly an unfinished crossword puzzle to Sam Mele during the chilly, damp, storm-ravaged Minnesota summer of 1965. He lacked enough fingers to count all the injuries to Battey. Offensive stars Oliva, Killebrew and Allison suffered injuries and extended batting slumps. A pitcher who the team considered releasing outright ultimately welded together the pitching staff for weeks. In an era of 25-man rosters, the Twins played the season with essentially 24. The new coaching staff conflicted so badly that pitching coach Johnny Sain moved from the coaches' room to dress with the players. Mele, accused of complacency by Griffith a summer earlier, was suspended and fined for charging an umpire.

In early October, before the World Series started, Mele had time to reflect in the cool of the evening, to enjoy the finishing canter after a fine race. Someone asked him to name his easiest decision of the season. The response was quick.

"Writing Zoilo Versalles' name on the lineup card every day."

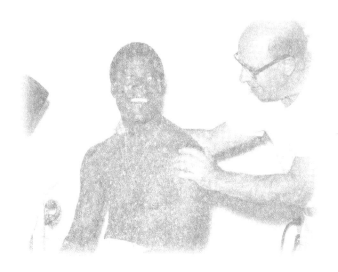

Jim Grant and George Lentz

FOUR

I considered Earl Battey and Lenny Green to be my friends,
but we couldn't stay in the same hotel. – Dick Stigman

The Boston Red Sox were the last major league team to integrate, but the Minnesota Twins were the last to house black and white players in the same hotel during spring training. Orlando's Cherry Plaza Hotel was the club's Florida headquarters. The multi-story building boasted high, wide windows that provided a glorious view of Lake Eola. The hotel's centerpiece was a large water fountain surrounded by extensive, tidy grounds, thick with vibrant flowers. Orlando was such a sleepy Southern town and the Cherry Plaza such a sedate setting that players walked about, chatted, and ate without autograph-seekers approaching them.

The Cherry Plaza served meals on heavy, white dinnerware emblazoned with "CP" inside a black circle. Each time Camilo Pascual ordered room service he kept a cup, bowl, plate, or saucer until he had a complete dinner setting that carried his initials. It was a swanky enough place that Walt Disney chose the Cherry Plaza for a 1965 press conference to announce exciting plans for a large amount of land he purchased in the Orlando area.

Twins infielder Frank Kostro recalled the Cherry Plaza had a pleasant atmosphere and good food, but some thought the rooms were small and modest. Kostro came from a mining family in Pennsylvania and as with many ballplayers of the era found most aspects of big-league life appealing. The Cherry Plaza's rooms were fine for him, but Kostro had some financially secure friends who visited one spring. "I told them the hotel was nice, but they moved out the same day they arrived."

Minnesota Governor Karl Rolvaag was also unimpressed with the Cherry Plaza, but for a more noble reason.

Rolvaag pressured the Twins to leave Orlando and train in a more progressive area that had loosened its grip on segregation, but the franchise had a 10-year contract with the city of Orlando to train at Tinker Field, a contract Griffith said he signed with the understanding that integrated, first-class dining and hotel accommodations would become available in Orlando. Griffith also maintained the organization had tried for several years to integrate its spring training hotel, but the Cherry Plaza would not change its policy. Griffith was adamant about staying there because, laughable as it now seems, he claimed there were only two first-class hotels in Orlando. Neither accepted blacks.

Club officials thought strides were made in 1962, when they persuaded city officials to end segregated seating at Tinker Field. More progress was announced in '63, when all Twins' players rode the same bus and stayed in the same hotel on the road. Previously, the team's black players had traveled to away games in a station wagon.

"Coming from Nimrod, Minnesota," Dick Stigman recalled, "every hotel looked good to me, but I remember the black players couldn't stay with us. There wasn't any resentment from the black players toward us about this. It's the way it was. It's a sad thing now when you think about it. I considered Earl Battey and Lenny Green to be my friends, but we couldn't stay in the same hotel."

Coach Hal Naragon recalled it similarly, and added the players would even joke about the segregated housing arrangement, which did not exist during the regular season. In Orlando, the black players didn't have to suffer bed checks at the Sadler Hotel, as could be the case at the Cherry Plaza. The Twins had no black coaches, so no one was at the Sadler to enforce a curfew. Naragon recalls Battey and Green would tease the white players about this, and the white players would return mock indignation, or kid the black players about having it so good. This coping mechanism had its limits.

Battey spoke of a need to integrate the team's spring hotel head-quarters before 1965, while remaining complimentary about accommodations at the Sadler. Battey maintained the rooms at the Sadler were as good as any he stayed in during the regular season, which of course contrasted with Griffith's opinion about the scarcity of fine lodging in Orlando. "We want this to be no reflection on Henry Sadler's business," Battey said. "The Sadler has a good coffee shop and there are three or four good restaurants for Negroes in Orlando." But Battey and Green wanted the black players to be treated like the white players.

Rolvaag wanted it, too, and appointed a three-member board after a Minnesota commission ordered a public hearing on the matter. The result could have been a court order to change the Cherry Plaza's policy, but by March of '65 the hotel integrated. It was Jim "Mudcat" Grant's first spring with the Twins.

Grant's hometown of Lacoochie was about 60 miles west of the Cherry Plaza, but Grant was not thrilled about spring training in his home state. He had joined the Twins after a 1964 mid-season trade from Cleveland, so he had spent each previous spring in Arizona. Grant encountered little prejudice in Tucson but said he knew the "superior feeling" of the people in Florida. His wife had accompanied him at other spring trainings, but he was reluctant to bring her to the Cherry Plaza. Because he was a ballplayer, Grant was treated fairly well. There were some demeaning incidents, such as the time he stepped into the Cherry Plaza lobby wearing his best suit and a tie only to have a man call, "Hey, boy, are the rooms filled here most of the time?" Grant was vocal about inequality, as Mele learned that spring, and history showed Grant not only refused to turn the other cheek, he could be provocative.

Near the end of the 1960 season with Cleveland, Grant – a scat-singing jazzman with an off-season nightclub act – stood in the bullpen and ad-libbed the final words to the Star Spangled Banner, "This land is not so free; I can't go to Mississippi." Indians' coach Ted Wilks objected. Grant told Wilks, who lived in Texas, that Russia was better than Texas. Wilks made a racial comment that angered Grant. A confrontation was averted, but Grant was so enraged he left the bullpen.

Cleveland manager Jimmy Dykes later called to have the right-hander prepare to enter the game. Dykes supposedly did not know Grant had already dressed in the clubhouse and left the park. Dykes fined and suspended Grant, saying there was no circumstance under which a player should leave the park without permission.

Grant apologized to both Dykes and general manager Frank Lane. Wilks apologized to Grant and pitcher Don Newcombe, who was in the last year of a career in which he became the first man, black or white, to win the Cy Young Award (and if the honor had been accorded in each league in 1965, as was the case starting in '67, Grant would have been the second black man voted the honor). Newcombe accepted the apology, but Grant would not, saying he was "sick of remarks about colored people." Wilks' timing was especially bad. Weeks earlier, Baltimore manager Paul Richards supposedly used a racial slur against Grant when Richards thought Grant was throwing at Oriole third baseman Brooks Robinson. News reports indicated Richards later admitted to the remarks, and Grant conceded he pitched inside to some Oriole batters, but Grant said the common practice of pitching inside hardly warranted racial slurs.

The season was nearly over when the bullpen incident occurred, and some teams might have waited it out and then sent Grant elsewhere in a quiet, holiday trade in late December. Cleveland, however, was the first team in the American League to sign a black player, and Grant had an enjoyable relationship with the club. He worked year-round for the Indians and even after his trade to Minnesota appeared in a public relations capacity for Cleveland. Grant was still on the Cleveland roster the spring after his suspension. Wilks was reassigned to work with minor league pitchers.

As with fans, reporters enjoy an engaging, entertaining personality such as Grant, and some beat writers continue to mine that source even if it has traveled on. The first time reporters approached Mele in the spring of '65 for a response to a controversial remark was after one Minnesota reporter obtained a quote from former Twins' pitcher Pedro Ramos, who was in camp with the Yankees. Ramos was a colorful character with blazing speed who liked to challenge swift position players to match races. At one point in his career, he was unbeaten for more than three seasons. He had the confidence of a Great Dane and liked to stir up the day, such as when he bet former teammate Pascual during the spring of 1965 that the first one to make it to the World Series would win $500 from the other.

As the tedium of spring training took hold in late March, Ramos announced to reporters that teams such as Minnesota have players who "work individually for themselves," and the Yankees won because they played as a team. This came on the heels of the Versalles incident with Mele and just before a Cleveland beat writer telephoned Grant about life with the Twins. Grant was quoted as saying, "I'm not trying to put the rap on Minnesota, but the Twins' organization – and I'm not referring to Sam Mele – is generally concerned about only a couple of players. The rest of us are just around. I'm sure the front office isn't aware of the special treatment, they do it subconsciously. They [Allison and Killebrew] don't ask for it, and don't want it. They are wonderful, fine players, but they get it."

Grant's words did not seem caustic, and in fact a rumor had long circulated that Allison was Griffith's nephew or son-in-law, because some fans thought management was never critical of Allison's play. It was true that Allison and Killebrew were among the players invited to events that Griffith hosted, but it was Allison, Killebrew and others – such as Camilo Pascual and Billy Martin – whom wealthy fans and business people wanted to meet, and even reserve players such as Don Mincher might find themselves at such events. When the Twins took their public relations road show to Alaska before the '65 season, Battey and relief pitcher Bill Dailey joined Killebrew and Allison. None of this made Grant's remarks less controversial.

The Indians were known as a fun club where a star was treated like any other player. Grant thought the same approach would make the Twins a better club. (Even during the franchise's days in Washington there was talk of tension, some racial, and lack of camaraderie in the clubhouse. As was the case with many clubs, there would be similar problems in Minnesota before the '60s ended.)

Mele was not happy when the news of Grant's remarks filtered to Minnesota and Orlando, and Griffith sharply denied Grant's charges. Mele handled it masterfully. He kept out of it. "We had Earl Battey, Camilo, Harmon, and Bob Allison. They took care of whatever problems came up like this," Mele recalled. "Camilo was a tough guy, and he would approach Versalles or Ramos and explain how it was. Everyone respected Harmon and Earl. Bob was six-foot-four, 230, or whatever. You weren't likely to go up against a man like that."

It was reported at the time that Mele spoke with Grant alone and then called a meeting with the three players. Mele and Killebrew recalled the three players resolved the situation themselves. "Bob, Mudcat, and I handled it. I don't recall that Sam had any part of it," Killebrew said. "It became a sore spot and an issue, but we talked it out. Mudcat was a great teammate, and he had a terrific record against us when he played with Cleveland, so it was nice to have him pitching for us. And he liked the fact we scored runs for him. It wasn't a big problem." Forty years later, Allison had passed on, but Killebrew and Grant remained friends.

A sparkling extrovert, Grant owed much of his outlook and personality to his mother. Grant's father had died when Jim was two, which left Viola Grant to rear seven children and accept domestic work in the lumber town of about 1,000 people. Table meat was possum instead of steak, but Viola ensured the family's tattered clothing was always clean, and she had a heavy influence on Jim, who was charming and free-spirited. He had no middle name but wanted one, so when a friend thought Grant looked Irish and suggested Timothy, Grant was amused enough by the Irish remark to take the name.

Grant worked at a lumber camp to help pay bills. He escaped by earning a football scholarship to Florida A&M. A Cleveland scout knew of him from Florida semi-pro baseball leagues, where Grant was an infielder, but the baseball scout lost interest when the young athlete opted for college. Grant became a running back at Florida A&M, but he left the school midway through his sophomore year because of financial constraints. He moved in with an uncle so he could take a job in New

Smyrna, near Daytona Beach, and soon the Cleveland scout learned Grant had left college and tracked down the youngster.

Grant arrived at a tryout camp for hundreds of prospects in Daytona Beach in '54. He carried a borrowed glove and spikes but wore a flashy white sweater. Friends called him "Coochie," for his hometown, but one of the many stories regarding his nickname is that someone thought Grant was from Mississippi and called him "Mississippi Mudcat." That was the end of "Coochie," and after two weeks in camp it was nearly the end of Mudcat. His hitting was a cut below what it would take to make the major leagues as a position player, and the Indians didn't know what to do with him; they just knew he was an athlete and kept him around.

One day they put him on the pitcher's mound, and he struck out a dozen batters in an intra-squad game. The Indians offered him a contract to play in the Northern League at Fargo-Moorhead, where he pitched with his brother, Julius "Swampfire" Grant. Mudcat went 21-5. He didn't reach 20 wins again until 1965.

Grant was the dean of the Indians' staff at 28 and was struggling through a series of bad outings in the middle of the '64 season when Cleveland made him available. The Twins landed him for pitcher Lee Stange, infielder George Banks, and $75,000. It was the most Griffith had paid for a player. The trade immediately solved one of Griffith's problems: Grant was 67-63 in his career, but 26-9 against Griffith's franchise, so just having Grant on his side couldn't hurt. Adding to Grant's appeal was that athletic ability.

Mele was an enthusiastic reader of manager biographies and managerial strategy, and although he foremost wanted pitchers who could pitch, he enjoyed the luxury of having pitchers who could handle a bat. There was no designated hitter, and many starting middle infielders were weak hitters, which made runs dear. Managers occasionally asked some pitchers to pinch hit and pinch run. The Twins were deep in such athletic pitchers. Pascual, Grant, and switch-hitting Jim Perry were among the better hitting pitchers in the league. Pascual was the best of the lot.

He had played infield almost exclusively as a youngster and dreamed of making it to the big leagues as a shortstop. Pascual loved to hit and run the bases, but Joe Cambria told him his best chance to make the big leagues was as a pitcher. He put the ball in play often for a pitcher, drove in 80 runs in his career, and was named Cuba's outstanding athlete of 1959. When Pascual won 20 games for the first time in 1962, Mele said if Pascual was trailing by no more than two runs after the seventh inning he would not remove him for a pinch hitter. "He was often better than the guys I had on the bench," Mele recalled, "but Calvin would still kid me that Camilo must be related for me to leave him in there like that."

Rookie pitcher Dave Boswell, who hit .316 in '65, joined Pascual, Perry, Grant and Kaat to give Mele one more small edge. It wasn't a given Mele would send in a pinch hitter for them if their turn in the lineup arrived in a close game. Mele was confident enough to hit-and-run with Pascual, and he used Kaat as a pinch hitter three times in '65.

In addition to those many athletic pitchers, the 1965 Twins' staff had two other welcome ingredients: an experienced core staff, and a great coach.

Former Dodger general manager Branch Rickey, one of the game's better judges of baseball talent, said a man didn't really learn to pitch until he neared 30, and one look at Minnesota's roster of hitting pitchers would have brought a grin to Rickey's face. The trade for Grant meant the Twins entered the '65 season with Pascual at age 31; Grant at 29; Perry, 28; and Kaat, 25. Kaat was considered a student of the game and wise beyond his years. Perhaps more importantly, the Twins had pitching coach John Sain, a man who said he didn't learn to pitch until he neared 30. Sain's impact on pitching staffs was such that New York Yankee third baseman Clete Boyer was standing around the batting cage before a series with the Twins in August and wondered aloud to reporters, "When you vote for the manager of the year in the American League, whose name you going to write in? Sain?" Boyer knew Sain's value.

As with many of the Twins, the six-foot-two, white-maned Sain was a Havana native – Havana, Arkansas. He was the Yankees' pitching coach when the franchise won three straight pennants starting in 1961. After Yogi Berra was named Yankee manager in 1964, Sain said he didn't think his former teammate had the temperament to become the manager of men who had been his teammates, so Sain priced himself out of a job during contract negotiations. Even Billy Martin, who eventually clashed with Sain in Minnesota, said Berra would "have to be mean at times, and I don't know if he can do it." Berra lasted one season. Yankee pitchers circulated a petition to bring Sain back when the team struggled in the middle of that '64 season. Whitey Ford was both pitcher and pitching coach that year, but Ford felt the call for Sain was no knock on him. Nothing came of the petition, but Ford was among those who signed, and with good reason: in 1960, the Yankees thought Ford would be better off with more rest. Ford went 12-9, his worst season in which he started at least 20 games. An advocate of a four-man pitching rotation, Sain arrived in New York and made sure Ford got the ball every four days. He went 25-4 in '61, and won 66 games in three seasons under Sain.

Sain was also an advocate of positive thinking. His pitchers would routinely comment that even if they had the worst outing of their careers, Sain would find something positive to say about their performances, even if it was something as seemingly trivial as fielding a bunt well or holding runners on base. Ford had a particularly bad outing one day and sat by his locker with his head down. Sain gave him some kind words and left Ford sitting there with the often heard, "The sun will be up tomorrow." Ford laughed when he awoke the next day. It was raining.

Sain was 46 and in demand as a coach when Griffith lured him from his business ventures during the winter of 1964 for the relatively high sum of $25,000. Sain was in a position to call his own shots, because he had business interests outside of baseball. His independence carried into the game. Sain felt a pitching staff belonged to him, and he protected his pitchers and implemented his own program. It was easy to see why managers would perceive Sain as too independent, or even difficult, but pitchers did not view him that way. Sain was called a psychologist, as much as a pitching coach, and he maintained a coach could do nothing by himself. Sain believed it was the player who had to piece together his own game and believe in his ability. There was nothing unilateral about working with John Sain, and he maintained that he learned as much from the pitchers as they learned from him. He tried to analyze each pitcher's abilities and envision how he would pitch if he were that man.

Jim Kaat, who had one of the longer careers in major league history, reflected that Sain had a unique approach compared to other pitching coaches he knew. "So many guys were successful as pitchers, and they would come in as a pitching coach and mean well, but they had one way of doing things. There was no one like John. He didn't have a particular style or method. He would suggest something to me and something different to Camilo or Jim Merritt." Catcher John Sevcik compared Sain to a good golf instructor. "He'd look at what a guy had and try to figure out how to improve that. John would work with a pitcher's strengths, rather than try to get the guy to do it his way."

The downside was most managers felt that Sain gathered a team's pitchers under him in what was essentially an exclusive club. Pitchers, by nature, tend to band together, and Sain preferred that managers not meddle with his program. This created what many managers perceived to be a team within a team and a group they could not reach.

With hands in his back pockets, Sain would stroll in the outfield among the pitchers during batting practice, when pitchers typically run in the outfield or chase fly balls. He would pause here and there, asking and answering questions. He was the opposite of someone such as Martin, the extrovert, and Sain didn't push advice unless approached. He involved himself with position players only when invited. Martin would not hesitate to advise a pitcher, despite the fact this was not part of his job with the Twins during that championship season. It wasn't until the '70s, when Sain was with the White Sox, that a manager devised a way to involve Sain more deeply with the entire club: Chicago manager Chuck Tanner made it one of Sain's jobs to hit balls to players in pregame drills, which suggested to Sain the entire team was part of his responsibility.

Pitchers were so fond of Sain that the Yankees' Jim Bouton and the Twins' Al Worthington said he was the best pitching coach ever, and Kaat caused a furor when the Twins fired Sain after the 1966 season.

Kaat told Mele it was nothing personal, then wrote a letter to a newspaper and ripped the Twins for firing Sain, specifying the move was the equivalent of the Green Bay Packers firing Vince Lombardi. Considering the source, this was very high praise. Kaat branched into business ventures in his 20s, became a pitching coach when he ended a playing career that spanned four decades, and eventually grew into one of the nation's more insightful baseball broadcasters.

After Sain joined Detroit for the 1967 season, Tigers' 20-game winner Denny McLain said he did not know Sain but insisted he must be a great pitching coach if Kaat went so far as to publicly defend Sain. "Kaat's not the type of guy to pop off." Under Sain, McLain won 31 games. No one has done it since.

Among the pitchers who had their best seasons under Sain were Grant, Ford, McLain, Bouton, Earl Wilson and Wilbur Wood. Kaat had all his winningest seasons under Sain. After winning 25 games with Sain as his coach in '66, Kaat later reached 20 wins in consecutive seasons with the White Sox while Sain was there. Sain was pitching coach for five pennant-winning organizations, and his theories affected major league teams decades after he retired from coaching. Leo Mazzone, pitching coach of the Atlanta Braves during their long reign of post-season appearances that started in 1991, called Sain his "guru." Mazzone applied Sain's theories to the Braves' pitching staff, which was as formidable as any staff of that era. John Sain understood pitchers – and life as a pitcher.

After being released by numerous low-rung minor league clubs, Sain debuted with the Boston Braves in '42, missed three years to World War II, and emerged from military service to win at least 20 games for three straight seasons. He won 20 games four times in an 11-year major league career, and if even a small percentage of pitchers handled a bat the way Sain did, there would never have been a designated hitter rule. Sain was a career .245 hitter who not only hit over .345 twice, he did something remarkable at the plate: he almost never drew a walk and almost never struck out. John Sain put the ball in play. In 1946 he batted 104 times without walking or striking out. In his career, Sain had 856 plate appearances, walked 24 times and struck out 20. Hall of Fame second baseman Nelson Fox was one of the better contact hitters in the history of the game. Fox always struck out fewer than 20 times in full seasons, even if he had 650 or so plate appearances, but even Fox had to admire Sain's ability to put the ball in play. It is, however, pitching for which Sain is remembered as a player.

With the Boston Braves, Sain was part of baseball's most famous short rhyme: "Spahn and Sain, and pray for rain." It was the Boston fans' mantra for the '48 season as the pitching-shallow club successfully rushed toward its first pennant in more than 30 years. But eventual Hall of Famer Warren Spahn won just 15 games that season while Sain led the National League with 314 innings pitched, 39 starts, 28 complete games and 24 wins. That was long before free agency, when players struggled to get a couple extra thousand dollars from a club. Sain was unhappy with his contract all season, and midway through it did something unconventional. He told the Braves' general manager he wasn't pitching any more unless the club wrote a new contract. Club officials were flabbergasted, but they ripped up his contract and wrote a new one.

Sain was unconventional as a pitching coach as well. He advocated a throwing program that involved frequent work at low throttle – about 40 pitches on a warm day – very little running, and not talking to reporters about any new pitch a man was developing. Most pitching coaches asked pitchers to jog and run sprints with the idea strong legs are the foundation of pitching. Sain thought coaches asked pitchers to run because they didn't have much of anything to tell them about pitching.

He believed frequent throwing strengthened both the legs and the arm, so there was little need to run if a man didn't want to. In spring training, pitching coaches might tell reporters about a pitcher who was developing a new pitch, which implied the coach was earning his money by teaching and strategizing. Sain wouldn't broach the topic of new pitches and suggested his pitchers follow that lead. Why give the hitter an edge and tell everyone? Let the hitter find out for himself. He criticized the habit of promoting young pitchers with limited experience from the minor leagues and expecting them "to develop into big winners at 23." Sain thought younger pitchers were less likely to accept coaching advice or adjust quickly to major league hitters. He was an innovative thinker in many other ways.

Sain instituted the practice of charting pitches in Minnesota – the type of pitch thrown, its location, and what the hitter did with it. All teams now chart each pitch thrown in a game. Sain correctly predicted in the early '60s that it would become typical to see three pitchers in each game. Even though Sain worked hard to become a nine-inning pitcher during his career, he concluded throwing nine innings not only put a terrific strain on a man's arm, but the more times a hitter faced a pitcher in a single game the more likely it was for a hitter to be successful. A hitter's job would be far more difficult, he said, if the hitter had to face a starter, middle reliever, and closer, each of them fresh, and each with naturally different pitching styles. In addition, Sain said it was easier for a pitcher to bounce back from just a couple innings of work rather than eight or nine.

Sain inherited an engineer's thought process from his father, an automobile mechanic. He learned to fly airplanes with Ted Williams during World War II, owned a plane, and applied this mechanical inquisitiveness to flying and pitching. He was fascinated with how spin affected a baseball, studied the ballistics of pitching, and tried to convey this information to pitchers in the form of suggestions, not commands. He even developed a device that players called a "spinner," which served as a visual aid while he presented his theories. The device was a baseball pierced by a dowel that allowed him to spin the baseball different ways. This information was perfect for Mudcat Grant, who mainly threw a fastball.

Grant had an uncommon, no-windup motion that became the norm in the '90s. It was a herky-jerky delivery that began with the ball in his glove in front of him, a downward pump, and then a second pump as he twisted to his right and pulled the ball from glove to throw. Early Wynn, his pitching coach in Cleveland, tried to smooth that delivery, but Grant struggled. He didn't blame Wynn for suggesting the adjustment; Grant said he just couldn't make the change and returned to his old motion. Then he met Sain. What Sain gave Grant was not a new delivery but his theories on spinning a baseball, and Grant suffered greatly learning these theories.

Sain had plenty of time to spend with Grant early in training camp because Pascual and Kaat both held out for better contracts. Sain began to teach Grant a "fast curve," a pitch thrown with a loose wrist that was harder than a sweeping overhand curve but resulted in a bigger break than a slider. The ball had movement, but it caught more of the strike zone than an overhand curve because it moved diagonally through the zone. Kaat recalled there wasn't any particular magic to it, and each pitcher might grip the ball a little differently, depending on what worked with the man's delivery.

Grant pitched six shutout innings in his first two spring outings and then started to throw the fast curve in game situations. He was hammered repeatedly, and Mele told the press he was concerned. In reality, Mele knew established pitchers often experiment in the spring because these veterans are guaranteed to go north with the team, so the words were just for the newspapers. The words were easy to buy: at one point Grant allowed 29 hits and 14 runs in 21 innings. Then the team broke camp, and Grant soon began to thrive in Sain's four-man rotation, an arrangement long misunderstood.

There was an era in baseball when most teams' top pitchers were theoretically scheduled to pitch after three days' rest, but even when this four-man pitching rotation was common, some teams did not advocate it, and today the format has been replaced by a rotation of five pitchers. However, five starters have long been necessary because, unlike today, baseball teams once played frequent doubleheaders. A four-man rotation was not practical when doubleheaders piled up. There were also 24 scheduled days off in 1965, compared with the 20 built into today's schedules, and there was only one domed stadium. Between the days off and rainouts, it was a rare pitcher who religiously started on three days' rest through the entire season. Grant and Kaat carried a heavy pitching load for the '65 Twins, but each enjoyed at least four days' rest before a start at least a dozen times, so pitching on three days' rest was not a season-long routine.

On the other hand, pitchers were not coddled. If a starter was battered early and departed, a manager might start him again in a couple days. Grant had an outing in which he didn't last an inning and was back on the mound two days later to start the second game of a double-header. It was also common for Kaat to ask for the ball in a couple days if he was blown out of a game early. Still, with no designated hitter in 1965 and a plethora of weak-hitting middle infielders and reserve out-fielders, pitchers could also afford to challenge more batters, rather than nibble at the corners. After all, it's not the number of innings pitched that tires a man's arm, it's the number of pitches thrown. Early in the '65 season, Grant wasn't throwing enough, and that also affected his performance.

Trench coat spring weather, coupled with frequent scheduled days off in April, placed Kaat in the odd position of starting two of the Twins' first three games, yet he had four days' rest between starts because the club's first three games spanned nearly a week. It was no strain on Kaat, but it left the other starters idle. Grant had not pitched for more than a week, and the weather made it difficult to throw in the bullpen. He lasted only three innings in his first regular-season start. He didn't get out of the first inning five days later. The Twins won both of Grant's starts, however, and then headed to Chicago, where criticism greeted them.

A Chicago reporter ripped the Twins' fielding, claiming reserve first baseman Don Mincher, a powerful hitter, couldn't break into the lineup because he was so poor defensively. The reporter had written that a pitcher like Grant had no business starting a game against the White Sox, one of the favorites to win the American League pennant. Grant had struggled badly in his career against the White Sox, going 3-16 against them as a Cleveland Indian. Billy Martin presented the article to Grant before the game.

"I won't say the article pitched a three-hitter for me," Grant said, as he and the Twins ended April with a 7-0 shellacking of the White Sox, "because I felt I was about ready to win one anyway. But I think something like that prods you to a little greater effort."

It was already the second shutout by a Twins' pitcher in 1965, after the staff managed only four shutouts during the entire 1964 season, and it was the first of Grant's six league-leading shutouts. He had nine in seven previous seasons. The Chicago reporter apologized to Grant after that game, which was wise: in Grant's first 27 innings against the White Sox in 1965, he allowed 14 hits and a run. Grant went 21-7 in 41 games in 1965 and twice appeared in relief.

The Twins were assaulted with injuries as July ended, but after the All-Star Game in mid-July there was a stretch when Grant took the mound every four days and won each time out. He was 10-3 after he won on Thursday, July 22. Four days later he beat Baltimore as the Twins gained a four-and-a-half game lead over the league. Grant got his third win in nine days when he beat Baltimore the second time in a week – and beating the same team in a week is always a difficult task for a pitcher. Grant developed tendonitis in both knees, kept taking his turn in the rotation, but altered his delivery to take pressure off the joints. It didn't affect him, as he improved to 13-3 in his next turn, then followed that outing with his fourth win over Boston that season. Grant won five times in 17 days.

Grant was clearly a different pitcher after going 34-37 the previous three seasons, but he claimed otherwise. He maintained there was no "new Jim Grant" and said he just had a good offense behind him, which seemed believable on the surface. He had reeled off four straight wins after arriving in Minnesota the previous summer but was as lucky as he was good. He had a shutout in which he allowed 13 hits, and in those four wins the Twins averaged nine runs and 15 hits a game. The Twins weren't often scoring that well for him in 1965, yet everyone but Grant insisted he was a different pitcher. He beat Chicago 4-1 in early May, and Sox third baseman Pete Ward wondered where Grant's high fastball had gone. "He used to challenge you with high fastballs. Now he's got a good sinker, slider, curve, change of speed." White Sox first baseman Moose Skowron said he saw only one fastball all day, and Grant's former catcher in Cleveland, John Romano, said, "This isn't the Grant I used to catch. He never had a curve when I caught him."

Grant said he never thought about spinning the ball until he met Sain. Suddenly, Grant had a curve ball that was breaking low, not up by the shoulder like an overhand curve, and this made it harder for the hitter to pick up the ball. Sain shrugged off public compliments from Grant. Mele praised Grant for sticking with Sain's new pitches in spring training. "He went out to learn something and stayed with it. A lot of guys might have dropped it when they weren't getting the batters out, but Grant worked hard and stayed with it."

Sain's positive effect could have been categorized as coincidence if Grant had been the only pitcher to improve, but a pitching staff that was considered suspect during spring training began to surge under Sain. The team earned run average at the All-Star break was a full run lower than in '64. As that All-Star break approached, White Sox manager Al Lopez said the Twins' fate hinged on their pitching, which he noted was the same group of pitchers as last year "but it's better pitching so far."

Sain's personal reclamation project was Jim Perry, who was a teammate of Grant in Cleveland until he joined the Twins in the middle of the '63 season. The older brother of future Hall of Famer Gaylord Perry, Jim was a crew-cut, six-foot-four right-hander who won 18 games in '60 before his production fell to the point that the Twins didn't know how to get rid of him in the spring of '65. There was talk of trading Perry, selling him, demoting him, waiving him, or releasing him outright. Sain had liked Perry's arm and mental makeup when Sain coached the Yankees, and he often thought Perry just needed more rotation on his pitches. Sain convinced Griffith to keep Perry despite the fact that in the entire 1964 season the North Carolina native started one game for Minnesota, failed to complete the first inning, and pitched a career-low 65 innings.

There was weekly chatter about getting rid of Perry from the start of the 1965 spring training, followed by a reason to keep him around a bit longer. It was clear there were separate factions on the topic of Jim Perry.

Late in spring training, Hal Naragon and Sain were working with Perry when team vice-president Joe Haynes wandered over and pulled them aside. Haynes indicated Houston had expressed an interest in Perry. Haynes wanted an opinion from the pair. Sain liked the expression "down the road," and told Haynes, "I think we ought to hang on to him because we might need him down the road, and if it turns out we don't, by then he might have a little more trade value." The three watched Perry as they talked, and it was clear to Haynes, a former major-league pitcher who was regarded as a keen judge of talent, that Perry had made progress with all his hard work. Sain's assessment made sense. The trade talk ended.

Perry was aware of the trade talk, and it should have seemed like he was observing his funeral, but Perry kept the tombstones out of his eyes and his head down and worked. He later said rumors of the team moving him bothered his wife and friends more than it bothered him.

Perry established himself as the Twins' most reliable long-relief man in June, just about the time the bullpen became a huge asset. Perry was instrumental in the bullpen's reliability, and he soon stepped in to prop up the starting staff.

Pascual was struggling by late June despite an unbeaten record, and he went on the disabled list in July with a torn back muscle. Kaat missed a turn with a muscle strain. The Twins had already installed promising rookie Dave Boswell in the rotation, but he would soon develop tonsillitis, then mononucleosis. In a gamble to refresh a wilting staff, Mele started relief pitchers Bill Pleis and Mel Nelson. Pleis was a very effective left-handed relief pitcher who hadn't started a game in two years and Nelson was a converted outfielder with control problems who ended the season 0-4 on a club that won 102 games. Pleis and Nelson struggled in their starts, going a combined six innings. Perry came out of the bullpen to pitch three innings of effective relief each time.

Jim Perry was 4-0 in relief and difficult to ignore as July began. The club would face six draining doubleheaders in a 23-day span. Perry hadn't completed a start for two years, and his longest outing of the summer was not quite six innings – which was still nearly twice as many innings as he pitched the first six weeks of the season. Because his game outings were brief early in the season, Perry kept working alone on the sidelines and working with Sain.

Mele finally started Perry on July 5 in the second game of a double-header. Only one runner reached third base as Perry threw a seven-hit shutout to keep his club in first by a game and a half. Perry beat the Yankees 4-1 on four hits in eight innings five days later. On his next turn, he won 5-2 against the California Angels, one of two teams to play at least .500 ball against the Twins in '65. In Perry's first four starts he allowed three earned runs in a little less than 34 innings. Perry said from the start of spring training he went to the bullpen and "threw and threw and threw," even though it was always to a catcher without a batter in front of him. He figured he'd get a chance one day, and wanted to be ready when it happened.

Starting Perry did weaken the bullpen. Perry, Worthington, and Klippstein were 13-6 in the team's first 72 games, so the trio had more than a quarter of the team's decisions. But the club needed another starting pitcher to carry the game to the bullpen, and Perry did. He finished the season behind only Grant and Kaat in wins, going 12-7 with a 2.63 earned run average yet didn't become a full-time starter again until Martin took over as manager in '69.

One of Martin's first managerial moves was to install Perry in the rotation, which was ironic because in '65 Martin was one of the people who thought Perry couldn't help the team. Martin thought Perry was not a competitor and didn't have the stomach for pitching because he was always nibbling at the corners rather than challenging hitters with fastballs and throwing inside. It was a matter of personalities. Martin was a hard drinker who was always in the face of his competitors. Perry didn't drink or smoke and was considered a gentleman. Before he became Perry's manager, Martin didn't seem to understand the competition, the challenge, for Perry was to hit his spot on the corner with a slider, rather than pop fastballs past hitters. And Perry could hit his spots.

If pinpoint control exists for a pitcher, Perry had it. He pitched nearly 3,300 innings in the big leagues and walked fewer than 1,000 batters. When Martin eventually became the Twins' manager, he realized he needed Perry pinching those corners. Perry won 20 games in

1969 and a league-leading 24 games in 1970. He had never been a head-hunter, someone who threw under a man's chin, but as his career developed he was more inclined to pitch inside if a batter seemed to be digging in a little too deep in the batter's box.

Jim retired in 1975, and by the time Gaylord retired in 1983, each Perry brother had won a Cy Young Award. At the time of Gaylord's retirement, their 529 victories made them the winningest brother pitching combination in the game's history.

Sain claimed he never had a pitching staff like the '65 Twins, where at some point every man stepped up and contributed. And he said no man worked harder on that hard-working staff than Perry, who used Sain's mechanical mind to his advantage.

Relief pitcher Garry Roggenburk later said Sain devoted considerable time to every member of the pitching staff, not just the team's front-line pitchers, and of course that democratic approach to the staff made each pitcher Sain's ally. Veteran John Klippstein was enjoying a wonderful season under Sain and maintained Sain was not only a great teacher, "but he sticks up for the pitchers through thick and thin." That habit led to a vocal showdown between Sain and Martin in Kansas City, an altercation that was the first step down the road to Sain's departure from the Twins.

The Twins were playing a Fourth of July game in Kansas City the day before Perry's first start. Pascual couldn't finish the third inning – after starting 8-0 he failed to exceed four innings in each of his next four starts. Jerry Fosnow replaced him in the scoreless game, and Kansas City's Ed Charles greeted him by tripling in a run. Jerry Zimmerman was behind the plate for Minnesota with the Twins now trailing 1-0. Zimmerman anticipated a squeeze play, with Charles heading for home on the pitch and batter Mike Hershberger bunting. Zimmerman called for a pitchout, guessing correctly, but Fosnow threw the ball too low and too close to the plate, rather than high and outside the strike zone. Hershberger laid down the bunt and Charles scored. The inning ended with the Twins trailing 2-0. When Fosnow reached the bench, Martin barked to no one in particular that mistakes such as that could cost a team the pennant.

"Martin, it just isn't that easy," Sain announced. Martin glared. The pair knew an argument in front of the players was bad form, so they cooled slightly and went at it in private after the game, with Martin telling Sain never to show him up, and Sain telling Martin to lay off his pitchers. Sain thought Mele should have supported him. Mele was a more of a big-picture man who considered long-term results, and the long-term result of the '65 season was that the Twins won the pennant.

Sain moved his equipment from the coaches' room and dressed with the players the rest of the season. Mele privately suggested to Martin that he stick to coaching base runners and infielders, which did not sit well with Martin, who was sometimes a rattling link in the chain of command. But Martin understood where he was in the chain. Second baseman Jerry Kindall recalled, "I don't think Billy ever crossed Sam, but when he didn't agree with Sam it must have taken Bill a great deal of patience."

Sain and Martin had been teammates with the Yankees in the early '50s and were never the best of friends, but it is easy to understand how even coaches are affected in a pennant race. Neither the manager nor the coaches can hit, pitch, or field for the players, but at least the manager usually has the last word. For six months, all Martin and Sain could do was hope, cajole, coach, and teach. The All-Star break was nearing when Martin and Sain clashed, but with six Twins named to the American League squad and the All-Star Game scheduled to be played at Metropolitan Stadium, the respite was diluted. In fact, the All-Star Game was played on a Tuesday, and all the Twins except those named to the All-Star team participated in a Monday morning workout at the Met.

The two coaches had confidence in the team, but both saw the injuries mount, and injuries could grease the brass ring and cause it to slip from everyone's grasp. Killebrew would soon be lost, but even opposing managers believed that wouldn't sink the Twins. Senators' manager Gil Hodges pinpointed the Twins' mooring when he said the team could survive an injury to Killebrew, because the offense could still produce runs without him, but Hodges said the Twins were done if Versalles went down. It was clearly Martin's job to keep the shortstop on his MVP path. White Sox manager Al Lopez had already underscored the importance of the Twins' pitching, which was mainly Sain's responsibility. Certainly, there were now expectations on both Sain and Martin.

After their confrontation, Sain had issues with Martin but survived through the '66 season. Bullpen coach Hal Naragon tried to act as mediator, according to player accounts, and got caught in the middle. Eventually, both Sain and Naragon grew further away from Sam Mele. Naragon was once Mele's golfing partner and right-hand man – Mele chose Naragon to run the team when Mele was suspended for charging an umpire a few days after the All-Star break.

Naragon had worked for the Griffith organization for eight years, but after the '66 season he and Sain were released, and both immediately signed with the Detroit Tigers. Griffith was a fan of Sain and did not want to let him go to Detroit. Mele demanded it, insisting Sain no longer communicated with him. Griffith could have fired Mele, but that would essentially mean Sain would have to approve any manager Griffith hired. If Griffith did allow Sain to approve a new manager, the man might want to bring in his own coaches anyway, which could mean both Martin and Sain would depart, and Griffith was certainly grooming Martin as the Twins' future manager. Griffith had little choice.

"Sam did a good job with that team, and it was tough on Sam the way the coaching situation turned out," Naragon would say later. "I know John and Billy had many conversations after that, so it wasn't like they didn't talk, but things just kind of came between us all."

Bob Allison called a meeting after Sain and Martin argued. The Twins congregated at the players-only gathering in a hotel room and discussed the caliber of talent on the team. They treated the difficulties between Sain and Martin not as a distraction but as something over which they had no control. They decided the controversy was not going to affect their play or their chance at a World Series appearance and post-season checks.

"The players were not caught up in all of this," Rollins recalled. "We just decided to throw all that stuff out the window. We knew we had a lot of talent and decided to just go out and keep playing the way we had."

Despite the coaching friction, which didn't become public knowledge until after the '66 season, the Twins prevailed to win the 1965 American League pennant, an example of how personalities of talented, determined people don't always need to mesh for success to occur. A clash between Martin and Sain, both strong-willed, territorial men, seemed inevitable, but peace would have reigned a little longer if Martin had kept quiet on July 4 in Kansas City after Fosnow's mistake. Martin's outburst proved to be unnecessary.

Oliva hit a three-run homer in the sixth, and Killebrew added a two-run shot in the ninth. Klippstein pitched perfect ball for four innings, striking out five. The Twins won, 5-2.

Jim Kaat

FIVE

I tell you, when I see that later in the paper, 'Pascual traded for a dozen bats,' I hung my head, I'm so embarrassed. – Camilo Pascual

Weather was the worst part of the 1965 baseball season in Minnesota. Rain hummed endlessly. Nearly 40 inches of precipitation made it the second-wettest year in the Twin Cities since 1891. Strangling rain and spring snowmelt collaborated to make the state a disaster area in April. Minnesota Governor Karl Rolvaag wore his navy blue Twins baseball cap with that overlapping red and white TC logo as he inspected flood damage around the metropolitan area the morning of opening day.

Fans had just endured the state's coldest March since the turn of the century and would soon be treated to the state's coldest September in almost 100 years. Tornadoes in May and June caused $131 million in property damage. Then there was the petty aggravation of the clocks. Saint Paul went on daylight savings time while Minneapolis remained on standard time, leading residents to claim a Minnesotan was someone with snow in the driveway, water in the basement, no roof on the house, and no way to tell you what time it was.

Twins' officials were concerned about the drop in 1964 attendance, and the weather was now conspiring against them. The team usually drew well on the road, but that was not where the money was. The team needed to draw well in Minnesota, and just preparing the stadium and field for the 1965 season was going to be a chore.

Pipes had frozen during the winter at Metropolitan Stadium, so crews repaired plumbing in restrooms as opening day approached. Other workers cleared snow and ice from tunnels beneath the stadium, sometimes using pickaxes to break apart the ice. They shoveled mud from the concourse, plowed the parking lot, and used flamethrowers to burn rye grass off the dirt portion of the infield. A 10-inch snowfall, just days after a bigger St. Patrick's Day blizzard, coated the field, then the cycle of daytime thaw and nighttime freeze left ankle-deep snow beneath a thin layer of ice. Ten days before opening day, each step brought a crunch as the ice gave way and boots sank into the powder beneath; it was like walking on a field of white creme brulee. Workers cleared three feet of snow from the windward side of the field and accelerated the ice melt on the playing surface by spreading black dirt over the snow and hoping for sunshine. The snow would melt five times faster if it absorbed rays from the sleepy sun that squinted rather than glared.

It was a baseball stadium where football games were played, so the Minnesota Vikings required portable stands that left their evidence in the turf. Ground crews patched the scars, constructed the pitching mound and painted over the football yard lines that were still on the field from the previous autumn's National Football League games.

Morning dawned on the season-opener, and Jim Kaat had to locate a helicopter so he could pitch against the Yankees. The spring thaw had caused flooding of the Mississippi and rivers south of Minneapolis – where Metropolitan Stadium stood. This left the ballpark inaccessible from some directions. Kaat, Rollins, Dick Stigman, and Bill Bethea spent the night before the opener south of the ball yard in an apartment complex that stood on high ground in the suburb of Burnsville, which was largely undeveloped land with rudimentary infrastructure. The players found themselves essentially stranded on an island. They had missed a welcome-home dinner the previous night, and the travel situation was no better in the light of opening day. Kaat and Rollins were scheduled to be in the starting lineup, and Bethea had to catch a plane at the airport to fly to his minor league assignment. The players left for Met Stadium and drove into congested traffic, so Kaat left the car and walked toward the source of the problem, which hit him like a month's worth of bad news: the bridge was flooded.

"I was saying to myself, 'I'm supposed to pitch today. What am I going to do?' " Kaat recalled. He thought about the situation on his walk back to the car and decided to return home to call Paul Giel at WCCO radio station. The Winona, Minnesota, native and former Minnesota Gopher football star was a teammate of Kaat's toward the end of Giel's modest professional baseball career. Giel now worked for the high-profile Minneapolis radio station, and Kaat knew the station had rented a helicopter for its news coverage of the flooding. Arrangements were made for the helicopter to airlift the players to the game. They boarded the chopper by twos in a schoolyard, flew to the stadium parking lot, and were on the field late in the morning, little more than two hours before game time.

Mele originally named Pascual to start his third-straight opening day. He had won at least 20 games in 1962 and 1963 before dropping to 15 wins in 1964. Unsure about a move of Allison to left field and Killebrew to first base, Minnesota fans and media were pinning considerable hope on the dapper 31-year-old, who combed his thick, black hair straight back and always seemed to dress sportily in casual sweaters.

The right-hander had pitched well in Florida but never more than six innings in any of his outings. He experienced arm soreness as camp ended. Kaat stepped in for the prestigious opening day start.

Pascual and Kaat each had contract disagreements with Griffith during the winter and held out the first part of camp, which meant a late start for each. Pascual had grown accustomed to these delays – this was his third salary holdout in four seasons. It was a successful negotiation tactic for him. Pascual was the team's highest-paid pitcher at $46,500 in '64, but his record fell from 21-9 with a 2.47 earned run average in 1963 to 15-12, 3.30 in '64. Griffith considered him to be a culprit in the Twins' poor showing and expected him to take a pay cut for '65. Pascual argued he had led the league in strikeouts three of the four previous seasons, and although he did not lead in '64, he recorded his second-highest strikeout total since the team moved to Minnesota. Pascual also argued, correctly, that the bullpen lost four of his leads, and seven of his defeats could be traced to unearned runs allowed by the team's poor fielding. He had pitched better than his record, allowing two or fewer runs in 16 games, but he walked off the mound having won just eight of those.

Like most owners of major league franchises, Griffith was a notoriously hard-line negotiator who had another list, this one filled with reasons why Pascual should take a pay cut – the typical result when a player's most visible statistics, such as won-lost record, tumbled in the era before free agency. Lesser known was that Griffith had his generous side. In '56, Pascual lost 18 games, yet Griffith thought Pascual had pitched better than his record and gave him a $1,000 raise, something Griffith had never done for a pitcher with so many defeats. Pascual eventually avoided a pay cut in '65 and settled for the same salary he earned in '64, but it turned out Griffith guessed right on the trend of Pascual's career. Pascual was still a very capable pitcher when healthy, but he pitched seven more seasons after 1964 and never again won 15 games in a season. Kaat was another story.

Five years younger than Pascual, Kaat's best days were ahead of him, and certainly his league-leading 25 wins in 1966, still the club record, would have gained him a Cy Young Award that season The honor was instituted in 1956 to designate the game's best pitcher. Unfortunately for Kaat, as was the case with Grant in '65, it wasn't until '67 that dual awards were presented, one for the best pitcher in each league. This meant in successive seasons before 1967, two Minnesota pitchers lost the honor to Los Angeles' Sandy Koufax. Kaat would later say he had no ill feelings about this. The lay of the land was there was just one award, and if it came down to Koufax or Kaat, the award was certainly going to Koufax, whom Kaat praised as the far superior talent. But Koufax's career was a sprint and Kaat's a marathon. Kaat played 25 seasons to Koufax's 12 and won nearly 120 more games. Kaat still holds the Twins' record for career wins and is argued to be one of the better pitchers not in the National Baseball Hall of Fame.

Kaat was justified in his first battle against Griffith for more money in '65. He sought to nearly double his salary to $30,000 and eventually settled for about $4,000 less. He was a bright, hard-working left-hander – despite holding out in 1965 he threw for 30 minutes daily at Rollins College near the Twins' spring headquarters in Orlando.

He reached his full physical stature slowly in Zeeland, Michigan, about three hours' west of Detroit. Townsfolk knew Kaat loved baseball. They would comment it was a shame Jimmy was so small. Kaat's idol was Bobby Shantz, a five-foot-six left-handed pitcher who won the first three Gold Gloves awarded to a pitcher for fielding excellence. Ultimately, Kaat's small stature as a youth was an advantage. Most pitchers who advance to the major leagues get by with an overpowering fastball in high school and then learn to pitch when they climb the professional ladder and realize most good hitters can hit most good fastballs. Kaat learned how to pitch rather than overpower batters at a young age because he wasn't big as a youngster and didn't throw hard. He sprouted about four inches to six-foot-three the summer after he graduated from high school, and suddenly he had size in addition to guile.

He was an intimidating presence on the mound and a fine athlete. Mele said Shantz was the best fielding pitcher he ever saw until he saw Kaat, and if awards are a barometer Mele was correct. Kaat easily passed Shantz to win a record 14-straight Gold Gloves at a position that is difficult to field well.

A pitcher stands about 55 feet from the batter as he completes his throwing motion and tries to regain his balance. Some pitchers follow through and then raise their heads to look at the catcher's mitt, but Kaat was one of those who followed the ball all the way into the target, and he made sure to finish in a position that left him squarely facing the batter. Pascual pronounced his name "cat," and he had that quickness. At point-blank range to a batter, though, anything can happen.

In 1962 during a game in late July, five-foot-eleven, 175-pound Detroit outfielder Bubba Morton scorched one of Kaat's pitches. The ball hit the wet grass at Metropolitan Stadium and skidded. The ball spurted over the web of Kaat's glove and crushed his lips into his teeth. The pitching mound was 15 inches high at the time, and Kaat now stood six-foot-four. Second baseman Bernie Allen walked over to Kaat, who stood on the mound with his hand over his mouth. The shorter Allen looked up at Kaat's hand, and when Kaat pulled it away all Allen could see was blood and the roots of Kaat's teeth; he had lost two of them on the play, chipped another, and eventually required surgery. Both Allen and Killebrew recalled looking at the baseball and seeing bits of Kaat's teeth in the horsehide.

Allen had scheduled a party at his home that night, and he remembered the festivities were in full swing when the doorbell rang. Allen opened the door and there stood Kaat. Allen had not expected Kaat to be in any condition to attend the party.

"What are you doing here?" Allen asked.

Kaat looked down at Allen. "I was invited, wasn't I?"

Kaat later said thoughts of the painful event never crossed his mind in subsequent games and never affected his fielding. He didn't even miss a turn in the rotation after the injury. Pitching on three days' rest, Kaat won 5-2 on a five-hitter despite eight stitches and a plastic guard in his mouth, in lieu of front teeth. He discarded the guard after five innings because it bothered his breathing, batted four times, got two hits, and easily handled a couple line drives back to the mound. The 23-year-old sat on a stool near his locker after the game and said, "I've never felt this tired in my life."

He was big, strong, and tough, but although he once fanned nineteen batters in a minor league game, Kaat never became an overpowering pitcher in the majors. Someone such as Sandy Koufax averaged more than a strikeout an inning during his career, and Kaat struck out about one every two innings. Even in his younger days, Kaat's strikeout totals were less astounding than the low number of walks he allowed. It was Pascual who could dominate hitters. He was Griffith's established ace with that curveball, the one pitch Pascual never wanted to leave back at the hotel. But handing Kaat the opening day assignment was not a step down for Mele. The move also signified a changing of the guard: from that point on, the better pitchers in the franchise would carve their reputations in Minnesota, not Washington.

Sain told Kaat the pressure games for a pitcher were his first All-Star Game, first World Series game, and any opening day. Kaat had a better reason to feel pressure: he hadn't beaten New York for years. His first major-league win had come against the Yankees in 1960, when he played for the Washington Senators. Kaat allowed four runs – one earned – through seven innings of three-hit ball before manager Cookie Lavagetto pulled him. Kaat went in to the clubhouse for a shower, Jim Lemon hit a three-run homer, and the Senators rallied for four runs in the top of the eighth against Whitey Ford. Kaat had a 5-4 win.

Teams coveted pitchers who could beat the Yankees. In fact, the reason Mele was traded to Washington in 1949 was because Red Sox manager Joe McCarthy wanted Washington fastballer Walter Masterson, who had good success pitching against both Boston and New York. Lavagetto wrapped himself in the hopeful notion Kaat was a Yankee-killer and started Kaat often against New York. Kaat was 1-9 against the Yankees as the Twins opened the '65 season.

Kaat's opening-day performance off a camel hump surrounded by the patchwork, quilted turf at Metropolitan Stadium suggested he was invigorated by the helicopter ride, winds that vibrated through the ballpark, and a 44-degree thermometer reading. He allowed six base runners and three earned runs in nine innings. The Yankees contributed five errors. With an out to go in the game, Kaat's first win of the season – first over the Yankees in three years – hung in the air as Joe Pepitone's cotton-candy pop fly arched benignly toward third baseman Cesar Tovar. He dropped the ball.

The Yankees tied the score, and about 15,000 fans, who were headed for the exits, harvested thoughts about whether to endure more chill or go home. Those who stayed until the bottom of the 11th saw Tovar atone for the error with a two-out, bases-loaded single to win the game.

The rookie had entered in the third inning to play third base after Rich Rollins injured his knee. Tovar handled five chances flawlessly before he dropped the sure out in the ninth. It was the Twins' third error, the eighth error of the game, and the type of fielding Twins' fans were accustomed to. And cynical about. They had cheered with derision when Killebrew cleanly handled a ground ball for his first play of the season at first base since his shift from left field.

Minnesota fans have long embraced the play of good-fielding first basemen. Their adoration of good glove men at this position did not begin with bubble-gum blowing Doug Mientkiewicz in 2000 or hometown boy Kent Hrbek in 1981, or even Rich Reese, a modest-hitting glove man whom Billy Martin complimented and criticized into a career high .322 batting average in 1969. Flashy-fielding first basemen began in Minnesota with Vic Power. The facetious cheers aimed at Killebrew were clearly intended to show the fans' love of the seven-time Gold Glove winner, who was traded to the Los Angeles Angels with Lenny Green in 1964. Power was blowing bubbles at first base long before Doug Mientkiewicz arrived.

A muscular, balding Puerto Rican, Power was a Midwestern idol from the time he joined the Twins in '62. He drove a Cadillac, was outwardly appreciative of women, and loved Minnesota. He had made previous major league stops but disliked playing in Cleveland and hated Kansas City, which he deemed racist. He was ostracized in Puerto Rico because he changed his name from Pellot and was considered wealthy and arrogant. So he abandoned his tropical paradise homeland in the winter to stay in Minnesota and make public relations appearances for the Twins. A dark-skinned man in a largely white community, he found he could visit a Minneapolis restaurant such as Café Napoli, which still stood on Hennepin Avenue four decades later, and be assured of walking out with no check. He was embraced by his neighbors in an area not far from Versalles' temporary lodgings with the Stiehms, a trendy area near inner-city Lake Calhoun, where even today mostly white people boat and swim. People invited his family to their homes to eat or went to Power's home to visit him and his family.

"In other places they just want to see me play ball, then forget me," he said. "You don't feel like you belong."

Minnesota Twins fans adored Vic Power so much that when it became apparent before the 1964 season the Twins would need to find a place in the outfield for Tony Oliva, which would push either Killebrew or Allison to first base, letters of protest besieged Griffith. He was in San Diego during the winter when a cab driver recognized the Twins' owner. The cabbie explained he was a Minnesotan who wintered in California, and if Griffith traded Power, the cabbie said, he would never set foot in Met Stadium again.

Vic Power was flamboyant in a part of the country known for stoicism. Mediocre at stealing bases, he stole home twice in a game while playing with Cleveland, seemingly only because he could. In the field he caught the ball with one hand, a practice which later became typical, but during Power's playing days was considered to be dogging it, showboating, or both.

First base is the only infield position tailored for left-handers, because their throws to other bases track inside the base paths and are less likely to hit runners, and footwork for a left-hander allows a quicker release. Casey Stengel said Power was the most graceful right-handed first baseman he ever saw. Power made infielders better, explaining to them it was always preferable to throw a little low than a little high. Power could stretch toward a low throw and the ball would reach his glove a blink sooner than if he had to reach up and back for a high throw. He explained the difference between those throws was as much as three steps for a runner, and that could easily make the difference between out and safe.

Power played such a deep first base that he told the infielders to just throw the ball to the base rather than expect him to be the target. It was confusing at first. More than once, infielders triple-pumped before throwing, as they awkwardly hesitated because Power was not at the bag. Eventually, the infielders adopted Versalles' attitude: "I throw the ball. If he isn't there, it's not my fault." But Power was always there.

Because of repeated leg injuries, Killebrew would never exhibit that range defensively, but he handled 18 chances flawlessly in the 1965 opener and was good enough in the field that he hardly deserved the fans' mockery. Killebrew was a considerably better hitter than Power. Still, fans were disappointed when the likable Power was traded, and they were also very anxious about the team's chances as the season began. Their response to Killebrew's play emphasized the end to those days when Twins' fans were satisfied that Minnesota had a big-league ball club. A myth persists about those Minnesota fans even today.

The 1965 Minnesota Twins drew patrons from towns and cities all around the upper Midwest, fans who lived perhaps more than 100 miles away, before interstate highways made motorists indifferent to that distance. Fans had to plan a trip to Bloomington in advance, typically ordering their $1.50 to $3 tickets through the mail weeks before the game. Because of that advance commitment, and the fact these were hearty, largely Scandinavian and German descendants, it is recalled that fans gladly endured bitter weather to watch sporting events at Metropolitan Stadium. In reality, weather strongly influenced attendance. There was one exception in 1965, and it was not opening day.

Club officials anticipated a record turnout of 25,000 for the 1965 season opener, based on advance sale of 14,000 tickets. Flooding and brisk weather cut walk-up sales to 1,000. Kaat and his mates weren't the only people in Minnesota isolated by floods, so the lower attendance was not surprising. The team played to many small crowds, particularly in the spring, and in fact the lowest single-game attendance in team history came during that championship season. Grant was trying to become the American League's first 1965 20-game winner on a late September Monday against Kansas City and future Hall of Fame pitcher Jim "Catfish" Hunter. It was 19-year-old Catfish against Mudcat, who was obviously the bigger attraction at the time. Far more exciting was the fact the Twins' magic number was down to three, which meant any combination of wins by the Twins or losses by the White Sox that totaled three would result in the Twins' winning their first pennant. Today, this would be a desirable game to attend in any big-league city, but in 1965 a paltry 537 patrons walked through the turnstiles in Bloomington.

There had been some concern about the Minnesota franchise's long-term viability in the state before the season began. Although the Twins' attendance in 1964 easily exceeded the magic mark of a million, it was a drop of about 200,000 from the club's league-leading attendance in 1963. The Milwaukee Braves were scheduled to move to Atlanta after the 1965 season, and Kansas City was struggling at the gate and would eventually move to Oakland. There was national media speculation about Major League Baseball's ability to survive in the upper Midwest and local concern about keeping Met Stadium updated.

Construction of the Met had been completed in 1956, and the minor-league Minneapolis Millers originally used the field. By 1965, the Met – often referred to as an erector set because of the patchwork stages in which it was constructed – was more than a decade old and required additional seating and other upgrades to keep big-league fans comfortable. There was concern where the money would be found to complete the upgrades. Additional seating in left-field was scheduled for completion by the mid-summer All-Star Game, but the Minnesota Vikings were footing that bill – in exchange for reduced rent – because it would be prime football seating. The seating accommodations that stretched toward the outfield down the third base line were just wooden bleachers instead of permanent seating, and in fact no upgrade ever was made there.

A pre-season media poll indicated nearly 70 percent of those asked had "some" or "a great deal" of interest in the Twins and Major League Baseball, but this wasn't to be confused with optimism or clicking turnstiles. Only three percent of those polled thought the team could win the American League pennant, and one in four expected the team to finish fifth in the 10-team league, a notch above their 1964 standing. By mid-July, the team would come to captivate the state, but fans were skeptical early in the season.

The Twins were not only well above .500 as June arrived, but the team had flirted with first place almost since the start of the season. They mostly spent May tied for first place or a half game on either side of the league lead, yet there was widespread discontent among fans. Five straight months of awful weather couldn't have helped their mood, but fans joined the media outcry for the Twins to make a trade when the team briefly dropped to second place in late May. Fan complaints reached the point where pitcher Dick Stigman asked, "What do people want? The ball club is good enough to be in second place, so why do we need help and have to make changes?" Days later, with the team in first, Rich Rollins reflected the players' irritation and said, "The spirit on this club right now is terrible. We don't have a bad egg on the entire roster and everybody gets along. They could make a trade, bring in somebody who doesn't get along, and upset everything."

The camaraderie in the clubhouse was crucial to the team. Forty years later, many of the surviving team members talked to each other as frequently as once a week, and many saw each other at least annually, maintaining friendships that began during the summer of 1965. "Sure, there were times when you got a little hot under the collar," Bob Allison recalled at a team reunion in 1986, "but in all we just had a great blend of personalities."

Some of the players didn't think it was entirely by chance the team overflowed with good character. It has been observed that the Twins placed a premium on citizenship as well as talent as far back as the early '60s, and with just two owners in more than 40 seasons it's entirely possible that continuity at the top of the organization could be part of the reason for this. Relief pitcher Garry Roggenburk recalled the Twins scouting him while he was in college, and he specifically noted the club's interest went beyond his athletic ability. "The Twins were big on that topic of your background. They didn't seem to want someone who wasn't going to fit into the clubhouse."

Although the fans and media fretted, the players began to think something special was in the making. Of course the opinion that carried considerable weight didn't belong to the fans or the media; it belonged to the manager, and Sam Mele was finding himself in a very positive mood. When the team rallied to win after Tovar made his costly error in the opener, Mele said it was the kind of game the team had lost the previous season. Martin didn't always mirror Mele's ability to respect the fact players make mistakes, but the rookie coach came to Tovar's defense.

"Since it was his first major league game, Cesar was a little excited," Martin said. Tovar responded by saying he would have none of that. The Venezuelan spoke English well, and said he waved off Versalles, yelled, "I got it," saw Versalles back away, and then the ball bounced off Tovar's glove. No sun in the eyes, no wind, no excuses. "I just messed up the play. Sure, I knew that the tying run was heading across third base at the time. I had to get a base hit. You could never find a better spot to make up for an error."

Before Tovar's game-winning hit, with the bases loaded and one out, Mele showed confidence in light-hitting Saint Paul native Jerry Kindall and did not pinch hit for the second baseman. Since breaking camp in Orlando, Mele had tried to show his players he believed each had something to contribute, despite the fact he was taking more control. Previously, Mele often let his players decide whether to hit and run, bunt or steal, but he found them reluctant to initiate any of this for fear they would be criticized by fans and media if it failed, so Mele pushed the buttons and took any heat. There was no heat coming from the owner's office. Griffith, who had missed his first season opener because of various health problems including phlebitis, was delighted with the team's early play and praised Mele for the way he had handled Versalles in spring training.

"This stroke by Mele was the finest psychological move since we moved to Minnesota. I've preached to Sam since he took over as manager to take the money off the players if they don't perform, so I'm glad now to see him get a lot tougher. I think the fine straightened out Versalles and woke up the entire team."

Spring training is supposed to be the time when ballplayers are light-hearted, but for much of the spring the team seemed like a clenched fist. Once the season and the winning started, the palm opened. Kaat said he would have loved the opening-day win, particularly against New York, but shrugged it off with the prediction "sometime during the season I'll get one I didn't deserve." Jerry Fosnow got the win in relief. It was the first of his three wins that season, his only wins in the major leagues, but he joked how he had nineteen to go to reach the coveted 20-win mark for one season.

Fosnow's name didn't appear often as the day's hero in '65, but soon a different name appeared daily as the star of the game and, as Mele noted, games the team would have lost in 1964 quickly began to go their way. Even Tovar was repaid for his error as the Twins improved to 6-1 heading into the last week of April.

In the top of the 10th inning during a game in Detroit, catcher Jerry Zimmerman replaced Battey, who had been injured. On a 40-degree night, the light-hitting Zimmerman drove in the tie-breaking run; it was the first time in his big-league career he could recall driving in the game-winner. Then Tovar brought home an insurance run when poetic justice struck after he hit a little pop fly to Jerry Lumpe at second base. Lumpe misjudged the ball, and it hit him in the face. Griffith was criticized for obtaining only the rookie Tovar in 1964 off-season trading and was further criticized when Tovar dropped Pepitone's pop fly in the opener. Now the veteran Lumpe, whose name surfaced in trade rumors dating back to Griffith's days in Washington, had made a similar error. It proved such plays could happen to any player, but because Tovar made his error in the home opener before Twins' fans, they remembered Tovar's mistake and continued to wonder about the team's defense.

It was too early to know defense would be less important than the club's tenacious bench, good pitching and timely hitting. For fans who wanted to see the cup as at least half full, the first outings by Camilo Pascual gave them encouragement.

Fans and the media believed the 31-year-old with the electric curveball would need to shine for the team to succeed, and he was meeting expectations. Pascual hit his second career grand slam and threw a two-hitter in his third start of the season, part of his 8-0 start. That streak was disrupted when torn shoulder muscles were diagnosed, but for a brief span the right-hander – once traded for baseball bats – was enjoying something quite unfamiliar: he was a winning pitcher. He had long been a better pitcher than his won-lost record, but pitching for the Senators meant life with a losing record. He was 4-7 in his rookie season of 1954, and until Pascual ran his record to 5-0 in '65 he spent his entire career looking up at .500. He beat Kansas City 6-4 in late May of '65 to get over .500, where he stayed for the remainder of his career.

Like so many of the '65 Twins, Pascual didn't blame misfortune on others, partly because he never forgot how delighted he was to be playing in the major leagues and partly because he understood winning doesn't rest on one pitcher. When he beat Kansas City to rise beyond .500 for the first time in his career, he gave his teammates credit. He threw 145 pitches in eight innings, allowed six hits and five walks but only one earned run. After the game he said, "A man has to be living right to win one like that. I want to tell you, my friend, for the first couple of innings I feel like a stranger on the mound. I have no coordination. My fastball goes everywhere and my curveball goes behind somebody's back after one pitch."

Pascual said he was a six-inning pitcher for much of his career despite being blessed at a young age with a curveball so wicked that the Chicago Cubs' Don Zimmer returned from the 1961 All-Star Game and announced to his teammates, "Boys, I have seen the best curveball – ever." Pascual was often so dominating that he was unhittable for a few innings. In '56, his third season in Washington, he pitched perfect ball for four innings in eight of his 27 starts and was perfect for five innings in three of those. The curveball bit and dipped more when Pascual was younger, but it was a hard, overhand curve that would cause him to tire in the late innings, and he struggled to make use of his fastball in tandem with the curve. As the game wore on and Pascual tired, hitters would wait for the fastball.

Then in 1959, team vice-president Joe Haynes, a former major-league pitcher, taught him to throw a slower curveball to keep hitters off balance. At the same time, Pascual learned to keep his fastball lower and throw it off his curve. He went 17-10 in '59, the year Killebrew and Allison arrived in the majors to stay, and was 100-76 from that year through 1964. Battey arrived in Washington in 1960, just in time to catch the 15-strikeout game in which Pascual eclipsed the Senator franchise record held by Walter Johnson. Battey said Pascual was the best pitcher he ever caught, and Battey caught 300-game winner Early Wynn.

Other teams coveted Pascual through all the losses. Griffith constantly declined overtures, many from the Yankees. It was rarely difficult for Griffith to turn away from the offers as the packages typically included players such as the Yankees' Tom Sturdivant, Johnny Kucks, Jack Reed, or Fritz Brickell, players with either short, undistinguished careers or one or two nice seasons amidst a backdrop of mediocrity. It would have been less embarrassing for Pascual to be traded for these men than it was for him to remember the trade engineered by Al

Campanis in the Cuban Winter League when Pascual was 17. Campanis, who was a career executive for the Dodgers until he made unfortunate racial comments concerning baseball on ABC-TV's "Nightline" in 1987, was managing Cienfuegos in 1951 and saw the 17-year-old Pascual pitch. Campanis was in need of a right-handed pitcher, and manager Mike Guerra of Marianao indicated the deal could be done for a dozen bats.

Pascual later said, "I tell you, when I see that later in the paper, 'Pascual traded for a dozen bats,' I hung my head, I'm so embarrassed.

"But they were good bats."

The best bats weren't of much help to hitters against Pascual in early 1965. He had learned he didn't need to fill those 3-2 counts and was often coasting, winning once early in the season on 105 pitches, and another time after throwing just 93.

It was comforting to fans and team officials because Kaat was not pitching particularly well, the team didn't have an established fourth starter in Sain's four-man rotation, and Tony Oliva was off to a slow start after a tremendous '64 season, when he became the first rookie to win a major league batting title. Allison jumped to his typical hot start at the plate, but was adjusting to his move to left field, a position he termed "lonely." Killebrew was getting comfortable at first base, but as April ended he had yet to hit a home run. He had never gone that far into a Twins' season without one.

Finally, he hit one and drove in all three of the team's runs in a win over Chicago the first weekend in May. He said he hit the homer for his fifth child, Erin Elaine. The next day, with no game scheduled, walnut-sized hail pelted the Twin Cities as Killebrew flew to his home in Oregon to see his two-day-old daughter. He returned to Minnesota in time for one of the state's more devastating storms.

Tornadoes bedeviled the Twin Cities area for six hours on May 7 in what is still considered the most costly summer storm in state history in terms of loss of life and financial damage. The storms killed 13 people, injured hundreds, shredded homes, and tossed around cars like spare change. In a nearby small town, wind sucked one farmer from his barn. He was crushed and died. There was $20 million in damage, and 4,000 citizens were left homeless. Adding to the insult were the looters, who hampered cleanup work. Already during the spring a dozen Minnesotans had lost their lives in the worst recorded flooding of the Mississippi. Now, once again, fans had more to worry about than the fate of their team, which was two-and-a-half games behind Chicago.

The Twins played exciting baseball in May and enjoyed a 19-12 record during that first full month of the season, but attendance was off by 100,000 compared to the previous season as June began. It was unusual to play to a crowd exceeding 10,000, let alone 20,000. The money for the club was on the road. The visiting team in those days did not split the gate but received 28.5 cents per admission. Even in Kansas City, where Charlie Finley's Athletics were usually struggling on the field and at the gate, the Twins drew more than 13,000 one game, a larger turnout than they were playing before at the Met.

The biggest paydays for the owners came when teams trotted out their newest promotion – Bat Day. Each child who attended a major league game accompanied by an adult received a free, 30-inch Hillerich & Bradsby Louisville Slugger baseball bat. After playing to crowds of six or seven thousand at home each game, the Twins started May in Chicago, playing in a doubleheader battle for first place before a Bat Day crowd of more than 42,000 fans. The club was clearly a contender and a drawing card in other cities. A mid-June swing through Detroit, Chicago, New York, and Cleveland was expected to draw about 300,000 fans, but in one day the team took a huge bite out of that forecast. The Yankees staged their first of two Bat Days, and 72,244 fans appeared to see Killebrew homer in both ends of the Twins' doubleheader sweep, the first doubleheader sweep by a Griffith franchise in New York since 1924. The huge crowds in New York were a financial windfall. Griffith was accustomed to banking about $300,000 in road gate for the season. He pulled more than a tenth of that out of New York alone, and the Twins' share of the gate during the club's 14-day road trip equaled what it normally drew in twice that many road dates.

The popularity of Bat Day exceeded bobblehead doll promotions that surfaced at major league ballparks in the 1990s. Bat Day began without extensive thought in 1953 after a man who acquired merchandise of bankrupt companies bought the inventory of a failed baseball bat company, then sold the bats to the St. Louis Browns. The Browns' idea to give bats to fans was a success, despite the fact some of the bats were not even finished. The promotion eventually took a strong foothold in the American League in 1965, when the Twins played to four Bat Day crowds that totaled nearly 195,000, including their own promotion. The effect on attendance in Metropolitan Stadium could not have been forecast when the team staged its Bat Day on a Sunday in early June. It was the one day of the entire season when awful weather could not keep the fans away.

The Twins were averaging 9,400 fans a game to that point in the season, just 2,000 more than the Washington Senators, who routinely had such poor attendance that D.C. managed to lose not one but two franchises within 11 years. Bat Day was a marketing gimmick intended to prop up attendance, but the scenario for the promotion at Metropolitan Stadium was not ideal. The lowly Senators were the opposition, which certainly was part of the plan. It's common in baseball to stage a promotion on a date when the home team plays an unattractive opponent, but the Senators fit that definition a little too well. They were worse than expected, arriving in Minnesota the first weekend in June batting less than .230 as a team. The pitching staff owned a painfully high earned run average.

Players had sat around the clubhouses for three hours the previous day, dreaming the horizon would be wiped dry long enough to play. That game was postponed. The sky was gray as a wet sidewalk on Sunday, and Bat Day began in a downpour. When Twins' officials saw ribbons of soggy fans in front of the ticket sales booths, however, it would have taken incessant cascades of water to postpone the game. Umpires did interrupt play for about 15 minutes during the early going, and in most cases they would have called the game, but in most cases there would not have been nearly 31,000 fans at a Senators-Twins game under these conditions. Of that total, 18,000 fans stood in line in the pre-game Sunday morning rain to buy tickets at the gate. The club purchased 10,000 bats at 68 cents each and had another 2,000 in reserve. The Twins gave away every bat.

So the promotion's effect was such that the Twins held Bat Day in early June on a day that was damp, cold, and windy – as it had been in the state for two weeks; the opponent was awful. Yet Met Stadium was packed with the biggest crowd of the season, 13,000 more than the previous high, and even about 6,000 more fans than the Twins played before during the franchise's first game in Minnesota in '61.

The irony of Bat Day was that light-hitting Jerry Zimmerman, a man who would hardly serve as a Louisville Slugger spokesman, hit a pitch from Washington's Phil Ortega 402 feet for his first major-league home run in the Twins' 11-2 win. The uncommonly high number of witnesses provided the reserve catcher with an appropriate flash of fame. Two of Zimmerman's nine minor league seasons were played at Met Stadium with the Minneapolis Millers, yet he had never hit a home run at the Met before he smacked Ortega's pitch. Zimmerman's home run once again followed the theme of the season, in which a reserve with a modest career had his day.

Zimmerman showed little power in the majors and hit only 31 home runs in the minors, but when Mele was formulating his approach to a running game in spring training, he expressed his dissatisfaction with the team's penchant for the long ball at the expense of hitting to the opposite field with runners on and said, "In some cases I'd rather have Jerry Zimmerman at the plate, just to do something with the ball, than some of our home-run hitters." A few weeks before Zimmerman hit his homer, Mele thought about making him his starting catcher. Battey was battling injuries at the time, and Zimmerman eventually did catch 39 of the team's first 70 games. The Twins won 31 of those.

Mele thought Zimmerman was the best defensive catcher in the league. Pitchers on the Twins' staff parroted Pascual, who said he didn't care which catcher was behind the plate. Few pitchers had the fine fortune to throw to two excellent catchers. Zimmerman was a good target behind the plate despite his height. He knew how to get low and stay low to allow the umpire a good view of pitches, which was more important in the American League, where the umpire stood behind the catcher rather than in a crouch inside the plate, with his head nearly alongside that of the catcher. By getting low, Zimmerman allowed the umpire behind him to get low, too, and to see the low strike better. He said he preferred the American League strike zone and its position of umpires behind the catcher. "I can remember Frank Dascoli," Zimmerman once said. "If I turned my head, I'd bump into his head. And he liked garlic."

Zimmerman was a terrific mechanical catcher and more talkative than Battey, who was considered laid back. Because Zimmerman didn't hit much, he really had to take charge of a game and coax a pitcher toward his strengths.

Battey was a bull at six feet, 230 pounds. Zimmerman was six-foot-two and just 185 pounds, but he was as tough as Battey. In late June, Battey left one game when a ball struck him on the ankle. A few days later Battey dislocated the middle finger on his left hand because his habit was to curve the middle finger of the catching hand through the space above the band on the back of the catcher's mitt. One day a ball caught the exposed finger. So Zimmerman stepped in to start all games of a home series against Detroit, a particularly ugly series in that the bullpen was called upon to pitch nearly half the innings played.

The starting staff was ailing, and Zimmerman caught nine different pitchers in the series, didn't make an error, and played both games of a Sunday doubleheader despite a pulled back muscle. Minnesota won three of the four games to maintain first place by a half game.

When Zimmerman had a good game, teammates would tell reporters, "Make sure to talk to Zimmy," who was quite popular in the clubhouse. Reporters wanted to talk to Zimmy about his first major league home run on Bat Day, but Zimmerman was happier about the fact he was seeing more game action than he had in years. He just didn't think one home run was that big a deal. He shrugged it off, and insisted, "Any man with a bat in his hands has a chance to hit one out."

COOL OF THE EVENING

Bob Allison and Sandy Valdespino

SIX

You can't look over your shoulder for someone to help you.
You do it yourself, because if you don't, there isn't time
for anybody else to do it. – Bernie Allen.

A cobra strike from the heart of the lineup is how the '65 Twins' victories are commonly remembered. The memory is inaccurate. Mele responded to the team's conga line of injuries with so many different lineups that his players called it Sam's shake-well system: shake and pour out a starting nine. And it was successful, with men who were not stars emerging as the heroes du jour. When it was all over, the Twins voted a portion of World Series money to a record 37 men. In an era when some managers could chisel their starting lineup on a dugout wall and reserves camped on the bench for weeks, Mele worked into the mix players such as Joe Nossek, Bernie Allen, Sandy Valdespino, Mincher, and Zimmerman almost as much as manager Tom Kelly did with his bench when the Twins won the World Series in '87 and '91. Even so, winning the '65 pennant was not a 25-man effort. The Twins took three catchers north from spring training, but one was a rookie who barely played.

It was evident late in camp there were two promising first-year players on the team. Because of the Vietnam War, the possibility existed that a player could be called into military service, so a new rule allowed each team to select a "designated player" who could be promoted from the minor leagues, then demoted without asking waivers. The Twins designated future Hall of Famer Rod Carew, who never played with the club that year. Catcher John Sevcik, another rookie, was kept on the roster all season because he had signed a contract that offered enough of a bonus that rules stipulated he spend his entire rookie season in the major leagues. The owners designed the rule to discourage each other from tossing large bonuses at young, untested players, but as with most such owner-induced financial restraints throughout baseball history the concept wasn't particularly successful: if a youngster showed enough promise, there was usually money available for him.

Any attempt to demote Sevcik would risk losing him, and Griffith believed Sevcik was too talented to expose to the waiver wire and venture a claim from another team. Sevcik was a standout football player at the University of Missouri, but his love of baseball kept him from considering any other athletic career. Retaining Sevcik on the big-league roster harbored some strategic merit. Battey was often injured and on thyroid medication, so the team needed insurance for Zimmerman, but instead of sitting through his own nicks, Zimmerman pulled taut all the slack.

Sevcik would approach Mele now and then about a start, keeping things light and picking a spot when the opposition was starting a fine pitcher, such as Cleveland's hard-throwing Sam McDowell. "C'mon. McDowell is starting tonight, you've got to put me in there," Sevcik would plead, almost always to no avail. In early August, 23-year-old John Sevcik sat in the bullpen under the scoreboard in right-center field at Met Stadium. He hadn't played in well over a month. The Twins-O-Gram, the portion of the electronic scoreboard that conveyed messages to fans, paid homage to the catcher with the lighted display: "Sevcik is here, sittin' and a watchin' and a waitin.'" Sevcik doubled once in 16 at-bats spanning 12 games that season and never played in the majors again.

So Mele worked his way to the World Series with essentially a 24-man roster. The organization was overloaded in spots such as first base and lean in the middle infield, but Mele had great lineup flexibility because Bernie Allen and Rich Rollins could each play second or third. Jerry Kindall was capable of playing all four infield positions. More importantly, Killebrew could play outfield, third, and first and was willing to shift for the team's benefit. In fact, Killebrew was statistically the team's utility player, which was unusual if not unique for a power-hitting franchise centerpiece. Don Mincher played more games at first than Killebrew in 1965, and Rollins more at third.

It was difficult for others to insist on a steady spot in the field when Killebrew was willing to play where it helped the team most. Among the position players, only the catchers and Versalles were assured a familiar patch of turf. Don Mincher, who complained loudly about lack of playing time in spring training, worked out at third base, offered to catch, and played one game in the outfield. Allison sometimes found himself at first base, and Oliva played some center field. Every day was a game of musical chairs, and while no one wanted to push or shove, no one wanted to remain standing when the music stopped. In late June, Rollins was left standing.

His average had inched up to nearly .240 after a poor start, but he was not producing offensively as he had during his three previous seasons in the league, and Rollins was only an average fielder at best. He had once said, "There's always someone waiting to take your place. Baseball is the most insecure profession I know." There was suddenly a mountain of truth in his remark.

Griffith hoped Bernie Allen in the minor leagues could give the team more production and better defense at third. Allen had been playing the position exclusively on minor-league rehabilitation assignment in Denver and was hitting more than .430 when the Twins brought him back. A 26-year-old former Purdue University quarterback, he had taken the Twins' second base job away from Billy Martin in '62. Allen was an exceptional athlete and capable second baseman but did not hit with the type of power most teams expected from a third baseman.

Allen surrendered his No. 1 jersey number to Martin when Martin joined the team as a coach on the field. Now it was Martin's turn to do Allen a favor and help him return to the playing form of his '62 rookie season. They had been in spring training together as players in '61, when Allen was battling Martin for the starting second base job. Allen didn't know what to expect of the situation, and one day he hopped on the team bus for a road game in Florida. "Hey, rook, right here," Martin shouted to Allen, patting the empty seat beside him. "Sit right here." Martin proceeded to fill Allen's head with information, and by 1962 Allen was not only starting, but starring for the Twins. It appeared the franchise had the second baseman it had sought for decades.

Allen's offense dipped some in '63, and he struggled early in '64 before going on a hitting tear after Memorial Day, but in mid-June he suffered severe ligament and cartilage damage to his right knee when Washington's Don Zimmer slid into him at second base on a force play. Allen had played football through college and never suffered a severe knee injury, and then it had happened on a seemingly innocent force out. Zimmer's rolling block into Allen cost him nearly a year of big-league play, but Allen later said he never blamed Zimmer. Allen recalled that Versalles' casual throw to him at second meant he had to keep his foot on the bag until Zimmer was on top of him. Today Zimmer's rolling block into Allen's legs would be considered a little aggressive. In the early 1960s, it was the norm.

Allen was recalled from his Denver rehabilitation assignment in June of '65, but Killebrew knew Mele wanted Mincher's bat in the lineup and offered to move to third on at least a platoon basis so the left-handed Mincher could play first base against right-handed pitching. Mele had promised Killebrew during the off-season that he would not move him from one position to another, but Killebrew could sense what Mele was thinking, so he initiated the discussion, even though it also meant his friend Rollins would see significantly less playing time.

"I'm not trying to take anybody's job," Killebrew said, "but I know the manager wants to get Don's bat in the lineup on occasion. A fellow 27 years old with that much talent should be playing. Now is when he has to play if he's going to go anywhere in this game. I offered to help out at third if Mele wants it that way. I didn't feel too much out of place over there."

Decades later, Killebrew still thought about Rollins when recalling the move, saying, "I felt bad about it for Rich. He was a good little player." Allen felt the same.

Allen was a friend and business partner of Rollins, was signed by the same scout, shared the same birthday and lamented the notion people hoped he could take the rest of Rollins' playing time. "It's a funny feeling, because I'd like to see both of us in the lineup, like it was before," Allen said at the time. "I'm sure Richie feels kind of strange, too." But Versalles was slumping offensively, although he had matured enough that he did not drag his slumps into the field, and the team needed an offensive boost as it felt the hungry breath of Chicago on its neck. Mincher was capable of providing it.

Mincher was a spare part in spring training, and a squeaky one. He was six-foot-three, 220 pounds with a sense of humor. He maintained that when he retired he planned to go into farming because he wanted to grow corncob pipes. If a group of players intended to meet at a specified time, Mincher would announce, "OK: let's Simonize our watches." After consecutive seasons as a role player in which he hit a combined 40 home runs in barely 500 at-bats, Mincher was tired of sitting while Killebrew or Allison played first base.

Mele liked Mincher as a powerful bat off the bench – although Mincher enjoyed little success as a pinch hitter beyond belting a home run now and then. Mele saw no way for Mincher to bump aside Killebrew or Allison and mentioned the possibility of a trade early in spring training. A rumor even started that Boston, which had dim prospects of success in '65, would take Allison and Mincher in a trade for Carl Yastrzemski.

A future Hall of Famer, Yastrzemski hadn't showed much power to that point in his career, but he had already won a batting title. Mincher could solve Boston's problems at first base, and Allison would fill Yastrzemski's spot in left field. It was, however, just a rumor, as the Red Sox knew what they had in Yastrzemski. Mele said years later that if that trade had been on the table he would have favored it.

The rumor began because Yastrzemski had played with the Red Sox minor league affiliate in Minneapolis, and a Minneapolis sports columnist had the habit of starting rumors by suggesting local sports teams were interested in a player if the athlete was born in Minnesota, attended school there, or played minor league sports in the state. The reporter had started a rumor a few seasons earlier that Killebrew would be traded for Yastrzemski. Players immediately recognized when these news reports were just vapor. Still, it's interesting to wonder what might have been: the Twins probably would still have won the '65 pennant with that trade, and most likely would have won in '67 as well, when Most Valuable Player Yastrzemski led the Red Sox to the pennant over the Twins on the final day of the season. With Yastrzemski in a Twins' uniform beside Killebrew and Cesar Tovar – who were second and seventh in MVP voting that season – Minnesota probably could have counted on being the 1967 American League champion.

No trade came for Mincher, only rumors, so he complained during spring training to an Orlando television station. Mele had already dealt with the holdouts of Kaat and Pascual, faced encounters with Versalles and Grant, endured Ramos' remarks from the Yankee spring training camp, and lived with the constant speculation that Martin would replace him. Now Mincher was complaining. Mele knew Mincher had a legitimate complaint.

The Twins had slick-fielding rookie Rich Reese in camp, and Reese and Killebrew were getting the at-bats. After 19 spring games, Mincher had played a few innings here and there and had come off the bench to hit three times. "I'm no more ready to play now than I was the first day of spring," Mincher complained. "What the heck, the extra men get only five to 10 swings a day in batting practice. And they started this trade talk about me during the winter and early in the spring. It wasn't my idea."

It can certainly be said Sam Mele reacted to problems on an individual basis. He confronted and fined Versalles after his languid play and loudly stood his ground after the incident, daring Griffith to support him or fire him. He let the players quell the rippled waters when Grant made his remarks of favoritism. Mele had another approach for Mincher: he took his side. Mele said he admired Mincher for speaking up for himself. "I want my players to want to play. He has to realize that Killebrew has to make a switch from the outfield to first base. We have to get Killebrew ready for the season. We know what Minch can do, and it's not a matter of him having to fight for a job. I don't want to trade Mincher."

Mele knew Reese was destined for the minors despite a .600 spring average and Mincher would be with the big club, even though he was batting .176. Mincher's thoughts cooled, and he responded by volunteering to work out at any position if Mele would get him into the lineup. As is often the case when a team has one too many good offensive players, an injury quickly erases the surplus. Killebrew's dislocated elbow in August did just that. Low-key Mincher greeted the news that he was the regular first baseman with understatement typical of so many on the team. "I'm willing to oblige with a home run, or help out wherever I can." He finished the season with 22 home runs in just 346 at-bats, an average of one every 16 trips.

How Mincher came to the organization is a platinum fairy tale that exemplifies how one seemingly small transaction and its footnotes can change the course of a franchise.

In 1944, Clark Griffith paid $100 for the contract of the year's top minor league player, an outfielder named Gil Coan, who had been a minor league home run champion but went on to an undistinguished major league career. Griffith eventually traded Coan to the St. Louis Browns for outfielder Roy Sievers, who had been the American League's first rookie of the year in 1949. Griffith obtained him after Sievers struggled through four inconsistent and injury-filled seasons. Once Sievers pulled on a Senators' uniform in '54, he became an offensive player similar to future Twins' first baseman Kent Hrbek or '60s slugger Rocky Colavito. Sievers ripped 159 homers during his first five seasons with Washington, and he became a four-time All-Star.

Chicago White Sox owner Bill Veeck was convinced in 1959 that Sievers could ensure the Sox would win the American League pennant, and in late June Veeck offered $250,000 for the outfielder. Calvin Griffith had taken over the club leadership from his uncle, Clark, and was using the patented Griffith approach to trades. Clark Griffith knew it was a sellers' market when a contending team wanted one of his better players for a pennant run. "The Old Fox" always held out for the best possible prospects, and a little cash was always welcome. But Calvin Griffith often said that cash couldn't play in the field, and he had already traded veteran third baseman Eddie Yost during the winter. Griffith expected Killebrew and Allison to make the team in '59, and he decided a few veterans were needed to help the youngsters. Griffith identified Sievers as one of those veterans, so he rejected Veeck's overture. The Sox won the pennant anyway. Veeck remained convinced Sievers could help the "go-go" White Sox, who had little power, and Veeck continued to covet the outfielder.

Sievers, 32, still had a few good seasons left in him when Griffith sent him to Chicago for the 1960 season, but Sievers would never again produce anything close to the league-leading 42 home runs he hit in 1957. In return, Griffith got Battey, Mincher, and $150,000. It was all but a felony, even without the $150,000. The Twins became contenders almost immediately, and within five years the Griffith clan had an American League pennant. The Sox finished third and fourth before they sent Sievers to Philadelphia in 1962.

"I thought that was the trade that started to make us a winning ball club," Killebrew recalled years later. "Battey was just a great catcher. I don't think people realized how great he was until he was gone. Don was a fine hitter, and when I hurt my elbow in August he just stepped right in."

Griffith had not wanted Mincher in the deal, and if the trade had transpired as Griffith had hoped, it would still have been one-sided but might have kept the Twins from winning the 1965 pennant. Mincher had never played in a major league game, and the player Griffith desired was a light-hitting utility infielder named Sammy Esposito. The Sox considered Esposito to be a good fielder who could step in at second base if Nellie Fox suffered an injury or at shortstop if Luis Aparicio went down. The Sox were contenders, and they did not have to worry about filling major holes after winning the 1959 American League pennant. Sievers was essentially a luxury. But Veeck sensed that a trade for Sievers could solidify the team and put an end to Yankee dominance of the American League.

Griffith wanted Esposito because there was a notion in the organization that Versalles was a better player when there was another man who could threaten to take his starting job. There had also been complaints and doubts about Versalles from members of Griffith's farm system.

A former Senators player and minor-league manager from the red clay of Georgia named Ellis Clary, a man who reflected on his fielding ability as a player by saying "balls went through me like water through a screen door," had worked hard with Versalles in the Senators' system. He told Griffith that Versalles had so many bad habits in the field that teaching him to play defense "was like getting an alligator to play the piano." Mele recalled the Senators also had a man named Packy Rogers in their minor league system who struggled to keep Versalles under control. "He was a tough SOB," Mele said of Rogers, "and he called farm director Sherry Robertson one day and was so frustrated he didn't know what to do. Sherry told him to knock Zoilo on his ass. Packy told Sherry, 'I've already done that.'"

White Sox manager Al Lopez was adamant that Veeck not include Esposito in any trade for Sievers, and he got his way. The White Sox were proud of the fact they had managed to get Griffith to take Mincher, and the Twins can consider themselves fortunate they took him. If the acquisition of Esposito had led to trading or benching Versalles, it's unlikely the Twins would have won the 1965 pennant.

Earl Battey was expendable to the White Sox because Chicago had veteran catcher Sherm Lollar and two other fine catchers in their farm system, Johnny Romano and J.C. Martin. It was not common to be so deep in catching, and the Sox squandered their wealth in a disastrous off-season of trading. They sent Battey to Washington and Romano to Cleveland, along with first baseman Norm Cash. Cash became a star in Detroit, Romano was a productive catcher in Cleveland, and Battey solved the Senators' catching problems. And the Senators had catching problems.

Clint Courtney was considered the Senators' top catcher in 1959, and he threw out two runners all season. Midway through the 1960 season, Battey had nailed 25 runners, and in one game he stopped Chicago's Luis Aparicio and Jim Rivera in embarrassing fashion. Each player led the American League in steals at least once during their careers, but Battey threw out each by such a wide margin in the same game that they retreated to first base and were put out during rundowns. He got rid of the ball in a hurry, threw bullets, and had won three Gold Gloves by 1965. His fielding would have been enough, but he was also a deadly hitter and a good man in the clubhouse.

Mincher bounced between the minors and majors until '62, when his nine home runs in just 121 at-bats ensured he was up to stay. He had one sensational streak in '63 where he hit safely in 10 games, went 19-for-32 with eight home runs and 18 runs batted in. His home runs often came in bunches, and three times in that span he hit two in a game. The question as the spring of '65 arrived was: where could the club place an additional potent bat? The Twins had awesome power already. Battey was always capable of double-digit home runs. In '64, Killebrew lashed 49 home runs, Allison and Oliva each ripped 32, Jimmie Hall 25, and Versalles 20. When Killebrew moved to third base to get Mincher into the lineup the Twins had what they wanted and what the league feared: yet one more man who could win a ball game on a single swing.

As it turned out, a murderers' row wasn't as vital as dreamed because the 1965 Twins were no longer relying on power to win games. They won with pitching, base running, a bit more power than top contenders Chicago and Baltimore, and their tag-team of heroes.

On a Friday night in late June against visiting Detroit, with Pascual and Kaat ailing, rookie Dave Boswell took the mound in a quintessential 1965 Minnesota Twins baseball game. Killebrew and Oliva went hitless, Mincher played first base and went 2-for-3 with a home run, and Valdespino was in left field in place of Allison. Bernie Allen was back at second base. Minnesota trailed 3-1 in the seventh inning, and a loss would drop the Twins into a three-way tie for first with Chicago and Cleveland. It was one of the rare Bloomington nights that summer when the temperature topped 70, so there was a sizable crowd of nearly 27,000, many of whom remained skeptical about this team and as skeptical about Allen as anyone on the roster.

The Twins scored once in the seventh to pull within a run at 3-2. Johnny Klippstein followed bullpen mate Al Worthington as the pair contributed nearly four innings of two-hit, scoreless relief in support of the rookie Boswell, yet the team was a run short when the last out arrived in the bottom of the ninth inning. In an amazing display of patience by men who could tie a game on one pitch, sluggers Killebrew and Mincher each coaxed a walk with the count at three balls and two strikes. This brought Allen to the plate. Tiger manager Charlie Dressen responded with six-foot-two, 220-pound right-hander Fred Gladding, 29, who struggled with his control but was enjoying his second-straight season of excellent relief work.

Mele made a move, too, inserting Grant as a pinch runner for Killebrew at second base. With the count at two balls and one strike, a batter's count, Allen singled sharply up the middle. Mele had Grant and Mincher moving with the pitch and Grant tied the score, easing into home without drawing a throw. The throw went to third base. Mincher was hardly a fast man, but he advanced to third safely. Allen alertly whistled into second when he saw the throw going to third, which eliminated Detroit's chance at a force play at second base when the next batter stepped in. So far, the heroes had been Boswell, Worthington, Klippstein, and Mincher. Now Allen had tied the score. He was winning back the fans.

Rollins entered the game as a pinch hitter, and Gladding walked him intentionally to load the bases and set up a force play at any base. Mele sent right-handed hitting Joe Nossek into the game to hit for Klippstein. Nossek began to see more playing time as July approached, and was a very effective pinch hitter for Mele in '65 and '66. That June night against Gladding, Nossek swung for one of his cheaper pinch hits. Nossek was an aggressive swinger who didn't take many walks, and he quickly fouled off the first two pitches before taking a third full swing. The ball just dribbled past the pitcher's mound to Gladding's left, basically a very effective bunt. Second baseman Jerry Lumpe charged in to make a play. Mincher crossed the plate, Nossek beat the throw and the Twins won. Nossek and Allen, two men who would not combine for 50 hits during the season, were the instigators of another come-from-behind victory.

Allen had been in many crucial game situations as a college football quarterback, punter, and place-kicker and thrived on such pressure. He had waited months for the chance to feel all his nerve endings tingle again and more importantly to prove wrong the doctors who said he would never play baseball after his knee injury. In the clubhouse that night Allen distilled how important each man was and how impotent formal leadership, such as a team captain, becomes once the game begins.

"Nothing a ballplayer can do means quite so much as delivering when a base hit means something in the pennant fight," Allen said. "You can't look over your shoulder for someone to help you. You do it yourself, because if you don't, there isn't time for anybody else to do it."

Mele was beaming. He said no amount of masterminding could pull out a win such as that one over Gladding and Detroit. All the credit belonged to his players. Mele insisted the team had developed "a winning complex" that carried it through one tight spot after another, one injury after another. "The White Sox and Indians are snapping at our tails and we win the ball game in the ninth. And I'll tell you about Nossek: I don't care if it was a squib hit, he's ripping and cutting up there all the time."

Minnesota swept a doubleheader from the Tigers two days later. Mincher's home run in the eighth decided the first game and Nossek, playing third base in the nightcap, went 3-for-5 to raise his average in a modest number of at-bats to .341. He drove in Rollins with a two-out single in the 10th inning. A few days after Allen's long-awaited hit, he contributed a pinch-hit double that started a ninth-inning rally to help beat Chicago, with Grant working an inning in relief of Kaat. Allen was barely hanging on with the team and still running poorly from the year-old knee injury, so Mele used Boswell as a pinch runner after the double, and the pitcher scored the game's winning run. A storied comeback was not to be for Allen.

He played in only 19 games before the club optioned him to the minor leagues a few weeks later. When the Twins took the field for the first World Series game in Minnesota history, the starting second baseman was not Allen or Rollins or even Jerry Kindall – who played most of the team's games at second base that season. It was Frank Quilici, who didn't play even half the schedule. The Chicago native epitomized the kind of season it was for so many Twins who retired with modest careers.

Quilici played slightly more than 400 major league games, all with Minnesota and many as a late-inning defensive replacement for Killebrew at third. He was barely a .200 career hitter, but he had his defining moments as the season neared its end. Quilici scored the winning run in the game that clinched a tie for the pennant. He topped that in the opening game of the World Series, when he equaled a record with two hits in one inning and ignited an 8-2 rout of the Dodgers and Don Drysdale, who had finished the regular season with consecutive shut-outs. Quilici hadn't even seen the World Series the previous fall. He had been working on a tobacco farm in North Carolina trying to make ends meet. His 1966 season was spent entirely in the minors. In be-tween, he was a rookie starting seven World Series games at second base.

Quilici was in spring training with the team but had been shipped out before Versalles' incident with Mele. He was playing every day at AAA Denver when the Twins recalled him in late July. Quilici heard Versalles could be moody, and now he was to be his double-play partner. What's more, Quilici was replacing Kindall, who lockered next to Versalles and who considered Versalles to be his friend. Quilici gave the situation some thought and realized those who had cautioned him about Versalles' moody personality were all in the minor leagues. Maybe they didn't know how to handle the man. So Quilici took the lead and ap-proached Versalles.

"Hey, Z. You remember me from spring training?"

"Yeah," Versalles said, "but you didn't stick around too long."

Quilici said, "Well, you've been playing every minute of every game up here, and I've been playing every minute of every game in Denver, and I'm wondering if you'd do me a favor?"

Versalles was willing to listen, so Quilici asked if the shortstop would come out early the next day and take some ground balls.

"Let's talk after the game," Versalles said.

The Twins played a doubleheader that day. Quilici batted leadoff in the second game and smacked a double. He seemed to have some legitimacy to him, so Versalles approached Quilici in the clubhouse after the game. "Hey. Dago. I'll see you out on the field at 2:30."

The next day Martin hit a hundred or so ground balls and Versalles scooped them into his glove, fed double-play tosses to Quilici, and took throws from him, with Mincher anchoring first base. Versalles loved to show his stuff, and he would backhand the ball, underhand throws, flick them with a quick wrist, and even flip the ball to Quilici from between his legs. Second basemen don't all turn the double play the same way, and they don't all like throws in the same place. Versalles had played with enough of them to know. He went to Quilici and asked where he preferred to take the throw.

Quilici looked at him. "You've got to field it. You've got to throw it. Get it somewhere around second base and I'll take care of it."

Versalles loved the fact Quilici shouldered all the responsibility.

"He never gave me a bad throw," Quilici later recalled, "and he played some of the greatest shortstop I've ever seen played."

Quilici pushed aside a domino row of Allen, Rollins, Kindall, Tovar and Kostro to take the second base job. It was a battle royal typical of a franchise that could not find a man to hold the position and that had gone through more than a dozen second basemen since the move to Minnesota. Allen played about 300 games at second base in '62-63, which was as much of a lock as anyone put on the second base job dating back to World War II. Nine men played the position in 1964, which was a startling number even for this franchise. Twins managers often tried six or seven men at second base each season, and many of these managers had once been among the candidates. In addition to Quilici and Martin, future Twins managers John Goryl, Billy Gardner, and Cal Ermer played second base for Calvin Griffith, as did future third base coach Wayne Terwilliger, Killebrew, and Vic Power – who was a first baseman. Even Griffith's brother, Sherry Robertson, played second base for the franchise.

The team entered the '65 spring hoping Tovar could assume the role. He later became a decent second baseman and the most versatile quality player in team history, but Griffith was sorely disappointed to learn during spring training that the 24-year-old rookie was not adept on the double-play pivot. Mele was reportedly unhappy even before he saw Tovar play second base. Griffith's only off-season trade had cost Arrigo, who as a left-handed starting pitcher was a coveted commodity. Mele was further dismayed when Tovar failed to impress at second base, which forced him to audition so many men at the position during spring training that beat reporters referred to each choice as "the second baseman of the day."

Minnesota scouts had been regular patrons at stadiums around Florida all spring, trades were discussed, but no agreements were reached. Boston management mentioned Chuck Schilling to Griffith, and Washington was willing to trade Chuck Cottier, but Mele brushed that talk aside, saying, "We've got a few Cottiers of our own," a reference to good-field, no-hit middle infielders, a group which included the likely starting second baseman for '65, Kindall. At the time, Mele had no idea how accurate he was with his comparison. When the computer age dawned and it became possible to compare players statistically through software programs, two of the 10 players computed to be most similar to Kindall were Schilling and Cottier.

Kindall led the University of Minnesota to the 1956 National Collegiate Athletic Association championship with his smooth fielding and 23 home runs, then signed with the Cubs for a reported $50,000, a "bonus baby." He joined Cleveland in 1962 and saw the most playing time and best season of his big-league career. Cleveland general manager Gabe Paul traded him to Minnesota in '64, when Kindall's wife was expecting a baby and planned to spend the baseball season back in Minnesota. It was a difficult pregnancy, Kindall later recalled, and he asked Paul to see if a trade could be arranged that would allow him to play near his hometown of Saint Paul. The deal was swung shortly before Allen suffered his injury at second base.

"I watched that team come to town with envy when I was with Cleveland," Kindall recalled of the Twins. "Being from Minnesota, I longed to be part of that. Up and down that lineup, there were guys who just kind of took their turn carrying the ball club."

Killebrew said Kindall was the poster boy for the fundamentals in how to field a ground ball, which is what kept the infielder in the major leagues. Kindall wasn't a particularly good major-league hitter and tended to chase high pitches, which submerged his batting average in exchange for occasional power. He was a tall, thin man with long arms, and when he did get his whole bat on a baseball he could drive it a long way. He would have been quite passable at the plate if he put the ball in play more, the way top pinch-hitting reserves Sandy Valdespino and Joe Nossek did, but Kindall struck out about every four at-bats, a rate appropriate for a slugger like Killebrew but not for a light-hitting middle infielder.

Hitting coach Jim Lemon worked hard with Kindall and widened his stance in the hope of smoothing Kindall's habit of upper-cutting the ball. Lemon told the right-handed hitter to hold his lead, left hand tight to the bat and just cradle the handle with the right hand. Lemon tried to get Kindall to hit down on the ball to diminish the number of fly balls that became uncontested outs.

"I was Jim's project," Kindall recalled. "I played with three big-league clubs, and I was always a project."

Lemon had the ability to soft-sell the players he coached, and Kindall claimed to learn from the former slugger, but it didn't translate into much offense. Mele was a firm believer that it was impossible to teach a man to hit, and Kindall didn't make him a liar. "Slim" Kindall, six-foot-three, 175 pounds, played 125 games in '65, and despite a .196 batting average, he did reach base nearly three of every 10 plate appearances, so he had an on-base percentage that was borderline but tolerable for the era; yet he struck out 97 times in 342 at-bats. But as with everyone else on the Twins' roster, Kindall contributed to the misery of the other contending teams.

Killebrew dislocated his elbow on a Monday in August at home against Baltimore, after which Mele told the team it had not been a one-man show to this point, and he expected that would continue. Two days later, Kindall batted for only the fourth time in three weeks and became the 13th Twin that season to drive home the tying or winning run late in the game. Kindall had not played much because he had first been injured, and then Quilici was promoted and played capably. This put the Minnesota native on the bench.

Kindall hadn't hit a home run for 10 weeks or driven in a run for seven. Mele needed a pinch hitter with his team a run behind, and the choices were Zimmerman, Sevcik, or Kindall. Zimmerman's .217 average was the best of the bunch. Sevcik was batting .000. Mele split the difference and chose Kindall, mainly based on the fact that "Kindall hits the ball out of the park once in a while." As Kindall took his warm-up swings, Mele thought about how his uncle, former player and current White Sox coach Tony Cuccinello, would bring teammate Al Lopez over to the house when Mele was a kid. Lopez, 15 years Mele's senior, never refused Mele's questions or phone calls when Mele became a manager. Lopez once told Mele, "When you're going good, try anything: it will probably work." It did.

Kindall drilled the first pitch from Washington's Howie Koplitz on a line over the left-field fence to tie the score 3-3. Three batters later, in an interesting juxtaposition, home-run threat Jimmie Hall singled home Versalles for the winning run.

Kindall's hit wasn't a happy accident. Because the team had been playing at home, he had the luxury of extra batting practice, and because he hadn't been playing, he soaked up the extra work, heading out to the stadium around 2 p.m. each day. Kindall would corral another player or two who wasn't starting, and they would take turns throwing early batting practice to each other. There was usually a pitcher or two willing to do some running, so Kindall would recruit them to shag balls hit into the outfield. It was that type of work ethic among the reserves that helped the Twins win 30 of their first 110 games in the eighth, ninth, or extra innings and to come from behind to win 26 games to that point in the season.

Players knew their work would be rewarded because Mele knew how to handle a bench. Mele's experience as a player helped to make him an empathetic manager who went to great lengths to prepare his bench for game action. He had a good rookie season as a player in 1947; then former New York Yankee manager Joe McCarthy took over as Red Sox manager. Mele was not a pull hitter, so he took a short stride into the ball, went to the opposite field and hit better than .300 as a rookie. McCarthy criticized this approach one day during batting practice. Mele was 25. McCarthy was one of the bigger names in the game. Mele figured the man must be right. He became an entirely different hitter because of McCarthy, and then McCarthy sat Mele on the bench until he was eventually traded. Mele felt he never fully regained his old batting style and never hit .300 again. He was very conscious of this as a manager, did not mess with success, and went out of his way to ensure his players were prepared and understood the confidence he had in them.

"Sam was the best manager I ever played for as a utility player and pinch hitter," Frank Kostro recalled. "He would get you ready long in advance. He would come up in the dugout and tell me that if the other team warmed up a certain pitcher and that man got into the game, I'd be in there to face him. That helped me get ready mentally. There were other guys I played for who waited until the last minute and then would say, 'Let's get a pinch hitter up here.'

"Pinch-hitting is a tough job, especially on the road. At home, you can go out early and take extra batting practice, but on the road, that's the tough part. When it's the seventh day on the road and you get to Boston and have to face Dick Raddatz, that's tough."

It had become very difficult for contenders to focus on stopping one or two members of the Twins' lineup. Killebrew drove in the tying or winning run seven times before he was injured, and as Battey said, "Harmon makes us a first-class team." But Mincher, Hall, Oliva and Versalles drove in the tying or winning run four times each to that point, and Allison three. All four of Mincher's clutch hits were home runs. When the club lost Killebrew for a month in '63 it went 11-15. When Killebrew missed nearly two months in 1965, players such as Kindall took turns reaching deep for their best and the team went 28-19.

Allison stood in the clubhouse after Kindall's game-tying home run and told reporters the team found a different way to win each day. Allison said the team wasn't even invested in watching the scoreboard to see how other teams were doing because the Twins were too busy fighting to win each game to worry about the other teams in the pennant race. "Every game we play is a World Series game," he said.

It wasn't just the players who felt that way. Emotion immersed their families.

Dick Stigman was a crew-cut, six-foot-three left-hander from Nimrod, Minnesota, which lies northeast of resort-area Wadena in the west-central part of the state. He was 26 when the Twins traded for him in 1962. He won nearly 30 games his first two seasons, but in '64 Stigman's earned run average rose and the team failed to score more than two runs in eight of his outings. He fell to 6-15. Mele began the '65 season spotting him in as a starter, but Stigman was struggling in the role, always struggled a little with his control of pitches, and wins had become elusive.

The Twins moved into Detroit on a Friday night for a mid-June, four-game series, smarting from three losses at Cleveland. Second-place Chicago was the team to worry about for the moment, however. The Sox had played lowly Washington and completed a doubleheader sweep of the Senators. The Twins needed to beat Detroit in both ends of their doubleheader to stay in first place, and they needed to do it before a crowd of more than 30,000 in Tiger Stadium.

Grant received poor defensive support in the opener, and Mele went first to Worthington, then Fosnow and Pleis, before Stigman entered in the bottom of the ninth with the score tied 4-4. Stigman was throwing smoke, had control of his pitches, and retired the Tigers in order during the bottom of the ninth. Center fielder Jimmie Hall hit a sacrifice fly in the top of the 10th inning to put the Twins ahead, so Stigman went out for the 10th with a chance to get the victory. He struck out the first two Tigers before future Hall of Famer Al Kaline came to the plate against the Twins' tall, thin left-hander. Kaline routinely had more walks than strikeouts in a season, and Stigman considered the right-handed hitting Kaline to be the toughest man in the league to strike out. Stigman got Kaline to two strikes and threw a hard curveball. Kaline missed. The Twins ended up sweeping the doubleheader and retained first place.

Pat Stigman had made the trip to Detroit with her husband, who had not won a ballgame in two months. Like many of the wives, she was deeply invested in her husband's outings. She sat behind the visiting dugout in Tiger Stadium, peering over the roof as Kaline missed Stigman's curveball. Zimmerman ran out to the mound to congratulate Stigman, who then turned to walk off the field. As he approached the dugout with teammates running by, slapping him on the back, Stigman looked up and saw his wife.

Tears were streaming down her cheeks.

Al Worthington

SEVEN

Geez, I was mad, and maybe I wanted to fight him, but he was a lot older than me, so I just stood there, cursing the hell out of him. – Sam Mele

The club held first place from Memorial Day until June 28, when it suffered its worst loss of the season, 17-4 at home against the White Sox. First place seemed more like a shifting wind rather than the calm eye of a storm as the Twins went 16-13 in June and struggled to get wins from starting pitchers. The starters completed four games in that stretch, so the relief corps appeared 61 times in 28 games and compiled a 2.52 earned run average. The Los Angeles Dodgers had the best pitching in baseball that season with a 2.81 team ERA, so although June was a mere comparative slice of the Twins' season, the bullpen sparkled in a stretch when the Indians won 10 straight but could not break away from the league.

The last time Cleveland had won 10 straight, Mudcat Grant won three of those games. This time around, he was the man to end the Indians' streak, but for the most part the starters needed help. It was during this stretch, when the bullpen constantly plugged the dike, that Sain decided he'd never seen so many pitchers contribute to wins.

Mel Nelson, 28, pitched as sparingly as any man on the team, had an earned run average above 4.00, and struggled when he pitched on consecutive days, but he was remarkably effective in short-relief outings against three of the Twins' tougher opponents: Baltimore, Detroit, and California. The Twins were 29-25 against that group, and might have been worse without Nelson, who allowed only four runs against those teams in 31 innings. It was a decent bit of work for a man who started his career in the outfield and who had been released outright before the Twins picked him up.

The Saint Louis Cardinals had moved Nelson to the mound nearly a decade earlier, after minor-league manager Dixie Walker was impressed when he saw the outfielder throw batting practice. A six-footer from San Diego, Nelson displayed a strong arm, and it was his left arm. Left-handers were always in demand. Like Mudcat Grant, Nelson did not convince scouts he could hit major-league pitching, and it wasn't a unique practice to convert a position player to a pitcher, or vice-versa. Cardinals' minor league manager Dickie Kerr, one of the 1919 Chicago White Sox who was not involved in throwing that World Series, proved to be brilliant when he later convinced Stan Musial to convert from a pitcher to an outfielder, and it appeared Dixie Walker was similarly struck by genius for making Nelson a pitcher – at least for as long as it takes a man to throw nine pitches. The first nine pitches Nelson threw as a professional were strikes. Soon, hitters made frequent contact, and Nelson was just another man with a uniform in the very deep Cardinal farm system.

Military obligations pecked at Nelson's career in the early '60s before the Twins purchased his contract from the Los Angeles Angels during the summer of '64. Twins' scout George Brophy had followed the 28-year-old in the winter leagues after the '63 season. The Twins had turned their scouting attention to Latin American leagues, now that Cuba was closed. Nelson had tossed only the second no-hitter in Venezuelan League history that winter, so the Angels had high hopes for him, but Nelson couldn't make the big-league club in 1964 spring training. He was pitching poorly in Class AAA Hawaii when the Angels released him.

While watching Nelson in Venezuela, Brophy had noticed Nelson's tendency to tip his pitches. Nelson's fastball delivery looked different to hitters than the delivery of his breaking pitch. He had pitched primarily in relief, but the Twins made Nelson a minor-league starter with their top farm club in Atlanta of the International League in 1964. Nelson could get plenty of work by starting regularly, which would allow him to even out that inconsistent delivery. He responded by going 9-12 with a 2.96 earned run average.

Oddly, Nelson wasn't among the pitchers Mele called on to hit, even though Nelson had once been a capable minor league hitter. Nelson had driven in 112 runs with 27 homers during his final minor league season as an outfielder, but he admitted he regressed at the plate once he started to pitch. Nelson had a theory about the largely inept hitting produced by pitchers, a theory which made the small batting accomplishments of players such as Kaat, Boswell, Pascual, and Perry seem all the more impressive. "I think pitchers get poorer and poorer at the plate because they never get any batting practice," Nelson said. "Remember, hitting is practice, just like any other part of the game." It seems to be an overly simplistic explanation, but Babe Ruth, who converted from pitcher to outfielder, held an almost identical opinion regarding pitchers with bats in their hands.

Nelson, Jerry Fosnow, and Bill Pleis were a manager's dream – three left-handers in the bullpen to face the league's tough left-handed hitters such as Carl Yastrzemski, Leon Wagner, Norm Cash, and Vic Davalillo – yet the lefties saw the smallest amount of work on a staff that eventually had more left-handers than right-handers. Fosnow and Nelson had earned run averages above 4.00, but it was an indication of the bullpen's strength if they were the worst of the relief staff. Leading that bullpen were Al Worthington and John Klippstein, two men unlikely to recall their first shaves.

Klippstein was closing in on 38, and Worthington had turned 36 early in the '65 season. Careers were often short because surgery, nutrition, training, and other techniques that can caulk a man's career were mostly a shoulder shrug. After Klippstein pitched in the '59 World Series for the Dodgers at age 32, it would not have been odd for him to end his career, yet he started his 16th major league season in 1965. Sain said Klippstein still had the smoothest pitching delivery of any pitcher he'd ever seen, fluid as a willow in a windstorm. Worthington recalled that Klippstein's delivery "didn't seem to take anything out of him."

Worthington had a fastball that naturally slid sideways and sunk, and that movement caused hitters trouble. He also knew how to keep the ball low in the strike zone, which was particularly valuable in the National League where umpires were more inclined to call the low strike. He had pitched for the Minneapolis Millers, a Giants' AAA minor league team, in the mid-1950s under manager Bill Rigney, who recalled Worthington's arm had been resilient enough that he could start a game one day and pitch an inning of relief the next. Worthington broke into the majors in '53 with the New York Giants and threw consecutive shutouts in his first two major league starts. He was a capable pitcher, but after that glorious debut he never distinguished himself as a starter, and he progressively pitched more in relief until he adopted the role exclusively as a 30-year-old in 1960.

Griffith added Klippstein and Worthington halfway through the difficult '64 campaign, and in retrospect it appears as if Griffith was masterminding the blueprint for his '65 championship team. The reality is they were obtained to fill the void created by the failures of relief pitchers Bill Dailey and Bill Fischer. As was the case with Don Mincher, Klippstein and Worthington were a happy accident rather than part of a grand plan.

The Twins had very high hopes for Fischer and Dailey and expected them to be the key to the bullpen in '64. Griffith had obtained Fischer, a 33-year-old native of Wausau, Wisconsin, from Kansas City before the '64 season. The Twins didn't get nine innings out of Fischer. He entered a game in late May in relief of Gerry Arrigo, who had given up a two-out, game-tying home run to a Baltimore outfielder named Sam Bowens, the man who set the record for home runs by an Oriole rookie that stood for 20 seasons until Cal Ripken, Jr., broke it. Arrigo then threw three straight balls to the next batter before Mele had seen enough and brought in Fischer, who threw one strike before allowing the game-winning home run. It was Fischer's last pitch in the major leagues.

The Twins got more overall mileage from Dailey, who joined the Twins in '63 and quickly became the bullpen ace. The Indians cast off Dailey during 1962 to make room for Mudcat Grant, who was on active duty with the Army but had finally arranged weekend leaves so he could pitch. Dailey was a surprise after the Twins purchased his contract from Cleveland. Batters barely hit .200 against him as he earned 21 saves on a 1.99 earned run average in '63, leading Griffith to believe he had found an anchor for his bullpen. Dailey could not throw strikes the next season. He insisted it was physical and attributed it to a torn muscle in his arm. When the wildness continued, some thought he had developed a mental block that has troubled other players, including Steve Blass, the homesick rookie contemporary of Versalles. The inability to throw a baseball near the intended target became known in the early 1970s as "Steve Blass Disease."

Dailey was loosening before a game one day in 1964 and threw about 20 straight pitches that failed to come within reach of the catcher. He had been one of the league's better, if not the best relief pitcher in the game in 1963, and now Dailey could not throw a strike. Mele thought the problem was physical, not mental. Regardless of the cause, Dailey's wildness, coupled with Fischer's departure, spelled a bullpen collapse.

The remedy for injured arms when Dailey played was not surgery but different arms, so Griffith scoured for new commodities in the middle of 1964 and picked up both Klippstein and Worthington for cash.

Klippstein, a six-foot-one right-hander from Washington, D.C., was pitching very little for Philadelphia, his sixth team in five years. Griffith had learned the Phils needed a roster spot for 39-year-old starting pitcher Cal McLish. Calvin Coolidge Julius Caesar Tuskahoma McLish – the only one of eight children his father was allowed to name – was coming off the disabled list after three straight seasons of double-digit wins. Griffith sent one of his top scouts, 45-year-old former major league catcher Del Wilber, to assess Klippstein. Griffith knew the Phils would keep McLish rather than Klippstein, because McLish and Phillies' manager Gene Mauch were friends. McLish barely pitched again after the Phillies activated him. Meanwhile, Griffith got Klippstein for the $20,000 waiver price.

The curly-haired Klippstein looked and pitched younger than his years, and he threw exceptional ball the rest of the '64 season, even though he was winless in 33 games, the victim of poor fielding and inconsistent hitting.

Griffith still needed another relief pitcher to fill the rest of the '64 season, so he paid $25,000 to get Worthington from San Diego of the Pacific Coast League. It was a gamble on Worthington's morals that many teams were unwilling to take.

Typically, capable players with difficult reputations create a problem for a team in need. Will the contribution on the field outweigh any issues that might be created in the clubhouse? In Worthington's case, many teams shunned him because he was scrupulous as Gandhi. A deeply religious man who devoted much of his time to the Fellowship of Christian Athletes and other church-related work, Worthington sported a crew cut and an unwavering ethic, which cost him at least one stint in the major leagues.

There was a long period in baseball when it was not surprising to learn the home team was concealing a confidant with binoculars in the scoreboard or other ballpark location in an attempt to steal the signs a catcher flashed to a pitcher. The confidant would then relay that call to the batter. Only certain players were usually made aware of sign-stealing, because if a team traded a player who knew the secret, the player might talk to reporters. Exactly that occurred during the Minnesota bullpen's staunch efforts in June of '65, when the contending White Sox traded outfielder Jim Landis to the suffering Kansas City Athletics. Landis extracted his revenge for going from a pennant contender to guaranteed free time in early October by revealing the Sox were stealing signals, relaying the information through walkie-talkies.

There were always rumors about which teams were stealing signs, and in fact when Birdie Tebbetts managed the Milwaukee Braves, he and star pitcher Warren Spahn were vocal and public in their criticism of the practice. The Braves were once guilty of the same strategy, but when Tebbetts joined the organization and learned of the cheating he put a stop to it. Commissioner Ford Frick contended he had investigators looking into sign-stealing in the game, but Tebbetts all but called that a farce, which just resulted in Tebbetts being called in front of the commissioner to have his wrists spanked. The message was clear: stealing signs was part of the game.

Worthington was not originally privy to the fact the Giants were stealing signs during his second season with them in 1959. He had become a Christian since attending a Billy Graham crusade, after which he refused to use any profanity, so it was not acceptable to him when he learned the Giants were stealing signs. He approached Bill Rigney and painted his manager into a dugout corner by insisting the practice end. The Giants were in a three-way battle for the pennant. To release Worthington, who was having a satisfying season, meant questions would be asked, so Rigney ended the larceny and the Giants promptly lost three games. The Giants released Worthington at the end of the season, and he spent the early part of 1960 pitching for the Class AAA Minneapolis Millers. He did well as a starting pitcher in Minneapolis and had an earned run average of 2.04 when the White Sox picked him up.

The Sox were also stationing a man with binoculars in the scoreboard. Worthington learned of this escapade and complained to manager Al Lopez. Lopez knew Worthington could help the club, but he told his new relief pitcher this practice was not going to end. Worthington quit the team cold. He got back into baseball in 1961 and ended up pitching in the minor leagues for two seasons. Being in the big leagues did not consume him, and he happily and brilliantly pitched at Indianapolis in 1962, going 15-4. Worthington later recalled some of his minor league experiences as fondly as he did the 1965 season.

Worthington was a former Alabama college football player who dominated minor league teams during his banishment. Then Cincinnati took a chance on him in 1964. A disappointing start sent him to Class AAA San Diego before Griffith purchased his contract. Worthington was the bullpen ace the minute he pulled on his number 15 Twins' jersey.

He arrived in town at 1 a.m., and hours later allowed one hit in nearly four innings of work as the Twins won. He was a stoic presence on the mound, the kind of man players wanted to play behind when the game was on the line. Worthington fully understood it was supposed to be a pressure situation when he entered the game with a runner on base, no one out and a one-run lead but said he was unemotional about it.

He didn't change the Twins' wayward path in '64, despite allowing one earned run in his first 20 appearances, but it was evident Griffith had made two fine acquisitions in Worthington and Klippstein. They were older than Fischer and Dailey but proved to be more durable, and both had an immediate impact. Klippstein pitched 45 innings for the Twins in '64 with a 1.97 earned run average. Worthington won five games and saved 14 more in 72 innings with a 1.37 ERA. Whether this pair could continue to flourish in 1965 was a question, particularly given their ages.

When all teams headed for Florida in the spring of 1965, Kansas City dangled 30-year-old John Wyatt before Griffith. The Athletics wanted center fielder Jimmie Hall in exchange. Wyatt led the American League in appearances in '64 and had finished among the league's top five pitchers in saves each of the previous two seasons. Griffith re-sisted the offer, saying he didn't like the idea of trading an every day player for a relief pitcher. He added, "I hope we don't need relief that often."

In reality the bullpen was used much more often in 1965 than in '64. Mele had more confidence in his relief staff during the champion-ship season, and the four-man rotation influenced his choices at times. He suddenly had no problem using a quick hook. If a starter faltered, Mele knew he could patch together the rest of the game with the bullpen and that same starting pitcher would be on the mound again in four days, maybe sooner if the pitcher had departed in the first or second inning. Mele also knew that smart baseball men understood bullpens had become crucial.

The Dodgers had finished 11 games ahead of the Giants in 1963, and when the season ended, San Francisco farm director Carl Hubbell noted the Giants lost 17 games while leading in the ninth inning. Hubbell, a Hall of Famer who completed well over half his career starts, had come to recognize the game had changed since his pitching days.

He claimed San Francisco would have won the pennant if the Giants had Dodger relief pitcher Ron Perranoski on their roster and further stated Los Angeles would not have won the pennant without Perranoski.

Until Worthington and Klippstein arrived in the middle of the '64 season, Mele was reluctant to use his bullpen. The Twins had been near the bottom of the league in saves during 1964 as Mele stuck with his starters much longer than he often cared to. The strategy had worked early that season, as starting pitchers went all the way in 19 of the team's first 32 wins. All that work took a toll on the staff, but Mele stayed with his starters longer than practical because of his unreliable bullpen.

The Twins finished 1964 leading the American League in complete games, even though the team didn't play .500 ball. In 1965, the Twins' pitching statistics flipped, with the club second in the league in saves, but near the bottom in complete games. Twins' starters pitched every four days under John Sain, but they didn't often go the distance.

The bullpen was a family invention for Calvin Griffith. It was Clark Griffith who decided to use relief pitchers in the early 1900s, and since then managers have used their bullpens differently and increasingly. In 1965, men such as Worthington or Klippstein were not one-inning closers who pitched only when the team was ahead, as later became the norm. They often entered the game when the team trailed, and quieted bats as long as it took for their mates to stage a rally. Worthington or Klippstein might pitch at any time for Mele, even early in the game, and although each was sometimes called on to get just one out, Mele often used both right-handers in tandem, as he did in late July.

One day the team swept a doubleheader at Boston, with Klippstein pitching more than three innings in the opener before Worthington got the game's final out to earn a save. Worthington pitched more than two innings in the nightcap and got the win.

Taking the ball that often seems simple and effortless in retrospect, when all that remains are old box scores and lines of statistics, but it was often a chore, with do-it-yourself treatment. As the season progressed, Worthington's right arm showed the results of all that pitching. He was tired and sore and eventually missed most of September. Instead of complaining, he would return to the hotel room, fill the bathtub with hot water and soak his arm. Only his teammates knew.

What the fans and media saw were stretches such as the one late in July, when Worthington saved three games and won four others during a scoreless two-week period of pitching that helped the Twins' to a 22-9 record for the month. The string of successes left Worthington with nine victories to that point in the season, his highest total since he was a part-time starter in 1958.

Naturally, the Twins won a different way with a different offensive star in each of Worthington's wins, the oddest highlight occurring when Oliva, the team's best base runner, scored from second on an infield grounder. Oliva alertly recognized Oriole first baseman Boog Powell had lost track of the number of outs and thought the inning had ended, so Powell was paying no attention to Oliva as he raced home. It was a significant win over the second-place Orioles, as the Twins expanded their lead to six games. Worthington's formidable pitching streak to end July also meant fine bullpen performances put bookends on the middle two months of the season.

Kaat had helped the Twins finish May on a bright note with an 85-pitch, 6-0 win. The starters then hit a faltering stretch, and suddenly the bullpen was called upon often – through 100 games the starting pitchers would finish the job just 19 times. The relievers responded by leaving opposing hitters limp. The bullpen's surge started in early June, when Perry relieved Grant in the second inning of a game and pitched nearly six innings of three-hit ball to win for the third time in just over a week.

It was about that time when the players decided they had a reason to be confident and had grown irritated at the constant discussion of trades. Center fielder Jimmie Hall punctuated the team's irritation over these demands from fans and media by emphasizing the team had chemistry. "We're together and we're winning. There's no feeling like it. Man, I never played on a winner, a championship team. I mean, I'm hungry. So are the rest of them."

Lenny Green, who had lost his center field job to Hall and was now with Boston, agreed. "They're hustling, and now they're running like they should have been all the time. They're not waiting for someone to pop the ball out of the park. They're going after runs with everybody."

In addition to involving his bullpen, Mele truly was using his bench players, living up to a pre-season promise of giving his regulars more rest. He benched Battey and Killebrew for the first of a four-game series with Cleveland on a Monday night in early June. The Indians won 2-1, after which charismatic Cleveland outfielder Leon "Daddy Wags" Wagner shook his head. "The Twins have the best club in the American League when they use the first team, but when you rest Killebrew and Battey the same night you're taking the pressure off the opposing pitcher."

Wagner arrived at the park the next day and looked at the lineup illuminated on the Twins-O-Gram. "I see Mele is using my lineup tonight," he said. "Now Killebrew will hit a home run to beat us and my manager will probably blame me for talking Harmon back into the lineup." Of course, not only did Killebrew hit a home run, Battey also homered. Pascual fanned just three but won his eighth straight game, and Mele sent a message to the Cleveland clubhouse thanking Wagner, who went hitless, for the advice.

Birdie Tebbetts, Wagner's manager, told him, "I don't mind you giving advice, but do me a favor and get me a couple of base hits when you do."

It was a crucial series between two favored teams. The Twins hadn't lost a series all season, which was now two months old. The Indians had expected to be in the chase and thrashed to life after the teams split the first two games. The Twins batted .202 during the four-game series and dropped the last two games. One game slipped away because of the mischievous Tebbetts.

He was 54, a former catcher, and was said to have "linguistic elasticity." He missed part of the 1964 season when he suffered a heart attack, which seemed to have little effect on the playfulness he had displayed from the day he was named Cleveland's manager in November of 1962. Grant and Perry were pitching for the Indians at the time, and both attended the press conference at which Tebbetts was introduced.

Tebbetts glanced their way during his words to the media and joked, "I'd like to think you're better pitchers than your records show." The media enjoyed him, although some inside the game considered Tebbetts aloof. He and Mele were great friends, had barnstormed together, and were former Boston teammates. But as Billy Martin had shown when it came to former teammate Mickey Mantle, competitive men rarely let friendships rise above winning.

Kaat was motoring along in the third game of the Cleveland series in early June, and he took a 1-0 lead into the ninth inning. He was two outs from winning and had a two-ball, one-strike count on Rocky Colavito when Tebbetts called time and stepped toward home plate umpire Bill Haller. Tebbetts complained about a tear in one of the blue sleeves of Kaat's undershirt. It was a rare warm night that summer in Minnesota, but many pitchers wear a cotton undershirt with three-quarter-length sleeves regardless of the temperature. A baseball rule stipulates players must wear sleeves of approximately the same length, and the sleeves can't be frayed, ragged or slit. Tebbetts pointed to the hole on Kaat's left sleeve and also mentioned the sleeve was longer than the one on the right arm. Haller ordered the sleeve trimmed at the point above the hole. Mele walked onto the field and Tebbetts began to pump his fists at Mele like a boxer, which infuriated Mele.

"He's throwing his fists at me like, 'come on, I'll fight you,' " Mele later recalled. "Geez, I was mad, and maybe I wanted to fight him, but he was a lot older than me, so I just stood there, cursing the hell out of him."

Kaat issued a one-out walk to Colavito after the interruption. Third baseman Max Alvis came to the plate, and Tebbetts knew Alvis had already homered off Kaat during the season. Tebbetts had the matchup he desired. Alvis ignited a 1-1 fastball for a two-run homer, and the Twins lost. George Strickland, who had coached for Mele and now for Tebbetts, later said he never saw Mele as mad as he was that night. Mele took it out on his team after the game.

"Maybe we're going so good that we expected to have the opposition lie down and play dead. We didn't fight back against Cleveland.

We've hustled all year. If necessary, I'm going to start taking their money." Mele verbally ripped Tebbetts, saying Kaat always pitched well against Cleveland, and that Tebbetts pulled the stunt to unnerve Kaat, who claimed he was not upset by Tebbetts' actions. Kaat said he couldn't locate his pitches to Colavito, and his fastball to Alvis had not sunk, as it had all night.

Tebbetts was found in the clubhouse after the game, buttoning a pink shirt. He strained to his tiptoes to look beyond the shoulders of reporters, as if expecting Mele to appear behind the crowd. He explained to the writers that both shortstop Dick Howser and Strickland noticed the hole in Kaat's sleeve in the first inning. "I'm not excitable about those things," Tebbetts said, "so I said, 'So what?' But it was a strange thing. The hole just must have gotten bigger. And then in the ninth, with the Twins leading 1-0 and one out for us, that hole in the sleeve seemed very, very big. Now, that sleeve must be a big distraction for the hitters, so I did the reasonable thing and asked for the sleeve to be repaired."

As the interview with reporters ended, Tebbetts smiled and made a request: "Keep Sam away from me until he cools off."

Tebbetts ended up the focal point of the next day's baseball coverage, which prompted Kaat to approach Tebbetts and deadpan to the manager that it was terrible shame Alvis had been the hero, yet Tebbetts received all the headlines.

It was not unusual for a manager to throw himself into a game with the intent of affecting the outcome. Mele had called time during a spring training game that season when the Twins had runners on second and third against Atlanta with center fielder Jimmie Hall at the plate. The Braves were in the process of intentionally walking Hall, but Mele picked up a clue, called time in the middle of the at-bat, and conferred with Hall. Before the next pitch, Braves' catcher Gene Oliver stood, acting as if he was about to scoot out and take another pitch far outside the strike zone. Instead the pitch came down the middle of the plate and Oliver ducked down to take the throw. The Braves wanted to catch Hall with the bat on his shoulders as he waited for another intentional ball. Hall swung and won the game. It was only an exhibition game, but Mele was a competitor, and more importantly a student of the game. He did not like to be fooled.

Afterward, reporters asked Mele if he had anticipated the Braves' trickery, and if that was why he went out to talk with Hall. "What do you think I do in the off-season," he asked in response, "clip coupons?"

The better managers always filed away bits of knowledge. They could not play, but they could still affect the outcome of a game with their psychology. Mele recalled Tebbetts eventually explained to him why he decided to call time and see if he could make an issue of Kaat's sleeve. The ploy was based on advice Tebbetts had once received from former major league manager Joe McCarthy, who told Tebbetts, "Don't ever be in a hurry to lose a ball game."

It was a tough loss for Mele and the Twins, and reporters covering the game spent plenty of time in the clubhouses at Metropolitan Stadium, quizzing the players and managers about the incident. Colavito left as soon as he could and headed for the team bus to wait for Tebbetts and his straggling teammates to board and return to the team hotel. As Colavito waited, he saw Kaat emerge from the ball yard.

Players had to walk through the Met Stadium parking lot to reach their cars; there was no security to escort them, and wise fans always waited for the players to emerge so they could obtain autographs. A smattering of young autograph-seekers saw Kaat and chased after him. Colavito later said, "Jim had every reason to be mad and upset, but he signed for every boy who asked for his autograph. He showed me a little class."

COOL OF THE EVENING

Harmon Killebrew and Calvin Griffith

EIGHT

That was a nice home run you hit, daddy.
– Harmon Killebrew's son, Kenny

It had been a wonderful half season for Twins' fans, in a detached, make-believe sort of way. Then as the All-Star break approached in mid-July, people felt less imprisoned by weather and began to appear at Metropolitan Stadium rather than follow the team through radio, newspaper and television. The club had suffered the slowest ticket sales since the move to Minnesota, but in July attendance began to gain on the previous season's pace, largely because of delegations that always provided a healthy portion of the Twins' gate. These groups had been scarce in the aftermath of the violent spring weather, but now they arrived by the busload. Thoughts turned from the notion that the pennant chase was a mirage – in the end the Yankees always won – to the belief that for only the third time since World War II a franchise outside of New York just might win the American League pennant, and damned if it wasn't the Twins who seemed likely as any team to do it.

The daily high temperature was around 75 degrees as Friday and a three-day home stand with the Yankees approached. The previous Sunday had been the Fourth of July, with the Twins tied for first place. The holiday weekend was followed by the seemingly routine weather-related property damage. This time it was mid-week hail and 90-mile-per-hour wind that created havoc and scrambled parts of six small aircraft that were parked at a suburban airport. Fans had begun to accept the possibility of lousy weather, licked their five-cent stamps and dropped ticket requests in the mail. Advance ticket sales now established a solid base for the turnstile count as the fans clicked into Metropolitan Stadium with their transistor radios. Such a high percentage of fans brought along radios to listen to the games that one sponsor, Theo Hamm Brewing Company, targeted a segment of their commercials toward fans in the stands.

For the weekend Yankee series more than 135,000 invaded the Met, which in keeping with its piecemeal construction history featured new, additional seating. A double deck in left field contained 6,000 more seats, just in time for the All-Star Game that would follow the Yankee series.

About 30,000 fans saw the Twins win the Friday opener minus Bob Allison, who had suffered a chipped bone in his wrist when hit by a pitch earlier in the week. The season's theme of tossing off injuries to key players continued as the Twins managed their eighth-straight win and started to shake away from a clump of five teams that had been within two games of each other during the final week of June. The Twins had fallen a breath behind Cleveland as July began. Then Minnesota squeaked ahead by a game and a half when Allison went down on July 7. The Twins had a four-game lead – their biggest of the season – after winning the Friday series opener against New York.

On Saturday, three days before the All-Star game in Minnesota, clever Calvin Griffith counted a double gate as the Twins won the opener of a day-night doubleheader before losing the nightcap, their first loss in 10 games. Griffith had wisely lobbied to postpone the season's second game during April's rain and floods, despite protests from the Yankees, who claimed Griffith was more concerned about poor attendance than unplayable conditions. The league went along with Griffith, and that decision put a bulge in his wallet because Major League Baseball had a directive that stated postponed games could be made up as part of split doubleheaders. The postponed April game with New York was converted into the second game of the Saturday day-night doubleheader, so what might have been a crowd of perhaps 3,000 in April resulted in a huge mid-summer gate attraction, with more than 36,000 fans turning out for each game that Saturday.

There was a break of a couple hours between games to clear the crowd, wait for the parishioners from Church of the Assumption to sweep out the stands as they had since the club moved to Minnesota, and then admit ticket holders for the nightcap. The downside for the players was they had to spend more than 10 hours at Met Stadium, so the players hoped for a short day at the yard when Sunday arrived. It was getaway day for the Yankees, and players on both teams were eager to start the three-day All-Star break.

It was 78 degrees, and another crowd of about 35,000 appeared for the series finale that soft Sunday afternoon, settling into the stands to watch a pre-game ceremony in which Oliva received his Silver Slugger Award for winning the 1964 league batting title. Fans were in an upbeat mood over the presentation, the sun, and the fact New York had lost two of the first three games and was more than a dozen games behind the Twins in the standings, but the Yankees took the lead in the top of the ninth on a controversial play that disgusted the hometown crowd and caused the fans to drum long and hard on the umpires.

The game had been tied three times, first when Versalles hit his 10th home run of the season to make it 1-1 in the third. The scoring seesawed from that point before coming to rest at 4-4 in the top of the ninth when, with two out and Yankees on first and third, New York rookie outfielder Roger Repoz chopped a high, bounding ball down the first-base line. Pitcher Jerry Fosnow raced over and lunged for the ball as Repoz sped down the baseline, making contact with Fosnow en route to first base. The ball fell to the ground and home plate umpire Ed Hurley called Repoz out for interfering with Fosnow's ability to field the ball. It was the third out and the Twins ran off the field, hoping to stage a ninth-inning rally and go home.

Yankee manager Johnny Keane charged out of the third-base dugout and insisted Fosnow had possession of the ball but dropped it, an interesting assertion in that Keane lacked an ideal view of a play on the first-base side of the field from the visitors' third-base dugout. If Fosnow had dropped the ball, it would mean Repoz should be safe and the run that crossed the plate would count. Umpires rarely reverse a call, but

Hurley did just that after a conference with the first-base umpire. Hurley decided his view of the play had been blocked and deferred his call. Fosnow was ruled to have been in possession of the ball before it fell to the ground, and Repoz was called safe. New York's Elston Howard scored from third on the play, the run stood and the Yankees led 5-4.

Mele charged out and argued with more animation than Keane, but lost the argument. Fosnow maintained he never had control of the ball when Repoz brushed him, and that Repoz unquestionably had interfered. Hurley dismissed the Twins' appeal, and Mele told the umpires his team would continue the game under protest as the players were ordered back onto the field. Minnesota got the final out of the inning for what fans believed was the second time, and those customers remained agitated and dismayed as the team left the field again. Didn't the Yankees always get these kinds of breaks? The specter of Yankee championships remained with many baseball followers, who still considered the franchise a threat. Could this open the door? American League president Joe Cronin was in the stands, so fans howled at him in addition to the umpires and the Yankees.

Keane brought in six-foot-two, 220-pound Staten Island native Pete Mikkelsen to finish the game. As was the case with many players around the league, Mikkelsen was familiar to avid baseball fans in the region because he had pitched for Fargo-Moorhead in the Northern League as a 20-year-old in 1960. He became a standout high school pitcher after his family moved to California, but neither his fastball nor his breaking pitch seemed to be more than minor-league stuff. He threw a palm-ball for his change of pace, maintaining his fastball motion so as not to tip the pitch. He just held the ball so far back in his hand that the pitch did not have the velocity of his fastball and tricked the hitter into swinging early.

This had not been enough to gain him a major-league roster spot, but an arm injury in 1963 caused him to drop down from a straight overhand delivery. Suddenly his fastball started to dip most of the time. He was now a sinkerball pitcher, capable of inducing groundouts. It was only Mikkelsen's second season in the major leagues, but he had confidence in his pitches and himself, and along the way he was offered some good advice, which quickly became ingrained: the edge was his when he entered a game in the late innings. Batters didn't make any money taking walks in those situations; they were up there to swing that bat and drive in runs, so they could drive better cars. Mikkelsen decided if batters swung at his sinking fastball, they would hit it into the ground. Of course, the ball had to sink.

In the fifth game of the '64 World Series, 23-year-old St. Louis catcher Tim McCarver clubbed the rookie's 3-2 fastball over Mickey Mantle's head for a three-run homer that won the game in the 10th inning. It was probably the undoing of Yankee manager Yogi Berra, who had left-handed options in the bullpen but let the right-handed Mikkelsen pitch to the lefty McCarver. The Cardinal catcher also happened to be hot as a flaming sunrise in the Series, with seven hits in 16 at-bats. Keane was managing the Cardinals, so he was the beneficiary of McCarver's blast, which helped his team eventually win the Series in seven games. Keane sat in the dugout with a million-dollar view that day as Mikkelsen's fastball to McCarver failed to sink. During the off-season, Berra was fired, and Keane was offered the job of Yankee manager, a job that forced him to make some decisions regarding Mikkelsen.

Mikkelsen began the '65 season in a New York uniform before the Yankees demoted the bespectacled right-hander to Class AAA Toledo in mid-June with the idea of making him a starting pitcher. The demotion also occurred days after an incident in a Newark Airport bar in which Keane fined three Yankees and reprimanded two others following behavior that led to bartenders' refusing to serve the players further. The *New York Times* reported Mikkelsen was one of those reprimanded. He had been used exclusively in relief in 1964 and was among the better relievers in the league that season, but he responded to the experiment in Toledo by winning three of four starts. That included throwing a no-hitter on July 4, exactly one week before he took the ball for the ninth inning in Metropolitan Stadium. The Yankees had flown him more than a thousand miles, from Florida to Detroit, just days before the series with the Twins. He started against the Tigers, pitching respectable ball through five innings, but the experiment as a starter didn't last long. Keane used him for nearly three innings of relief in the second game of Saturday's split doubleheader, and Mikkelsen got the win.

He was making his third appearance in four days when he entered the game following the controversy with Repoz and quickly retired Versalles to begin the bottom of the ninth inning. Working a walk had become rare for the next batter, Rollins, but he coaxed a free pass, to the delight of Martin, who in his Yankee career often used patience to get on base late in the game so one of the Yankees' big bats could send him around the base paths. Pre-game honoree Oliva hit a fly ball to Repoz in center for the second out, with Rollins remaining at first base. Killebrew stepped into the batter's box. He had 15 home runs at the time, a low mid-season total for a man who was averaging 47 homers a season since the franchise had relocated to Minnesota, but he had worked hard to cut down his swing and drive the ball to the opposite field in Mele's go-go offense. Mikkelsen had faced Killebrew twice during the Yankees' win Saturday and induced groundouts both times. Mikkelsen first developed deep confidence in his sinker against Killebrew while auditioning for the Yankee pitching staff during spring training in '64. Killebrew drove numerous sinkerballs into the dirt in one exhibition game, and if Mikkelsen could handle Killebrew with that pitch, he stood to be a valuable weapon in the Yankees' bullpen.

It was Killebrew's habit to stand perfectly straight in the batter's box and take one or two gentle half-swings, then bring the bat back to his shoulder, his hands tight against his chest in the manner of a man trying to keep himself warm. He used a 33-ounce bat, about the norm for a major-leaguer, even though Killebrew was stronger than most. As the pitcher began his motion, Killebrew would push his hands and that narrow-grained bat away from his chest as if liquid had begun to leak from the bottom and he didn't want it to drip onto his shoes. His knees would flex and the number 3 on his back would stretch tight as his back rounded, but he stood perfectly still in that pose as the ball left the pitcher's hand. Then he brought his hands in and down and lashed at the ball, using his powerful hips to drive into the pitch. Unlike Henry

Aaron or Ernie Banks, Killebrew was not a wrist hitter; he was more like Babe Ruth. Harmon Killebrew took a vicious, lumberjack's cut at a baseball.

Mikkelsen worked a two-ball, two-strike count before Killebrew looped that swing through the strike zone and fouled off Mikkelsen's change-up. Mikkelsen had confidence in this pitch as well as his sinker, so he threw another palm ball, hoping the slugger would time the pitch incorrectly and swing too early. Killebrew took the pitch, which was called a ball, to make the count three balls and two strikes. The Yankees preferred not to walk Killebrew, which would move Rollins into scoring position and force right-handed Mikkelsen to face left-handed, streak-hitting Mincher, who was sizzling. Mincher had homered twice Friday and driven in three runs on Saturday. Keane had seen this situation before, last October, when Mikkelsen faced a hot-hitting left-hander with two runners on base. He certainly did not want to put Killebrew on for Mincher to recreate the scenario that led to McCarver's blast the previous October. In addition, Killebrew was right-handed, so the match-up favored Mikkelsen.

Yankee catcher Elston Howard called for a fastball to end the three-and-a-half hour struggle. There was a healthy breeze blowing toward Killebrew from left field; otherwise the belt-high fastball that never sank might have gone farther than 380 feet. It was the agonizingly loud smack of wood on horsehide that hit Elston Howard's eardrums. The ball jetted toward the stands, almost as if Killebrew had lit a short fuse on a Fourth of July pop bottle rocket. It was not the typical "Killebrew Fly" that featured a majestic parabolic arch. The ball was still rising when it crashed into the left-field pavilion.

Silence.

Had this happened? Had Killebrew hit a two-out, two-run homer on a 3-2 pitch to beat the Yankees heading into the All-Star break? Was this team going to the World Series? The crowd erupted, screaming, applauding and stamping its feet on the stands, as had become the custom when the Met Stadium regulars wanted to display their appreciation enthusiastically. The cantilevered triple deck behind home plate shook from the thunderous pounding. Killebrew circled third base as Rollins crossed home plate, then turned to wait and congratulate Killebrew. Two fans in straw pork-pie hats ran onto the field to aid the celebration as Killebrew planted a cleated foot onto home plate and headed for the dugout. Seven-year-old Kenny Killebrew was often in the Twins clubhouse, and he greeted his father as the players marched in.

"That was a nice home run you hit, daddy."

Killebrew enjoyed some watermelon as reporters surrounded him. He recalled hitting a game-winning home run a year earlier against the Yankees' Al Downing at the Met. It hadn't received much reaction. "I guess it's where we are in the standings that makes the difference," Killebrew said, but he did admit his 288th career home run was one of the "sweeter of the sweet. I knew when I hit it that it was going a long way."

The home run was considered the most dramatic "big fly" in the history of the Minnesota Twins until Kirby Puckett deposited Charlie Liebrandt's change-up into the Metrodome seats in the sixth game of the 1991 World Series against Atlanta. Killebrew's home run abruptly halted the days when fans called him "Harmless Harmon." He became the most loved Minnesota Twin in club history until Puckett came along, but during Kenny Killebrew's seven years, his dad's career could hardly be reduced to numbers on the back of a baseball card. Killebrew's career had twinkled and faded so often that carrying the team as a star ballplayer had to be simple compared to what he had carried since he left home in 1954 as a 17-year-old bonus baby. For starters, he languished in the major leagues for two seasons on the Washington Senators' bench.

Baseball owners have always been so eager to throw money at prospects that from time to time these monolithic egos decreed that a "bonus baby," a player who accepted more than a set dollar amount as a signing bonus, must either be carried on the major league roster or clear waivers before being sent to the minor leagues, but no team would risk exposing a player to waivers after giving him thousands of dollars. Supposedly, this rule would be so damaging to the player's development and such a burden on the big-league team that owners would contain their spending. The Senators, strapped financially, had always, and almost uniquely, managed restraint.

The Griffiths did not jump into the bonus market until Idaho Senator Herman Welker started to sit in Clark Griffith's box seats during Senators' games. Welker enjoyed chatting with Griffith about prospects. Most notably, Welker tipped Griffith to Boise, Idaho, native Vernon Law, who pitched 16 years in the major leagues. Griffith ignored the tip. One afternoon, Welker mentioned he was a friend of a Payette, Idaho, family that laid claim to good athletic bloodlines, and one boy was a remarkable high school shortstop. When Griffith stopped by Welker's office, the senator showed him newspaper clippings inked with words about the Idaho state semi-pro baseball tournament in which the kid had gone 12-for-12 in three games – with a sizable configuration of home runs, triples and doubles – to bring his batting average to nearly .850. The proportion of extra-base hits varies depending on the source for this anecdote, but the story of Harmon Killebrew is rich with enough homespun coincidence and tall-tale that it is appropriate he landed in Minnesota, a state that lays claim to Paul Bunyan.

One of the better pitchers in baseball history, Hall of Famer Walter Johnson, was born about 15 miles from Payette, Idaho. Johnson, "The Big Train," had been the player from that area the Senators had signed most recently – in 1907 – and of course Johnson not only went on to be one of history's more notable power pitchers but was considered to be one of the more likable, easy-going, virtuous players in a rowdy era for the national pastime. Killebrew had one of the more notable power hitting careers of his era, and although the job of baseball player was considered more respectable by the time Killebrew came along, he was thought to be exceptionally easy-going and approachable.

As with the Killebrew family, the Johnson family had roots in the Midwest, then migrated west. As with Killebrew, Johnson became a Hall of Famer, and as was the case with Killebrew, Johnson was not an instant success. And if the story were a Hollywood film, there would be an obligatory shot of young Harmon playing ball on a field. The camera would pull back to reveal the name of the ball yard. Yes, Killebrew played his early baseball on Walter Johnson Memorial Field.

Then there was the history and legend of Killebrew's grandfather and father. His grandfather, a Civil War veteran from Decatur, Illinois, was reputed to be the strongest man in the Union Army by virtue of being the heavyweight wrestling champion over all comers. The mere fact someone would suggest a fellow is the strongest man in the Union Army hints at some measure of validity regarding his strength, although Killebrew himself seemed to doubt the tale that his ancestor was so strong and could jump so high that he could clear the back of a standing horse. Killebrew's father, Harmon Clayton Killebrew, Sr., was a fullback who played for undefeated Millikin College in Illinois before transferring to West Virginia Wesleyan, where he was an all-America selection under Pro Football Hall of Fame coach Earle "Greasy" Neale, the only man to play in a World Series and coach both a college football team to the Rose Bowl and a professional team to the National Football League title. Clay Killebrew loved sports and participated in football at some risk, as he had lost the sight in one eye.

He urged his sons into football, baseball, basketball, and track. Harmon liked to tell the story of his mother commenting about the condition of the backyard grass, which suffered under the constant abuse of the Killebrew brothers during their various pick-up sporting games. Clayton's response was, "We're not raising grass here, we're raising boys." Clay Killebrew enjoyed strolling to the movies with his sons, stopping for ice cream afterward, and then challenging his boys to a footrace home. Harmon inherited his father's speed, so when baseball and football scouts visited Payette they noted his running ability, in addition to his strength. Eventually, Killebrew's lack of speed was a subject of teammates' jokes and even his own light-heartedness. He never tried to defend himself with the fact his speed quickly eroded because of various injuries to his knees and legs.

Clay Killebrew was in his 40s when Harmon was born and would not likely have lived long enough to know he had fathered a Hall of Fame baseball player, but he and Harmon never even had the opportunity to share the excitement of Harmon's first big-league contract. Clay Killebrew died in 1953 of a heart attack at age 59, when Harmon was 16.

Welker's newspaper clippings and stories of the thoroughbred backgrounds of the Killebrew men inspired Clark Griffith. He discussed Payette's high school athletic phenom with his confidant and current farm director, Ossie Bluege. Other teams were also learning about Killebrew, so Bluege used Welker's influence to gain a seat on an airplane to Boise, where Bluege rented a car. He arrived in Payette, which could just as well have been Minnesota in 1965: it was pouring rain and had been for days, so Bluege sat in his motel room wondering how to justify his expenses to the economical Griffith. The weather broke the next day, just long enough for a game to be played. Bluege arrived at the park to see Killebrew practice bunting the ball – something Killebrew was never asked to do during a game in his entire major league career – and immediately liked the way the kid handled a bat. Eventually, Killebrew hit a home run that cleared an 18-foot fence. Bluege stepped off the home run at more than 400 feet, well beyond the capability of many big-leaguers.

Most of Bluege's 18-year playing career, all as a fine-fielding third baseman with Washington, coincided with the career of Babe Ruth, so Bluege had a litmus test to use when judging Killebrew. Bluege was one of the more successful Washington managers during the half-century span in which the Senators were usually last in the league, so he knew baseball. Finally, he had been an accountant in the off-season during his playing days, so Bluege knew money, and he knew this signing would not come cheaply. But the Senators were going nowhere at the gate or on the field, and Griffith was ready to dive into the bonus market.

Bluege stopped by the Killebrew household the day after Killebrew tagged that mammoth home run and learned the high schooler was following in the footsteps of his father, a housepainter, and was over at the local school house with a brush. Bluege was not convinced the $30,000 bonus Griffith had approved would put Killebrew in a Senators' uniform. The boy certainly fit in around Payette, and the Mark Twain scene with classmates at the school reinforced that notion. Bluege's enthusiasm was further muted when he recalled the day he arrived and announced his presence in Payette. He saw Killebrew was pleased but certainly not excited. And Harmon was the youngest of four children, the only child now living at home. With one of his brothers serving in the military in Korea, mom was leaning toward the merits of college.

Killebrew had won 12 letters in high school athletics and was named to the National Scholastic All-American football team at quarterback. Unsurprisingly, he already had a scholarship to the University of Oregon to play baseball. Then there were the bats Bluege had seen in the corner of the kitchen when he stopped by the Killebrew home. The bats were from Ted Williams, and Bluege knew the Red Sox were the other team seriously chasing Killebrew. The Senators had no comparable big name to influence Killebrew.

After a family discussion that involved his oldest brother, Killebrew signed for $30,000 spread over three years, including $6,000 in salary and $4,000 in bonus for his first season. Bluege admitted the youngster would be better off in the minor leagues, but because of the bonus rule Killebrew would be stuck in the major leagues for two seasons. Killebrew later said the chance to go immediately to the big leagues helped sway him to bypass college, although he also reflected that, in his opinion, the bonus rule helped neither the club nor the player. Bluege expressed hope that Bucky Harris, who was managing the Senators at the time, could get Killebrew into the lineup frequently. Bluege thought highly of Killebrew and was adamant in his belief that the teen was a better prospect than the collegian for whom he was also bidding: 22-year-old Minnesotan Paul Giel.

Nine days later, Killebrew went from painting the high school in Payette to decorating the Senators' bench. He stood five-foot-eleven, weighed 185 pounds, with sandy brown hair that soon began to recede. It was a week before his 18th birthday when, walking on air, yet scared to death, he entered Bucky Harris' room in the Del Prado Hotel in Chicago to meet his manager. He played in nine games the first year and 38 games the next. Harmon Killebrew avoided being the prequel to the John Sevcik story, but it was not easy – on or off the field.

The teenager was strong, solid and displayed raw power in spring training in 1954, but he was just a kid breaking into the big leagues during a period when there were only 16 teams, and integration had made it more challenging to stay in the big leagues. Rosters had been opened to black players in 1947, so the competition to wear a major-league uniform was particularly keen, arguably as difficult as any time in history. Suddenly, there were far more candidates to play ball but the same number of teams. The Senators also complicated life by first trying the teenager at second base, then third, then first, and then outfield.

Killebrew married his high school sweetheart following his second and final season under the bonus rule. With the adult responsibility of supporting someone, he decided to play winter ball instead of heading back home to attend college classes. He could use the playing time after idling on the Senators' bench, and he hoped to play in Cuba, where the competition was better that Mexico. Unfortunately for him, a new rule was instituted that allowed only six players from one major league team, including Cuban natives, to play in Cuba's winter league. The Senators had met their limit, so Killebrew went hundreds of miles south of Mexico City to play in Cordoba. His winter season was cut short when his brother-in-law died. Killebrew returned home and soon expressed confusion about his future: he was married; he contemplated continuing his education; and although the recruit quota from his hometown was being filled by enlistments, the military draft in the post-Korean War era also drifted through his thoughts.

It wasn't as though there was a bright light drawing him into the game anymore. The Senators were not a good team. They finished in the top half of the American League only 20 times in 60 seasons, and during Killebrew's apprenticeship it was an accomplishment when the Senators didn't finish last among eight teams. The struggling organization wanted Killebrew in the majors in the worst way, and the fans certainly enjoyed those home runs, but sitting on the bench for his final teen years had limited his development as a player. On the positive side, there were some benefits to being exposed to the minds of these professionals. One of his early roommates was Johnny Pesky, born in Portland, Oregon – Killebrew's region of the country.

Pesky was an intelligent ballplayer who broke in with Boston in 1942, missed three seasons because of World War II, then resumed his

Red Sox career. Pesky played with an outfielder named Sam Mele, who met his future wife through Pesky.

Killebrew was always a good listener, and when Pesky spoke, Killebrew listened. Later, Washington manager Charlie Dressen had Killebrew room with coach Cookie Lavagetto, who drove home the point that all players drop into slumps, but good players learn how to correct the problem themselves. Lavagetto also provided first-hand detail on how Killebrew could work to break the habit of being a pure pull hitter, in Killebrew's case, driving everything to left field. Lavagetto was a pull-hitter as a rookie but eventually taught himself to get his hands through the strike zone ahead of the bat barrel and drive the ball into right field. Lavagetto knew Killebrew would eventually have to learn this to succeed against big-league pitching.

It wasn't until 1956, when Killebrew's bonus-baby sentence ended and he was sent to minor-league Charlotte, that he was able to see regular live pitching. He responded with 15 home runs in 70 games and batted .325. Killebrew was pressed into service in Washington briefly that season and teased fans with each of his first three hits, which were long home runs. Future Minnesota Twins manager Billy Gardner set the stage for another glimpse of what was to come from Killebrew after Gardner spiked Senator second baseman Pete Runnels during a game in Baltimore. Killebrew replaced Runnels and hit two long home runs, one over a wire barrier in center field that had been cleared just once before. He was still just a kid, 20 years old, and his share of poignant moments lay ahead.

One occurred in 1957, when the Senators were hurrying to catch a plane for Detroit after a game in Cleveland. The players were tired and rain was imminent, which made their bones more miserable, and what happened next made some of their hearts miserable. Traveling secretary Howard Fox intercepted Killebrew as he boarded the bus and told him to grab his bags. Killebrew was being sent to Chattanooga. Eddie Yost, who would eventually lose his third base job to Killebrew, helped him hunt for his bag as rain began to fall. Killebrew gathered his belongings, stepped to the sidewalk, and said he planned to walk to the train station. Looking at the sky, Yost suggested a cab. Killebrew declined. Players settled into their seats, the door closed, and as the bus pulled away, some of the Senators looked back to see the knot of a man slowly moving toward the train station in the rain, suitcase dangling from the end of his right arm.

Killebrew drove in 100 runs for the first time in his professional career after that demotion to Chattanooga. He led the Southern Association with 29 home runs despite the fact that the left-field fence in Chattanooga was very high and a very long way from home plate. A shoulder injury also limited his playing time and restricted what was still impressive offensive production. It seemed he was ready to move up the ladder, and in 1958 he was promoted to Indianapolis. He struggled badly. After barely 30 games he was back in Chattanooga, with *The Sporting News* graciously reporting that Killebrew "failed to hit the size of his hat" in Indy. The demotion happened just before his 22nd birthday. Killebrew was going no place.

Ossie Bluege stepped in to help.

It seems hard to imagine for most Twins' fans, because Ossie Bluege was always an old man to them. In 1984, a year before he died, Bluege appeared at the Metrodome for Harmon Killebrew Night. Killebrew had been retired for 10 years. The fringe of hair Killebrew had since his mid-20s had turned a distinctive white. Bluege remained trim, his frame a little bent. He had white hair and wore glasses. Bluege and Killebrew embraced before a crowd of more than 40,000, but the relationship seemed to be nothing more than scout and prospect, 30 years later. But Killebrew spent most of his life without a father, and another mentor, former University of Oregon ballplayer Don Dibble, died of kidney disease when Killebrew was 19. Ossie Bluege was not just the man who signed Killebrew to a contract; he had once been very much like Killebrew.

Bluege was a 19-year-old kid from Chicago in early 1920 with a dream of playing big-league ball. A player could earn as much as $6,000 a season in the big leagues, he boasted to his father, who replied, "Who's going to pay that kind of money for chasing a ball around?" His dad offered him a bookkeeping job at $35 a week, but Bluege signed a $200-

a-month contract to play in the Three-I League. Charlie Dressen was playing third base for Rock Island, so with his favorite position unavailable, Bluege played shortstop. He found minor league baseball fun for a while but was soon bored, rising in the morning with nothing to do before playing ball in the afternoon, and then taking in a movie at night. Bluege was living on nerves and feelings and lost all objectivity on his chances to make the major leagues, lost perspective on his talent, and decided to go home to be a bookkeeper. He was ready to pack his bags when his manager, a man named Bill Jackson, intervened.

Jackson told Bluege he could hit and run and field, and all the great things a lost youngster needed to hear. Jackson explained a bookkeeping job would always be there for him, but the big-league window opens briefly, and only a crack. Bluege wound up with an 18-year major league career – with a minor league stop playing for the Minneapolis Millers. In 1958, Bluege knew exactly what to say when Killebrew began to wonder if his future was back in Idaho.

"Ossie always had words of encouragement for me," Killebrew said years later. "He was just one of those guys with a good word, and I have to say there were not many of them like that around. I could always go have a conversation with Ossie and walk away feeling better."

The chat with Bluege and the return to Class AA Chattanooga, where Killebrew's friend, Bob Allison, was enjoying his second and most productive season with the Lookouts, was what Killebrew needed. Chattanooga was a step back, but the familiarity carried a comfort level. When he returned to the Lookouts after his chat with Bluege in late June of '58, Killebrew hit nine home runs in 41 games, occasionally facing Mobile left-hander Dick Stigman, who was on his way to winning 15 games in the Cleveland farm system.

They were both born in 1936, and each began his professional career in 1954, but illustrating the difference in their paths to the Southern Association is the fact Stigman started with Fargo-Moorhead of the Northern League, pressing up from the lowest rung of the minor leagues, playing regularly and honing his skills at each stop. Killebrew spent his first two seasons spectating because of the bonus rule. After their first two seasons in pro ball Stigman, who of course didn't even play daily because he was a starting pitcher, had played almost as many professional games as Killebrew. Stigman said he knew he had faced Killebrew in AA ball, but had no memory of any encounter. "There were a lot of good players in that league," Stigman said. "I knew about Harmon, but that was about it."

The bonus rule seemed to be more obstacle than honor, and it kept rearing its head.

Calvin Griffith assigned Allison to Cuba for the winter of '58, but Killebrew went to a sales job in a natural gas company in Ontario, Oregon. Killebrew wasn't allowed to play in Cuba because of his veteran major league status. Griffith was loud in his complaint about the rule that prevented him from sending Killebrew to the Almendares club for winter ball. Griffith also maintained Cuban fans would enjoy seeing Killebrew hit his majestic home runs, but Griffith's campaigning didn't change anything. There was a restriction that stipulated players who had spent 334 days with a big-league club in the United States could not play in Cuba. Killebrew had exceeded that with his two years of bonus servitude.

American players have loved wintering in Cuba as far back as Babe Ruth, who enjoyed the food, cigars, and gambling on the island at least as much as he did playing ball there. Griffith traveled to Cuba during the winter of 1958 and was surprised to find conditions were very livable and games were played in modern, well-groomed stadiums, with players allowed at least two days off each week. American players stayed in air-conditioned apartments and homes, complete with servants if they desired, but just as Cuban players had to adjust to the United States, American players had to adjust to Cuba. One notable difference at the park was the armed policemen and soldiers at each entrance who frisked fans as they passed into the ballpark, security vaguely similar to what would be seen at American stadiums in the next century. The island was a good place to spend the winter and a great place to play baseball. Hitters benefited from facing the likes of Pascual and Ramos along with career minor-league pitchers such as Tommy Lasorda. Americans also learned little things to advance their U.S. careers while playing in the Cuban league, which was highly competitive and could be cutting-edge when it came to instruction.

Allison won 11 letters as a high school baseball, football, track, and basketball star, then played two years of football at the University of Kansas. Despite all the coaching involved, it was in Cuba where he learned to improve his running style. He was an oak of a man with decent speed, and the momentum he generated was a fright on the base paths. After he arrived in the big leagues to stay in 1959, opposing middle infielders took no delight at the sight of Allison blotting out their view of the first baseman as he charged into second base on a double play. One player said it wasn't Walter Johnson who should have been called "The Big Train," it was Allison, who "looks like a runaway limited when he piles into you at second base to break up a double play."

Allison honed that running style in Cuba during the winter of '58, when Oscar Rodriguez, who managed the Almendares club, noticed Allison ran with his arms spread like the wings of a bird. Rodriquez contacted a friend, a Cuban track coach, to work with Allison on his form. Even after that, Allison still had a tendency to remain upright until he was just a few feet from second base. He had a football mentality, so he was conditioned not to fear the thought of contact. This intimidated middle infielders, but in baseball it meant Allison had to learn to slide. If he didn't, it would be just a matter of time before a middle infielder would force him to the base path dirt by aiming a relay throw squarely at his forehead.

Killebrew and Allison became teammates in Washington despite the fact Killebrew had been strongly courted by the Red Sox and Allison was shadowed by Yankee scout Tom Greenwade, who discovered Mickey Mantle and did the background work on Jackie Robinson. Allison and Mantle came from the same region of the country – Allison from Missouri and Mantle from Oklahoma, but Allison decided not to follow Mantle's path to New York because he thought it would be easier to reach the big leagues with the Senators. Whether Allison would have made it to New York to stay in '59 is hard to say, but he spent just four seasons in the minor leagues. The Senators jumped Allison from Class AA Chattanooga to the major leagues at the end of 1958, and he never did return to the minor leagues. Certainly, the Senators tolerated more from him than the Yankees would have.

Allison had a powerful arm and liked to show it off. Early in his career, he would often unleash throws to third base when he had no chance to catch the runner, which would allow the batter to advance to second base on the throw. The Yankees did not win pennant after pennant with that style of play. It was something the Senators had to accept, and in a way it was welcome. The Senators had been mocked for years by sports writers and fans for "a Venus outfield" – no arms – so even if Allison was a bit enthusiastic, at least the team finally had an outfielder who was capable of throwing the ball from the outfield warning track to home plate on one hop for perhaps the first time since the Senators acquired Sam Mele in 1949.

The competition for starting center fielder in Washington during spring training of 1959 was one indication the Senators' future was brightening. The battle was between incumbent American League Rookie of the Year Albie Pearson and the aspiring Allison. Pearson arrived late to camp, which gave Allison a chance to play. It was a visually disparate competition, if not a heated one. Albie Pearson, all five-feet-five inches of him, took one look at Allison in Florida and accurately assessed the future.

"He's a big one. He can run, he can throw, and he's got a good bat. I'm going to have to fight for my job."

Some players called Allison "Mr. America." He had thick, jet-black hair that formed a perfect widow's peak over the face of a Gentleman's Quarterly model, and hands that could engulf not just the handle of a baseball bat but the barrel. The physical differences between Allison and Pearson were even greater than they appeared in uniform, according to George "Doc" Lentz, the team trainer who also worked with the Washington Redskins' football team. Lentz called Allison "the strongest guy I ever worked on, and that goes for the Redskins, too."

Allison, 25, was soon the starting center fielder and Killebrew's roommate. Pearson was in Baltimore, traded for Lenny Green. By late July,

Allison had driven in 61 runs, nearly 30 more than Pearson's entire 1958 total. Allison hit 30 home runs in his rookie season, more than Pearson did in his nine-year career. Only seven of Allison's home runs came after mid-July, which became his pattern. He was usually off to a hot start each season, but as the season wore on the strikeouts became more frequent and his production typically slowed.

Allison and Killebrew, protected in the lineup by power-hitters Jim Lemon and Roy Sievers, captivated Washington fans in '59. The Senators had cleared the third base job for Killebrew by trading Eddie Yost to Detroit the previous winter. Killebrew had been destined to stick with the Senators because he was out of options and either had to stay with the Senators or be exposed to the waiver wire.

Lavagetto, a former Brooklyn Dodgers' third baseman, worked with Killebrew at third base during spring training. He helped improve Killebrew's fielding, but the youngster was hitting mainly singles and doubles. Griffith was expecting him to hit for power. Then the regular season began. Killebrew homered on opening day, and the home runs never stopped. At one point during the first weeks of play he hit seven home runs in eight days and by May 20 had piled up 15 home runs. Just months after *The Sporting News* had reported that Killebrew couldn't hit his hat size in Indianapolis, the publication was calling him baseball's "most exciting personality since Willie Mays."

Naturally, this success at the plate did not sit well with pitchers around the league. Killebrew was hit by pitches seven times that season, and found himself on the ground more often. One day in Detroit, 29-year-old Frank Lary, the Tigers' veteran ace, fired a pitch near Killebrew's skull. Killebrew pulled himself from his sprawl in the dirt and deposited Lary's next pitch into the left-field bleachers. As the scene was repeated in various parks, pitchers slowly curbed their enthusiasm for agitating the man.

The Senators still finished last, but it was an enjoyable season for fans who liked to watch home runs fly out of American League stadiums. Sievers, Allison, Lemon and Killebrew were tabbed "The SALK Shots," an acronym the media composed from the first letter of each man's last name, compliments of Jonas Salk, who had discovered the miracle of the day, the Salk polio vaccine. The team was second in the league in home runs as Allison hit 30 – 29 off right-handers – drove in 85, stole 13 bases and batted .261. Killebrew, two years younger than Allison, hit 42 homers and drove in 105 runs, a better season than Allison but once again the bonus rule would affect him: Killebrew had spent too much time on a major-league roster to be considered a rookie.

Allison traveled to Cuba with his wife and two boys following the '59 season. He was playing winter ball there when Kansas City sportscaster Merle Harmon called him in Havana with the news Allison had beaten out Cleveland pitcher Jim Perry, 23, for American League Rookie of the Year. Allison joked that the title for his season was "Allison in Wonderland."

Yankee manager Casey Stengel was less jovial. He greeted the news by grumbling that Allison should have signed with the Yankees, but Allison said few scouts thought highly enough of his baseball skills to offer a huge bonus, so he had been signed for only $4,000. Allison further countered by noting that until his last year at Chattanooga he had never batted above .256 or driven in more than 55 runs. He pointed out to reporters that an objective look at his minor-league record revealed just one decent campaign, his last one in Chattanooga. Even then, he hit just nine home runs. There was no hint that he would put up the power numbers he did in 1959. His 30 home runs for the Senators that season were one short of Ted Williams' rookie record – which Twins' center fielder Jimmie Hall would later break – and more home runs than Allison hit in four combined minor league seasons. In sum, his season surprised him.

"Would the Yankees have stepped me up to a higher classification each year the way Washington did?" he asked. "You see, I don't know the answers to such questions." But Griffith observed that Allison had played in pitchers' parks, in fact he played in pitchers' leagues, in the minors. The parks were so big in most of these cities that Griffith insisted veteran big-league power hitters would see their home runs become loud outs there.

In the swirl of conjecture and second-guessing, Allison was certain of one thing: he was tired. American League pitchers had tested him all season, throwing brush-back pitches that left him on his seat in the dirt. Because he had started off the season well in Cuba, hitting five home runs in a short span, pitchers – most notably his Senator teammates Pascual and Ramos – were putting him on his rear there as well. Allison cut short his winter in Cuba shortly after receiving the good news about his award, and the family returned to his hometown of Raytown, Missouri. His kids were sick, and the 25-year-old hadn't been home for more than a month at a stretch in four years, although he had taken a liking to Washington, D.C. He planned to move the family there for the 1960 season. It was Griffith's final season in Washington, as it turned out.

Allison was vocal in his displeasure when it was announced the Senators would move to Minnesota for the '61 season. He had rented a place to live in Silver Spring, Maryland, but said that short-term problem wasn't why he was unhappy. He had grown to enjoy the district, which would now have an expansion franchise. Allison expressed a desire to be a part of it and said, "Maybe in this disaster plan they're talking about to stock the new franchise, I could be retained here. I'd certainly like to be." Battey had recently moved to Washington from Los Angeles, and Lemon had taken up residence there after living in Roanoke, Virginia, for years. They were the only players living in the area, but only Allison made it known he really wanted to stay. He had expected to put down roots, get an off-season job in the region, and raise his family.

It's difficult to imagine Griffith satisfying Allison's wish by trading him for anyone on the expansion Senators' 1961 roster, and more difficult to imagine the early Twins without Killebrew and Allison – by the start of spring training in 1965 they had combined for nearly 300 home runs in the Twins' four seasons in Minnesota. "Killebrew and Allison" in the upper Midwest meant the same as "Mantle and Maris" in New York. But Mantle and Maris weren't defensive vagabonds.

As the '65 season approached, the Twins decided to move Allison to left field and Killebrew to first base. It was the fourth shift for Allison since '59. He began in center field as a rookie and was moved to right field for the next three seasons. In '64, Allison was at first base. Despite the fact he was an established veteran, Allison had arrived 10 days early at 1964 spring training to work out at first base. He was voted to the All-Star team by fellow American League players that season, although as with most first basemen it was his offense that earned him the recognition. Killebrew was struggling with an injured knee in the spring of '64 and didn't think he could take the twisting or quick stops and starts required in the infield, so he was moved to left field. Oliva was a rookie that year, and the Twins wanted him roaming right field. With Killebrew in left, this meant Allison would move to first, Don Mincher would remain on the bench and Vic Power would be traded.

Allison accepted the move to left field in '65, stating he liked the action in the infield and felt he was more involved in the game mentally, but he didn't really care where he played, as long as he played. It was a sound move for the team. There was more ground to cover in left field at Met Stadium in 1965 because the Twins' moved the fence back 15 feet before the season. Allison was a better runner than Killebrew and stood to do a better job covering that additional ground, and Allison had a far better outfield arm. Mele commented that runners had such little respect for Killebrew's arm that they would go from first to third on balls hit to left field. "How often do you see that?" Mele asked. "Virtually never."

In the infield, Killebrew had limited range, but had soft hands, an infielder's reactions, and an accurate arm. Frank Quilici remembers Killebrew's throws came into him softly, rather than heavily. "It was easy to turn a double play with his throw."

Killebrew is not recalled as a good fielder, but Cleveland's Leon Wagner summed up Killebrew's ability at first base during the '65 season. "People love 'Brew's home runs, but they see him on defense and he's kind of chunky and they don't think much of him there. But 'Brew has the good hands. I mean, he's not like Dick Stuart or guys like that," Wagner said in reference to the man who fielded so poorly he was nicknamed "Dr. Strange Glove." Wagner said Killebrew "catches the ball.

He's got to with a guy like Versalles throwing. Versalles is either going to put 'Brew in the Hall of Fame or kill him."

Moving Killebrew seemed to cement the notion that the Twins kept trying to hide him defensively. In fact, he was moved for the same reason Mele moved Vic Power to second or third base at times in 1963: he would be better defensively at the new position than any other first baseman on the team. Killebrew moved to third midway through the '65 season to get Mincher's bat in the lineup. The move was made not because Killebrew wasn't a good first baseman, but because he could play third base and Mincher could not. Even in Killebrew's rookie season, most baseball men believed Killebrew was best suited to first base, and during the course of his career he had a little better fielding percentage and a little better range than the average first baseman in the league. He didn't measure up that well defensively at third or in the outfield, but he was a good athlete and once had decent speed. Repeated leg injuries took a toll on his defense.

He had short, muscular legs from thigh to knee, and lost playing time to a pulled hamstring in 1960 and 1961 and a pulled quadriceps muscle in 1962. He injured his knee before the first game of the spring training in 1963, and he missed most of spring training and the early part of the season. He played with the injury, missed just 20 games, and led the league with 45 home runs before off-season knee surgery helped convince the Twins to leave Killebrew in left field for the '64 season and move Allison to first. By 1965, Killebrew and Allison showed fans and teammates they were willing to relocate defensively for the good of the team.

Those first four seasons in Minnesota also established the pair as the leaders of Minnesota's offense, which is certainly why most fans recall the pair leading the Twins to the 1965 pennant. But Allison hit just 23 home runs and drove in 78 runs in fewer than 450 at-bats in '65. Killebrew batted just 401 times with 25 home runs and 75 runs batted in. More refined statistical barometers were developed in the '90s that reveal both players had a huge impact on the team's offense when healthy, but Allison was injured before the All-Star Game and inconsistent in the second half of 1965. Killebrew's dislocated elbow limited him to just 42 at-bats after August 1. Fortunately for Minnesota, from July 1 until the end of the season, Tony Oliva, the 1964 batting champion who was honored the day Killebrew homered off Mikkelsen, collected 108 hits, drove in 58 runs, scored 58 more and batted .373. Oliva's performance in the second half of the season, with Killebrew on the shelf and Allison contributing in spurts, is the sharpest arrow in the quiver of those who argue Oliva, not Versalles, should have been the 1965 MVP.

Tony Oliva

NINE

"Always I hit. I don't see why this league is any different."
– Tony Oliva

Tony Oliva didn't have strings of strikeouts. He put the ball in play, treating walks as if they might induce a rash. His lone nemesis was "hitting in bad luck," the stretches when sharp line drives don't find the gap. No hitter is immune from these times when, as one player said, "You look at the field and it's one big glove."

Oliva didn't recall swinging the bat poorly at any time during the 1965 season, but the reigning American League batting champion was batting .230 after two months of play.

He stood slightly bent over with his feet in a wide stance, deep in the left-handed batter's box – so far back that it was a challenge to catch up to a left-hander's curve ball before it broke. He used an inside-out golf swing on fastballs and, as with most big-league hitters, could hit the belt-high pitch. But Oliva feasted on pitches low in the strike zone, which is where good pitchers work hitters and expect little damage.

"Low pitches that were balls," Oliva recalled, "I don't miss those."

Oliva stepped toward the plate on outside offerings and drove the ball into left field. As Stan Musial said when he first heard about Oliva, "Line drives to left field for a left-handed hitter? That's good." Oliva took his stride straight ahead, or a little toward right field, on inside pitches, and he pulled curveballs that bent into him from right-handed pitchers.

There were only two types of pitchers in Tony Oliva's mind during his early days with Minnesota: right-handed and left-handed. He attacked everything thrown at him, but he hadn't learned anything about the pitchers. One day early in 1964, Vic Power, or as Oliva called him, "Big Powder," discussed the merits of Mudcat Grant, who pitched for Cleveland at the time.

"Who is Mudcat? Who is this Mudcat?" Oliva asked.

"You got two hits off him yesterday," Power said.

Oliva got so many hits early in his rookie season, 45 in his first 102 at-bats, the national media noticed. He was unsure what to make of the attention.

"You can imagine it was tough for him," Mele said in 2004. "He had to learn everything all over again, the people, the country, the language. He had to hit off the best pitchers most of the time. It wasn't like today, when you might see some of a club's worst pitchers in relief quite a bit."

Mele was amazed that the young man could handle the culture and also hit a baseball the way he did. "I don't really know where he got it, if someone taught it to him or what," Mele recalled, "but he could wait and wait and wait on a pitch. Then they'd bust him inside and he'd pull that damn pitch down the line."

Killebrew said Oliva was the best off-speed hitter he ever saw, let alone played with. "You could throw Tony ninety-nine fastballs and then bring in one change-up and he'd lose it."

Oliva did have a simple secret to hitting, but he didn't bother to bore reporters with it, and he completely dismissed the subject to one national news magazine reporter with, "Batting is all luck anyway. You not lucky, you get no hits." In reality, Oliva believed the secret to hitting was hard work.

"When I played the game," he recalled years later, "some guys might miss the first round of batting practice. I never missed any batting practice. The main thing for my success was my work ethic. If you hit the ball good and they catch it, that's fine, but when you go into a slump, when you're hands are slow, that's when you have to work even more. The good hitters know when it's coming, and they go to the ballpark early and hit and hit and hit. I never liked to have a day off, I never wanted to miss any batting practice, because I always believed the more you work, the better you get."

It didn't look like work as he tore through his early years in organized ball. His minor league batting averages read .410, .350, 304, with a .365 tossed in during the winter of '63 in Puerto Rico. When Oliva was promoted to Minnesota briefly toward the end of the '62 and '63 seasons, he batted well over .400 in a few at-bats, just enough for everyone to see the damage he inflicted on a baseball. Not only did Tony Oliva not swing badly in '65, he hadn't swung badly for years. The Los Angeles Dodgers' scouting report on him before the World Series read: "Best breaking ball hitter on club. Good low fastball hitter. Can hit the ball out to all fields."

"Every hitter has got maybe a little weakness," Camilo Pascual said as he recalled Oliva decades later. "Tony could hit anything, and I think the only way you could pitch to Tony Oliva was up and inside the strike zone, and the problem with high-and-inside is you don't have much room there before it's just a ball. He was a good curveball hitter, and he could go out and hit a pitch that tailed away from him."

Twins' relief pitcher Garry Roggenburk used California Angels' pitcher Dean Chance as the quintessential example of pitcher bewilderment. Chance led American League hurlers in five categories in 1964, including a microscopic 1.65 earned run average, but he stood on the mound one day with a helpless, puzzled look as he watched Oliva reach for an outside pitch and drive it from the park. "Tony had the kind of arms that would go way out," Roggenburk recalled, "and he stood off the plate just a little and could hit to all fields. The next day, Chance and I were talking, and he told me that pitch Oliva hit must have been a foot outside. He couldn't believe Tony even got the bat on the ball, let alone hit it out of the park."

Oliva didn't have the strike-zone discipline of most hitters, let alone someone such as Ted Williams, who picked over pitchers' offerings like a kid who had been served vegetables. Yet the comparisons between Oliva and Williams rushed to print because Oliva started hitting the minute his career began. He won batting titles after his first two seasons in the majors, something no one else including Williams was able to do. Williams was an inch taller, 15 pounds heavier, and a more selective hitter than the six-foot-two, 190-pound Oliva, but before Oliva's knee surgeries piled up, Mele said strength was Williams' main asset over Oliva.

"Williams had a lot more power than Oliva because Ted was bigger and stronger," Mele said, "but as a hitter, Oliva isn't too far behind. And Tony was a much better all-around player than Williams."

Oliva could run, had a strong throwing arm and transformed himself from an awful fielder into a man who won a Gold Glove for his outfield play. As usual in baseball, it was the offensive part of Oliva's game that drew attention.

Despite his free-swinging approach to batting, Oliva averaged barely 50 strikeouts a year in the 12 full seasons of his 15-year career, all as a Minnesota Twin. Oliva struck out 64 times in 1965, led the league in hits for the second season in a row, and had a .491 slugging average. In more than 600 plate appearances, Oliva either put the ball in play or wound up on base nine of every 10 at-bats. "Tony is one of those hitters who doesn't draw a blank very often," Boston's Carl Yastrzemski said. Oliva never struck out more than twice in a game all season. He was so locked in at the plate as he chased Yastrzemski for the 1965 American League batting title that in one 16-game span Oliva struck out once while going 19-for-46 with 15 runs batted in.

Oliva also stole five bases in that stretch. Mele thought Oliva was the team's best base-runner and let him run at his discretion. Oliva thought about the Twins lineup one day. He asked himself, "Tony, why run? You'll get home quick enough anyway." After that, Oliva decided stealing bases rarely made sense on that team.

Mele often announced that Oliva was the best all-around player in the league, and Martin thought Oliva was the best hitter in baseball. The question as the 1965 pennant race wound down was not which American League team would go to the World Series, but who was the best hitter in the league that season: Yastrzemski, who captured the crown in '63, or Oliva, the '64 batting champion?

It was a rarity to bat .300 in 1965, when exactly three players in the entire American League reached that level. Oliva pushed his average to a season-high .299 with a week remaining in July, when Yastrzemski had a seemingly insurmountable 48-point lead. The 25-year-old Boston star hit well over .300 most of the season, and after June 15 he was never below .300. The hits were not falling for Oliva, however, and he was batting only .227 in late May. As June closed, Yastrzemski had a 65-point lead over Oliva in the batting race. Then Oliva put on such a relentless second-half charge that he easily out-hit Yastrzemski, .321 to .312.

Oliva began his hot streak in July, when he and Killebrew went on a damaging tear that helped the Twins win more than 20 games in a single month, something that has happened less than 10 times in club history. The Twins went 22-9 in July, Killebrew's last full month of the season before an elbow injury in early August. Killebrew did about two month's worth of damage in July, going 36-for-107 with nine home runs, 30 runs batted in, a .471 on-base percentage and a .626 slugging average. Oliva was 50-for-127 with four home runs and 24 runs batted in. He scored 36 runs, had a .451 on-base percentage and slugged .567. It was a soothing sight for Mele, but he did not expect to be watching from the press box.

Mele was ejected from a game against California four days after the All-Star break. He made contact during an argument with umpire Bill Valentine and received a five-day suspension and $500 fine. A widely published photograph of the incident showed Mele reaching his left arm under Valentine's jaw as Rollins and Kaat tried to intervene. It appeared Mele was striking the umpire in the jaw. Even Valentine admitted that wasn't the case. Mele was just reaching to grab Valentine. It was an unusually aggressive point in Mele's career.

The groundwork for Mele's explosion was laid earlier in the game, when he argued with second base umpire Bill McKinley after a close play at second base in which Rollins was called out. The following inning, California shortstop Jim Fregosi was called safe as the Angels got another call on that close play at first. Rollins was playing second base, and he approached first base to question the call. Valentine took off his cap for emphasis as he chased Rollins back to his position, telling him only the first baseman or catcher could argue the call. Irritated that Valentine was humiliating his player, Mele ran onto the field. Valentine greeted him by sticking a finger in Mele's face, at which point the manager began to shove toward Valentine as players restrained him.

Although Rollins was a fanatical worker who attacked the game, he accepted most umpiring decisions, so Mele was particularly irritated that Valentine was chewing out a player who caused little trouble. Mele typically had a similar perspective on the game, in part because one day his uncle, former major leaguer Al Cuccinello, provided an unforgettable lesson. When Mele was a teen, he returned home from a baseball game and tossed a fit because he had gone hitless in a doubleheader. He threw his uniform on the kitchen floor and complained how hard baseball was. His mother was an Italian immigrant who learned English quickly and was disciplined and bright enough to purchase a home in the United States as soon as practical. She scolded her son for being a quitter. Al Cuccinello went a step further.

There was a transom in the Mele household, so Cuccinello fashioned a noose and slung it over the transom. Cuccinello looked at young Sam and said: "There it is. Hang yourself." The point to keep things in perspective had been driven home. So Mele's mother was shocked when she saw the newspaper photo of her son straining into Valentine. "Sam almost never lost his temper, he was always patient," she said, recalling a boy who would walk to the East River and watch the water lap toward shore when he was upset.

Mele was unhappy he had overreacted. He apologized to Valentine and awaited the fine and suspension. He had been ejected from a game only twice in his four years of managing, and was "down in the dumps" when he returned home and revealed the day's events to his wife. "I told her the American League president, Joe Cronin, was in the stands and saw the whole thing. I told her I'd be fined a lot of money. Connie had been on *Jeopardy!* before and won some money, and she just laughed and calmed me down by saying, 'So what? I'll just get on *Jeopardy!* again.'"

It was tough for Mele to sit in the press box in the middle of a pennant race, but he said what he missed most was being in the dugout with the players, joshing and encouraging. He called managing a "lonely life," and although he remained in baseball for decades after Griffith fired him in 1967, Mele never had the urge to manage again.

Bullpen coach Hal Naragon took over on the field during Mele's suspension, which Oliva made tolerable. Mele watched from the press box two days later as Oliva collected five hits in a game, and he had another five-hit game a week later. Once, four of the five hits were infield rollers. In the other game, each hit was a wicked line drive. Defenses could not cheat on Oliva. He hit the ball everywhere.

"I always knew I had this confidence in me," he recalled after he retired. "I felt I could get a hit anytime I wanted, especially against a right-handed pitcher."

The biggest obstacle to Oliva's second batting championship in '65 did not seem to be "Mr. ABCXYZ" – as Oliva called Yastrzemski – or even hitting in bad luck. From the start of his career it was a struggle for Oliva to say healthy. He chipped a bone in the big knuckle of the middle finger on his right hand in Los Angeles early in the 1964 season, and after that it was difficult for him to grip the bat properly. The knuckle was constantly swelled to twice its natural size during the '64 and '65 seasons before surgery corrected the problem. Oliva analyzed the situation and realized the pain snapped at him only when he swung and missed, and he didn't miss that often. At least it didn't hurt when he made contact, which would inevitably affect his hitting.

The injury meant he had even more trouble holding onto the bat than usual. He wrapped the last two fingers of his bottom hand around the knob of the bat and would cradle the handle, rather than grind it with a death grip. When he was fooled by a pitch, the bat sometimes left his bare hands and twirled toward the field, foul territory, or even into the stands. After the injury to his middle knuckle, a big swing and a miss sent his bat into flight more often. He resorted to a knobless bat to take pressure off the finger, but that experiment failed. He tried batting gloves but preferred to hit bare handed. His 33-ounce, 35-inch

Louisville Slugger hit Killebrew in the on-deck circle once during the season, and Oliva was down to one bat on a late July road-trip – three others he had packed ended up in the stands, and fans kept them.

The pain was worse in the field than at bat. Oliva batted left but threw with his right hand, so each time he made a throw back to the infield a sharp stab of pain came with it. Oliva had a high tolerance for playing with pain and approached the hand injury with the same calm resignation he would exhibit with future injuries. He was regarded as a man who took life as it came to him, smiling and joking so often that *Time* magazine wrote, "His laugh explodes like a marble popping out of a bottle of ginger ale."

Baseball was more glamorous than most professions, so a man should have been smiling if he was in the big leagues, but baseball was also the only way for Oliva and many of his countrymen to earn a living away from Cuba. Oliva not only had to accept the pain of his injuries, he found it necessary to work through occupational hazards just like any other worker with limited options. Bob Allison could recover from the season's nicks and aches as a sales representative for Coca-Cola in the Twin Cities. Earl Battey drew an off-season paycheck from the public relations department of Minneapolis-based General Mills. Jim Grant, who once worked in a post office during the off-season, took his "Mudcat & the Kittens" song-and-dance nightclub act on the road. Minnesota companies did not eagerly pursue Tony Oliva, who during his early years in the country struggled with English to the point where Versalles said, "Tony talks so bad that he even says 'ain't' in Spanish." Oliva's fluency in Spanish could have been a launching point to an off-season job beyond baseball decades later, but in 1965 there were no corporate initiatives – or widespread need – to reach out to Minnesota's small and disperse Hispanic community.

A $50,000 salary was exceptional money in baseball in the early 1960s, and if a player was halfway to that figure he was doing well. Oliva made $7,500 his first season in the majors. If he went home to Cuba to work in the winter, he would not be able to return.

Castro's sports commissioner had ordered the confiscation of all property of Cuban natives in the major leagues who did not return to the island in the winter of 1961. Those who obeyed were almost exclusively minor leaguers from low classifications, and they did not leave Cuba again. The rest of the ballplayers traveled to Venezuela, Puerto Rico, Mexico, or the Dominican Republic to play winter ball. Jackie Robinson might have broken the color barrier in Major League Baseball, but more than a decade later Cubans still faced Castro's discrimination, in addition to whatever racial prejudice they found in the United States. Oliva was the first black man to win an American League batting title, but he was a black man during a time of civil rights unrest in the United States, and he could not return to Cuba to escape it.

"Because we couldn't go back to Cuba," recalled Sandy Valdespino, "we went to any cities where we could play in the winter. It would have been wonderful if we could finish playing baseball in the United States and go back to our own country to work, or to play ball before our friends and family. It would have been the most wonderful thing in the world for us and for the Cuban people to go back there each winter."

After four years of playing ball year-round, Oliva finally abandoned his winter baseball ritual during the 1964 off-season at the request of Calvin Griffith. Even though Oliva won the 1964 batting title, Griffith knew the injury to Oliva's hand was not improving and Griffith – never eager to pay for surgery – thought the time away from the game would help Oliva. The swelling did diminish as the American League Rookie of the Year took cortisone shots while first vacationing in Puerto Rico, then in Florida. He then returned to Minnesota, where he saw snow for the first time.

Oliva was a young man, 24 years old, unmarried, and did not own a home and traveled with all his possessions in four suitcases. Like Versalles and many Latin players he carried a record player for company. Oliva returned to Minneapolis with that luggage during early 1965 to live in a 12-by-15 foot hotel room. He didn't smoke, drank a beer now and then and didn't own a car, so a big night was a restaurant steak dinner followed by 10 hours of sleep. He hadn't seen his family in four years; gifts he sent back home were confiscated and his letters were censored. Now and then he managed to get a phone call through to his mother. He told his parents he would return home if needed, but his mother insisted he had such a great opportunity in the United States that he should remain there.

Oliva became bored if he didn't play baseball and said breaks from the game that lasted longer than a couple weeks created the loneliest times of his life. He claimed playing baseball almost 12 months a year might tax a pitcher, but a man in his early 20s should be able to play outfield nearly year-round. And early in his professional career, Oliva needed the experience.

By 1965, fans who watched the tall, slender, swift outfielder believed he was blessed with the innate ability to chase down a baseball and accurately rifle it back to the infield. Oliva was proud people believed that, because as late as spring training in 1963 he could neither go back well on a fly ball nor handle ground balls well enough to play in the big leagues. He was still learning the mechanics of throwing in 1963. Tony Oliva was trying to catch up to the skill level of other minor league players because he had hardly played any baseball.

He spent his early years in a rural area of the Pinar del Rio province in the northwest part of the island. His father loved the national sport of baseball, but Oliva played most of his baseball games with his nine brothers and sisters, father and friends on rural fields with bats carved from the lightweight, tough wood of majagua trees. Oliva was at a disadvantage compared to city kids because he spent his early childhood on beautiful rural plantation land where morning fog shrouds palm trees and nearby hills. Schools in such areas did not have baseball teams.

"I never saw a professional game before I played in one," Oliva said. "I listened to games on the radio. In my mind, I thought it would be nice to play for one of the Cuban teams. I never traveled too much and never thought I would have a chance to leave the country. Where I grew up, your dream is limited. If I lived in Havana, probably there I would have thought about playing American baseball."

He was a teen playing against men after his family moved to the city. He finally had the chance to play ball regularly, and he could hit the pitching of the older men because he had exceptional eyesight, strong hands and quick wrists. When he took up golf years later, Oliva found the ball rocketed off the face of his club. He immediately knew it was because of those long fingers and powerful hands. He had the physical tools to hit a ball with a stick, but the men in Cuban amateur games weren't there to coach him, so Oliva received little instruction.

Roberto Fernandez, a former outfielder in the Senators' organization, hailed from Los Palacios in the Pinar Del Rio province and saw Oliva in some ball games. Oliva could hit, so Fernandez delved into Oliva's character. He thought the 19-year-old could learn to field and adjust to the United States, with its rigors of travel and play. Fernandez recommended Oliva to Joe Cambria, who eventually saw the kid play once. He noticed Oliva would field balls in the outfield with one foot behind the other. That could be fixed. Cambria signed him in 1960 for assignment in the Twins' organization in 1961.

Oliva did not impress at the Twins' camp in Fernandina Beach, Florida, and there was a question about his age. Both Latin and American players have been known to adjust their ages downward to help their cause, as there is a vast difference in a good-looking 18-year-old ballplayer and a good-looking 21-year-old ballplayer. Oliva, conversely, was younger than his immigration papers stated because they were not his papers. The birth name of the man who won the 1964 and 1965 American League batting titles is Pedro Oliva, who feared immigration troubles would interfere when he tried to leave Cuba after signing with Cambria. Pedro's brother, Antonio, had a passport, however, so Pedro used it to exit Cuba. Pedro Oliva claimed to be 19, and Cambria had no reason to believe otherwise. But when the youngster arrived in Florida the passport showed his name was Tony, and that he was 24. The Twins' media department was so confused that its director, Herb Heft, listed Oliva's age as "somewhere between 19 and 24" in early player profiles distributed to reporters.

The Twins did not deem Oliva to be a major-league prospect when he arrived at Fernandina Beach. The organization saw it had a foreign player who spoke little English, couldn't field very well, and was of indefinite age. The Twins offered Oliva to Houston, which had no interest in making a trade or buying his contract. Minnesota released Oliva in April of 1961, just as the U.S.-supported, counter-revolutionary Bay of Pigs Invasion occurred. The heightened international unrest created a delay in returning Oliva to Cuba. He had no place to go, so he traveled to Charlotte to visit a friend, who was playing with the Twins' minor league affiliate there.

Charlotte's general manager was a man named Phil Howser, who attended George Washington University with Calvin Griffith and spent 39 years working for the Griffith family. Howser's name was synonymous with baseball in Charlotte. He was general manager of the minorleague Hornets when Killebrew, Allison, Rollins, and Allen passed through. Howser saw Oliva work out and was so impressed with Oliva's diligence and hitting ability that he convinced the Twins to stick with him.

The Twins took Howser's suggestion and sent Oliva to Wytheville of the Class D rookie Appalachian League, where he drove in 81 runs in 64 games. Oliva's .410 batting average was the highest of all minor league players in the country, and his .854 fielding average was about 100 points below unacceptable. Scout Del Wilber had observed Oliva "can learn just by watching," so Oliva was promoted to Charlotte in 1962, where he batted .350. He missed two weeks of the season when he contracted the mumps and missed winning the league batting title by a tenth of a point. He fielded much better.

Oliva and Mele each later agreed that Oliva's fielding problems were largely behind him after he spent the 1963 season under manager Jack McKeon with the Dallas-Fort Worth farm club. McKeon spent hours hitting ground balls to Oliva. Mele did the same when Oliva was in spring camp with the Twins. "Hundreds of grounders an hour, hundreds of fly balls," Oliva recalled. Mele would bring Pascual with him to the outfield and have the pitcher translate Mele's English into Spanish as he explained how to judge the ball off the bat and how take routes to balls, just as Dom DiMaggio once had told Mele. Mele pointed out that the ball hit directly over his head would be the toughest to catch. Mele talked about being aware of wind direction, and how to play balls hit into it. "He picked it up so fast I couldn't believe it," Mele recalled.

"When it wasn't my turn in batting practice, I would watch the best fielders," Oliva said. "In games, I would see players like Al Kaline, Roberto Clemente, study how they fielded, and watch Zoilo Versalles field ground balls. You could see how they played and say to yourself that you don't want to be less than they are. When I won my Gold Glove, it was one of the biggest things for me. I no play that much ball in Cuba as a boy, so I didn't know many of these things about fielding and I had to go out and practice. When I won that Gold Glove, I knew I had come from the worst to the best."

Unlike Killebrew's minor-league life, Oliva kept moving up the ladder with no demotions. When his batting statistics suggested he was struggling, men like McKeon could see he was swinging well but the hits were not falling. Oliva was batting .234 in early June after advancing to Dallas Fort-Worth of the Pacific Coast League. Reporters didn't see what McKeon saw. They asked about Oliva's low batting average. The outs were line drives, McKeon had noted, so he just replied, "Oliva has always hit. I'm gambling he will again."

Oliva also knew he was hitting the ball well. Eventually, the ball would fall. "Always I hit. I don't see why this league is any different." The league wasn't much different, but his life was.

Cesar Tovar, a 23-year-old Venezuelan, was on loan to the Dallas club from the Cincinnati Reds' organization. Even though their contracts belonged to different major league clubs and they came from different countries, Oliva and Tovar played on the same team, became roommates and friends off the field and rivals during games. McKeon once moved Tovar from his second base position to take Oliva's spot in right field after briefly benching Oliva to give him a break from the frustrations of watching his line drives become outs.

Tovar was in the chase for the batting title, which was only a mild source of verbal jousting between them because the pair rarely discussed baseball away from the field. But Oliva was so eager to challenge Tovar that when he returned to the lineup Oliva hit a hot streak in which he drove in 25 runs with 16 doubles. Oliva was a riddle for pitchers because he had no pattern. One game Oliva would hit a triple to right-center field and later drop a double short of the fence in left. He would be fooled badly by a pitch in one at-bat, then tee off on the same pitch the next time he went to the plate. He drove defenses into spasms with his aggressiveness, once scoring from second on a ball hit back to the pitcher. Best of all, he began to judge fly balls and snap up ground balls while on the run.

"I saw him when he was bad," Twins' infielder Frank Kostro recalled. "They were afraid to put him out there because he might hurt himself. He had a great arm, but he was so raw at first, so bad, that you never knew what would happen to a ball hit out to him. They hit fungoes to him all day. In a short period of time he got to be pretty good, then better than pretty good."

Oliva was capable of strong throws, but when he began playing organized baseball he used a sidearm motion and the ball hopped wildly toward its destination. McKeon helped Oliva adopt the habit of throwing overhand rather than sidearm, and Oliva eventually became so accurate that midway through the 1966 season he had made five throws from the outfield to home plate without the help of a relay man. The highlight came in Cleveland, when he swept a ball off wet grass and threw out Chico Salmon at home plate. Indians' manager Birdie Tebbetts called it "a play that couldn't be made. Nobody is going to pick up a wet baseball like that and throw out my fastest runner at the plate." Mele said Oliva became such a good outfielder that he had no equal at throwing to first base behind a runner.

When Griffith announced before the '64 season that Oliva would be his right fielder, writers, fans and even other baseball people wondered if he had solved his defensive shortcomings. Mele knew those problems were behind him. He saw Oliva hustled constantly, backed up plays, and concluded any remaining deficiencies in Oliva's defense would be softened, and soon erased, by the outfielder's willingness to hustle and work hard.

Detractors surfaced again when Oliva began the 1964 season by assaulting American League pitching. Would he continue to hit when pitchers saw him a second time around the league? Major league pitchers always adjust, and rookie hitters don't necessarily do the same. Mele thought back to the 1962 season when the club called up Oliva for a few September at-bats. He had stuck Oliva in the lineup against Cleveland's Sam McDowell, who threw harder than anyone in the league, but with such imprecision that he walked as many batters as he struck out that season. Oliva stood in and hit against McDowell, which impressed Mele to the point that when people asked if Oliva would hit the second time around the league Mele looked them in the eye and said, "Oliva will be hitting the second time around and the third time around."

Oliva later said McDowell happened to be one of two pitchers he hated to face. The other was Nolan Ryan. "They threw all over the ballpark, but McDowell, he threw ha-a-a-rd. You had to have an idea up there against them." McDowell and Ryan created nightmares for hitters with fastballs that approached 100 miles an hour, and early in their careers accuracy was compass point rather than pinpoint. Oliva stood in there against them, which made it easier to tolerate what was to follow.

After Oliva's white-hot '64 start, opposing pitchers put Oliva in the dirt four times with throws at his head, and he was struck in the shoulder once. In late May of '64, Oliva drove in a run during a four-run Minnesota first inning against Baltimore's Steve Barber. When Oliva batted again, Barber hit Oliva in the head on the first pitch, which split the rookie's batting helmet. Barber later argued he had thrown at Oliva's belt, and when Oliva heard that from reporters he responded if the pitch had been belt high it could not possibly have hit him in the head.

"First pitch up there, that's kind of tough," he said. "Maybe sometime our pitchers take care of it."

Oliva was taken to the hospital for X-rays and Barber was immediately warned, which brought an automatic $50 fine. That was not enough for Mele. He called a meeting and compiled a list of the seven pitchers who had thrown close enough to Oliva in the first two months of the season to knock him to the dirt. Mele bit off his words as he instructed the pitching staff to protect Oliva. He demanded that the knockdown pitches in the vicinity of Oliva's head would stop, and said the only way to stop it was for Twins' pitchers to retaliate.

Neither Oliva's hitting ability nor this high, tight pitching escaped the notice of national writers. *Los Angeles Times'* columnist Jim Murray wrote Oliva was a rookie "so good he may have to report directly to the Hall of Fame or form his own league with Willie Mays. Tony Oliva swings at a ball so fast that a National League pitcher in spring training observed, 'All I ask is that he wait till I let go of it.' Pitchers get a load of him and decide the only way out is homicide. Oliva leads the league in head x-rays."

In his career, Oliva became very familiar with all types of medical technology. He had seven operations on one knee in an era before arthroscopic options. He was still a .270 hitter in his last full season at age 35, and he later said if he had played after better surgical techniques were developed he might have played until he was 40. Certainly, he would have been more productive in the years he did play.

Even with the surgical techniques of the 1960s, he would have needed only a little luck to win three straight batting titles.

A car accident midway through the '66 season resulted in a neck injury that might have cost him his third straight title. He and Tovar were driving to Met Stadium in Oliva's Mustang when the car was struck and Oliva suffered a whiplash. He enjoyed some more X-rays and played that night, but had a stiff neck for months and could not turn his head without pain. He continued to play and watched his average plummet from better than .330 to .307. It cost him his third straight batting title as Baltimore's Frank Robinson batted .316, led the league in home runs, runs batted in and average in 1966.

The only two years Oliva failed to hit .300 in his first nine seasons were '67 and '68, when he missed a combined 50 games because of injuries. He still batted .289 each season, which hardly seems impressive, but that was about 40 points over the league average. During that two-year period, only five American League batters topped the .300 mark.

The injuries that tagged Oliva during his entire career were frequent. In '67 alone he suffered nine injuries, including nearly losing a finger when the cleat on the shoe of the Yankees' Horace Clarke came down on Oliva's hand as he slid into second base. Oliva also crashed head first into a steel railing during the '67 season, re-aggravating the neck injury he suffered during the car accident. He went to Rochester's Mayo Clinic to have the neck examined after the '66 season and then took treatment twice a week during the winter of 1966. Injuries to his knee resulted in several surgeries. He detested driving in Minnesota's icy, snowy conditions, but commuted daily from his suburban Bloomington home to rehabilitation sessions at the University of Minnesota near downtown Minneapolis.

The efforts were rewarded. He had four more straight seasons batting over .300, including another batting title in 1971, but even in that stretch he kept fighting injury and illness. In 1969, Oliva was batting nearly .340 when he developed "the stupid chickenpox" in mid-July and missed his first All-Star game since joining the major leagues in 1964. Oliva lost six pounds, missed nearly two weeks of play and went hitless in his first 16 at-bats after he returned. He finished the season batting .309, the second time in four seasons he had finished second in the league. He lost the batting title to teammate Rod Carew, who flirted with .400 the first two months of the season before finishing at .332.

Years later, Oliva recalled those times when he was "hitting in bad luck" and the line drives would not fall. He said he never really thought about winning batting titles, just hitting. But in his first six seasons, he won two batting titles, finished second twice, and third – by one point – another time.

Camilo Pascual and Earl Battey

TEN

"You could hear everyone's heart go 'bump, bump, bump' on the bench." – Jim "Mudcat" Grant

Doctor George Resta was a team physician for the Washington Senators and a friend of Camilo Pascual. Resta performed surgery on Pascual's damaged right shoulder at Doctors Hospital in Washington, D.C., the first week of August 1965. The original diagnosis was a benign tumor toward the back of Pascual's right shoulder, but surgery revealed three frayed muscles had snapped, like severed rubber bands, and formed an egg-sized lump.

Just as with Pascual's annual contract holdouts, it had become seasonal for him to miss playing time because of shoulder problems. Resta reasoned the damage he repaired likely started small and progressed into the lump, which might have accounted for Pascual's persistent shoulder miseries.

Some writers had intermittently reported speculation from baseball insiders that Pascual took "vacations" during his Minnesota days, all but portraying him as someone who thought he was good enough to miss a month annually and still win 15 or 20 games. Pascual called the talk "crazy." Considering contracts were awarded based on the owners' scrupulous review of statistics, particularly strikeouts and victories for pitchers, Pascual's rebuttal seemed believable: to miss five or six starts each season would cost him both victories and strikeouts. Resta's discovery was strong evidence that Pascual probably pitched through more discomfort than anyone realized.

Given the invasive orthopedic surgical techniques of the day, Pascual was to remain in the hospital while the Twins began a home stand against Baltimore. By the time Pascual shook off the fog of anesthesia, he was able to tune in the game on a Baltimore radio station. He listened as his replacement, a 21-year-old left-hander named Jim Merritt, carved his way through the Baltimore Orioles' lineup. It was Merritt's first major league start and an important one. The Orioles were just a handful of games behind Minnesota, and the Twins were already without 20-year-old rookie Dave Boswell.

A Baltimore native, Boswell had pitched increasingly and effectively until mononucleosis drove him to the 30-day disabled list in mid-July. With Pascual possibly lost for the season, Merritt was called to Minnesota from the team's top farm club in Denver. The Twins had previously recalled pitcher Garry Roggenburk, and the constant raids on the Denver team at one point left that club with only five pitchers. The sense among close followers of the league was that the Twins' pitching was in deep trouble.

There was mild astonishment around the American League when Mele decided to pitch Merritt against the contending Orioles rather than save him for eighth-place Washington a day later. The Twins would have a season-high six-game lead if they could beat the Orioles, so it seemed logical not to start a rookie. Mele, however, was high on Merritt. Blade-like and standing six-foot-two, Merritt was one of the last players cut during spring training. He showed remarkable poise, a nice repertoire of pitches, and an exceptional move on his pickoff throw to first base. It was a technique he had taught himself, and after just a few starts in Minnesota both scouts and opposing players decided Merritt's pickoff move was second only to that of New York's Whitey Ford.

Pascual listened to the radio as Merritt retired the first 10 Orioles he faced before Baltimore's Russ Snyder singled in the top of the fourth inning. An outfielder who made good contact but had little power, Snyder was still trying to regain his fine speed after missing most of the '64 season. He had broken a bone in his ankle while trying to beat out a bunt. Snyder had finished behind Allison and Perry in the 1959 Rookie of the Year voting, but his career path was not distinguished. Despite the recognition he received as a rookie, Snyder said he never traveled to spring training thinking he had made a team's roster. He had begun to see more playing time when Oriole outfielders Paul Blair and Sam Bowens began to slump. Snyder's increase in playing time around the middle of June coincided with the Orioles winning 12 of 14 games, which moved Baltimore within a game of the Twins.

Snyder was ready to test Merritt after breaking up his no-hitter. He had a big lead off first base when Merritt promptly picked him off base with a throw to Killebrew. Snyder ran toward second, Killebrew took a few steps after him before firing the ball to Frank Quilici at second base. Snyder reversed his field and brushed Killebrew as he retreated to first, where Merritt awaited. The pitcher had run to first to back up Killebrew and took Quilici's throw on the rundown, tagging Snyder for the out. But second base umpire Bill Kinnamon ruled Killebrew had impeded Snyder on the base path when the two made contact. Snyder was called safe. Merritt worked his way out of the inning and continued to cruise through the Oriole lineup against two of baseball history's more notable pitchers.

Oriole starter Steve Barber had departed the game early with a lower back problem and was replaced by Don Larsen, the only man ever to throw a World Series perfect game. Larsen, 36, matched up with Merritt and threw more than three innings of hitless ball before being replaced by Harvey Haddix. Haddix, nearly 40, was famous for having thrown 12 innings of perfect ball in 1959. It is often considered the greatest game ever pitched and more notable because Haddix lost. If that wasn't heady enough company for Merritt, the Orioles later sent in a rookie – eventual Hall of Famer Jim Palmer – to finish the contest. Merritt's first start was thick with footnotes, and in the sixth inning he became a footnote himself.

Snyder laid down a bunt in the top of the sixth, and from his hospital bed Pascual could envision the lanky left-handed batter as he dumped the ball to his left and tore down the first base line. Rollins charged in from third base to field the ball and throw to Killebrew at first base.

Pascual waited for the call and then heard himself say aloud, "Oh, my goodness." Rollins' throw had been off target, up the baseline toward the home plate side of first base, so Killebrew had to reach across the baseline for the ball, somewhat off balance. He tried to catch the ball and tag Snyder in one motion. Snyder was churning hard to first and his torso met Killebrew's outstretched glove. The crack of Killebrew's elbow snapping was heard in the dugouts. He dropped to the ground, writhing in pain with a dislocated elbow, an injury more commonly associated with a fall. The area swelled to twice its normal size almost immediately.

Trainer Doc Lentz rushed out and noticed the black and blue mark on the outside of Killebrew's left bicep. He had seen that bruise before. It was from a pitch that hit Killebrew four days earlier during Pascual's last start. Lentz began to examine Killebrew's swollen, hyperextended elbow and nearly had tears in his eyes as he thought about the injury's severity and its impact on the team's pennant chances. Lentz cursed and said, "I don't know when he's gonna be able to play again." Players watched Killebrew float off the field on a stretcher. Jim Grant later said, "You could hear everyone's heart go 'bump, bump, bump' on the bench."

The elbow joint was aligned, and Killebrew wore a plastic, inflatable splint to support the ruptured ligaments. The insulted blood vessels in the swollen limb resembled a devilish roadmap. He was expected to begin some light exercise by week's end, and doctors thought he might return to the lineup in 10 days. Instead, he missed seven weeks.

Killebrew recalled years later how his initial concern for the team migrated to concern for himself, as it became clear the Twins were going to the World Series, with or without him. Killebrew had never played in a World Series and was unsure if he would ever get another chance. What if the elbow didn't heal by October?

Killebrew was in his prime playing years at 29, and he was enjoying yet another terrific season. He finished the first half of 1965 batting .358 with runners in scoring position. He was tied for the league lead in home runs with 22, and led the Twins with 70 runs batted in when he injured his elbow. Killebrew had been the American League home run king in each of the previous three seasons, and he most likely would have done it again in '65. He missed nearly a third of the season and still finished just seven home runs behind the league-leader.

He faced weeks of extremely painful therapy as he worked to rehabilitate the elbow. The object was to bend it, and reaching the goal was unpleasant enough, but then there would be the matter of swinging a baseball bat. Because he was a right-handed hitter, Killebrew's left arm was the lead arm and crucial to his swing. Players can often tolerate a minor injury to their trailing arm, relying on the lead arm to pull through the ball. When Killebrew eventually was able to swing a bat, every cut he took at a batting practice pitch brought a pinch of pain. Hitting coach Jim Lemon stood by to coach and coax when Killebrew was able to hop into the batting cage for the first time. Lemon winced as he watched the process.

Killebrew and Pascual had been anointed as the team's hitting and pitching centerpieces entering the season. Now the Twins were without both men and clinging to a five-game lead with two months to play. Sports writers around the country indicated the Twins deserved the pennant if they could overcome this. Even without Killebrew, most opposing managers conceded the Twins were still the league's best run-making team, but no one had expected Allison to suffer through a two-month slump when that assessment was made.

After batting more than .400 in April, Allison struggled to hit .220 in May and June. He seemed to get back on track in July, but tumbled into a horrendous stretch in August and September. He was quietly nursing wrist and shoulder injuries and hit just .192 the final two months of the season, with a flimsy .295 slugging average in September. Sandy Valdespino was capable of that, and he was largely a singles hitter who stood about 10 inches shorter than Allison.

The season had begun with the scrutinized move of Allison to left field and the expectation Allison would hit like the All-Star he was in 1964. Instead, Allison finished the season with a career-low number of at-bats. Of his 114 strikeouts, 66 came after the pitch struck his wrist days before Killebrew hit his dramatic home run off Mikkelsen. Allison still made remarkable use of his 30 hits in the season's final two months, driving in 28 runs and scoring 26.

As the aching Twins prepared to start their first series without Killebrew, Mele called Washington Senators' manager Gil Hodges to confirm the Senators' proposed pitching rotation for the upcoming series, a courtesy that managers extend to each other. Mele began to complain about Battey having missed 28 games, Pascual's surgery, Boswell's mononucleosis, Allison's cracked wrist and recent injuries to Jerry Kindall's hip and Jimmie Hall's knee. Hodges was running a second-division ball club. He politely listened to Mele describe the ashes of his season, and then said, "Sam, you can't see it, but I'm crying for you." Mele had to laugh.

Mele called a meeting to remind the team it had not been a one-man show to that point in the season and that he expected that would continue. There would be more weight placed on Versalles now, because his right-handed bat was crucial in what had become a dramatically different lineup.

With right-handed Killebrew sidelined, the batting order would list heavily to the port side. Oliva, Mincher and center fielder Jimmie Hall were all left-handers, and only Hall hit as much as .240 against left-handed pitching that season. Then there was the impact to the bench. Mele had Rollins, an experienced right-handed bat, to use as a pinch-hitter when Killebrew played third base. With Rollins playing regularly at third base, there would be a hole on the bench. Mele knew teams would not purposely load up on left-handed starters to neutralize Oliva, Hall and Mincher. Left-handed pitching was always in short supply to begin with, and teams could not afford to juggle their pitching just to match up with the Twins.

That was fortunate. Left-handers were effective against Minnesota in the first few weeks after Killebrew went down, winning three of seven games. Considering the Twins played nearly .600 ball in August, it was a good showing.

The Twins' offense seemed good enough to keep the team winning, but Killebrew and Oliva were unparalleled in the league for their respective abilities – Killebrew for hitting home runs and Oliva for making contact and driving the ball with authority to the outfield gaps. It was certain when either was out of the lineup that their replacements would not be as good. The absence of either Killebrew or Oliva also affected the spots before and after them in the batting order. A man batting ahead of either would likely see better pitches, because no pitcher wanted to put a man on base with Killebrew or Oliva on deck. Since he drew so many walks, Killebrew's on-base percentage was actually a tad higher than Oliva's in '65, and both men were on base so often that anyone who batted behind them could count on a pitcher throwing strikes.

Killebrew's injury had other implications. Boswell and Pascual were each on the disabled list, and a new rule that season stipulated teams could have only two men on the disabled list after July 31. A player had to spend a minimum of 30 days on that inactive list. Boswell would soon be healthy and eligible to return, which would create a vacancy on the disabled list. Killebrew was expected to return in 10 days, however, so it would be foolish to assign him to the disabled list, where he would have to sit for a month. This meant Killebrew was occupying a roster spot as if healthy. The Twins were down to 24 men, and Sevcik was virtually never playing, so it was really 23.

Killebrew's injury propelled Rollins into a regular role again. Even decades removed from his throw following Snyder's bunt, Rollins recalled the play with obvious disdain, saying, "It certainly wasn't a strike, I'll tell you that." Rollins could empathize with the mental and physical anguish associated with a serious injury. Unable to relax for fear he might lose his job, Rollins once played third base – a position assaulted with wicked line drives and screaming ground balls – with a broken jaw.

He was called short, bow-legged and stubby-armed. He wore glasses for astigmatism in his right eye. The son of a Cleveland welder, Rollins had a cousin and an uncle who had played professional baseball. With that family legacy, his parents not only encouraged but indulged his ball playing, even though, as Rollins stated, "there were many times they could have used my help with the family treasury." He was a junior in high school when he first watched Vic Power play first base with the Cleveland Indians, but there was nothing to suggest he would ever be on the same field with Power.

Rollins graduated from Kent State and eventually taught school during the off-season. He looked like just another guy in Ohio, and he was supposed to be an obscure minor-leaguer in 1962. Instead he gained national publicity in the first half of the '62 season as a major league rookie. Rollins was earning $8,000 a year, a little more than the minimum salary, but entered the All-Star break leading the American League with 108 hits. The players, managers, and coaches voted for the All-Star teams then, not the fans, and Rollins received more votes than anyone, including Mickey Mantle. There were two All-Star Games that season, and Rollins started at third base in both.

In any era, sports writers are drawn to stories about rookies who sprint to a hot start, as if this individual will establish a new standard for ballplayers. Rollins was no exception and drew national media attention. He eventually settled in as a capable ballplayer, which was probably more of a story, because he had so many detractors along the way.

Versalles had contracted mumps during 1962 spring training. The Twins had two other shortstops in camp who were both ailing, so Mele inserted Rollins at shortstop. He wasn't a shortstop, but Rollins hit so well that he finished camp with a team-high .400 average that spring. Griffith and Mele had initially ticketed him for the minor leagues, but Griffith – who heavily influenced the composition of Twins' rosters – decided to break camp with Rollins as his third baseman. Rollins rewarded Griffith's support by improving on that .400 spring average. He batted nearly .500 in his first dozen games, and his first 20 hits included four home runs, two triples and two doubles.

As with numerous members of the '65 Twins, Rollins owed part of his development to Jack McKeon and Ellis Clary, each of whom managed Rollins in the minor leagues. McKeon immediately took a liking to Rollins and worked hard to find him playing time. Both McKeon and Clary focused on his fielding. Rollins thought all their help made him only adequate. "Billy Martin would say to me if I could field like him and he could hit like me, we'd both have made the Hall of Fame. I could hit the ball. I never felt like I was overmatched my whole career. I always felt I could hit anyone, not get a hit, but I could hit him."

He would have either won the 1962 Rookie of the Year Award or finished second to New York's Tom Tresh, but Rollins had not been eligible for the award because he had spent more than 45 days with the Twins in 1961. Tresh and Rollins had comparable seasons, with Tresh enjoying the advantage of playing in the media center of New York.

Rollins worked hard to hone his reactions and condition himself, which included playing handball with a national champion, whom Rollins could not beat. "And I was in shape," he said. He was one of the rare players of the era to stay in shape year-round. He worried endlessly about keeping his job, which might not have been such an obsession if the national media had not torn him down as quickly as it built him up.

National sports magazines asked in headlines during the '62 off-season if Rollins was a "miracle or a mirage." He claimed not to read these publications, but it was impossible to be unaware that writers were wondering in print if Rollins would be just a 40-watt success. The stories reflected opinions of the scouts who saw him play second base at Kent State and maintained he could not hit a curve ball or throw well.

Twins' scout and coach Floyd Baker did not agree. He signed Rollins, in addition to Bernie Allen and Garry Roggenburk. Those three Pennsylvania-Ohio boys had more in common than Baker, as they shared the same birthday, work ethic and positive attitude. Rollins was probably the worst natural athlete of the bunch, and probably the hardest worker. He stood five-foot-ten and sometimes managed to weigh 180 pounds. Rollins proved Baker was right in his prediction that a little dirt-pawing hard work could make Rollins a decent player. By 1962, Rollins could rip a curve ball and throw bullets from third base.

Rollins' 1962 season had already proved wrong the scouts who dismissed him at Kent State. As spring training ended in '63, Rollins was gearing up for a good season to prove wrong the writers in those glossy publications. Then a fastball from Detroit's Paul Foytack, the man who allowed the first of Roger Maris' 61 home runs in '61, fractured Rollins' jaw. Allen, Roggenburk and Rollins celebrated their collective April birthday with Rollins drinking baby food and supplements through a straw.

He missed about 10 games and could not stand it, so he decided to play, carrying wire cutters in the event he needed to free his locked jaws. Almost immediately he crashed into six-foot-four, 205-pound Boston catcher Bob Tillman. The collision at home plate loosened the wires. He played third base as unflinchingly, reasoning if he kept his head down and eyes on the ball he was less likely to take a shot on the side of his jaw. Boston third baseman Frank Malzone called Rollins foolish, saying it was not worth trying to get an extra two or three weeks of playing time at risk of serious injury. Baltimore's Brooks Robinson said he would never play third with a wired jaw. "Those smashes come hard down there." Rollins scoffed. Robinson once broke two teeth in batting practice and left the field briefly. "Robinson would play," Rollins said. "So would anyone else. I'm not the first one to do it."

Rollins beat the "sophomore jinx" with a good second season in the majors. His runs batted in fell from 96 to 61, but he had nearly 100 fewer at-bats than in his rookie season. He hit .307 compared to .298 the previous season. Because of those solid performances during his first two major league seasons, there was less reason for the Twins to panic when Killebrew went down. Rollins could handle this.

As Rollins moved off the bench, Killebrew began his rehabilitation back home in Oregon, and Versalles worked hard to emerge from a slump that saw his batting average fall to .228. Mele said his team had always charged back when bad news arrived, so there was no reason for him to have any doubts about the players now. The Twins did get one break when Killebrew went down, however. Minnesota was in the middle of a ten-game home stand, and better yet, Washington followed the Orioles into town, with Boston next on the schedule.

Versalles barely slept the night Killebrew was injured. He and his father drove to the airport late at night to pick up Versalles' uncle, and the trio returned to Versalles' home, where they talked until nearly dawn. The Twins had that doubleheader with Washington scheduled, so

Versalles finally went to bed. He was starting his third hour of sleep when Maria Josefa awakened him with the news she was in labor. Versalles spent the rest of the day at the hospital, before he drove to the ballpark. He had virtually no sleep and was purring about the birth of his fourth daughter. He went out and made three great defensive plays in the first game, once darting deep into the hole to his left and throwing out the runner. He said he couldn't recall ever ranging that far for a ball and getting an out. Gil Hodges had been singing a Versalles-for-MVP refrain for some time, and after the game he said, "Rarely a game goes by where he doesn't come up with some sort of great play."

Still, the Twins probably would have lost except that Don Zimmer, in the final year of his career and at this point a very poor fielder, booted a ground ball to third base off the bat of Versalles. When he recovered, Zimmer should have just held the ball, as he had no chance of throwing out the swift Versalles. Instead, Zimmer threw wildly to first, committing a double error on the play. Grant, who had been on first base, ran all the way home on the wild throw to give himself the deciding run in his 13th win of the season.

Mele gave Dwight Siebler the start in the second game of the doubleheader against Washington, about 24 hours before the right-hander's 28th birthday. Siebler had been recalled in mid-July after Boswell was diagnosed with mononucleosis. In his only start of the season, Siebler allowed three hits and three walks in just more than two innings. The Twins lost, 4-2.

The next day, after languishing on the bench and without a home run for 10 weeks, Kindall cracked his big pinch-hit homer off Washington's Howie Koplitz. With Minnesota trailing, Mele sent his pinch-hitter to the plate swinging.

It is expected that a .200 hitter batting late in the game with his team trailing will take a pitch. Mele figured Koplitz had heard about this and would throw a strike, hoping to get ahead in the count. Kindall slammed Koplitz's high, inside slider beyond the fence to tie the game in an eventual 4-3 win. Kindall was in the process of temporarily winning back the second base job from Frank Quilici, and in 10 days he would hit his final major-league home run, again a clutch smash in the top of the 11th inning to give the Twins a 4-3 lead.

These close games against Washington were not good news for Mele. With just a little luck, the overmatched Senators could have won three of four from the league-leading Twins, and the American League contenders would have been grinning over the notion the Twins could not win without Killebrew. Minnesota was playing .560 ball against the four teams behind them in the race, well below their overall mark of .638.

A good baseball team needs to beat the bad teams often or it will have to beat the good teams more often than it cares to. The Twins were beating the poorer teams, and 30 of the remaining 54 games on the schedule would be against the bottom half of the league, with half of their remaining games scheduled at home. As they prepared to leave Killebrew behind and embark on a 13-day road trip against New York, Cleveland, Detroit and California, Jim Perry sent them off in style.

Before nearly 26,000 hometown fans on a Sunday afternoon, Perry was within seven outs of a no-hitter when Boston's Felix Mantilla doubled about three feet beyond the reach of center fielder Jimmie Hall. Perry threw 112 pitches, 75 of them strikes, and finished with a two-hit, 8-0 shutout. Don Mincher, the streaky offensive player, was capably filling in for Killebrew at first base. He had gone 3-for-4 in the Friday win over Boston, hit a two-run home run in Saturday's win, and then drove in three runs in Perry's masterpiece.

Perry's win against Boston meant a three-game sweep against the ninth-place Red Sox as the Twins improved to 14-1 against Boston. Even though they had not played great baseball, the Twins had clicked off six straight wins since Killebrew was injured. Those opponents were not contenders, but it was the major leagues, so it was never automatic, a point Killebrew drove home one day as he watched a game from the press box. "It looks easy from up there," he noted.

In a fitting goodbye to Met Stadium there was one more injury before the team headed to the East Coast. Oliva's bat slipped from his grasp during one of his at-bats during Perry's gem against Boston and struck a fan.

It was after the opening game of the road trip in New York when New York writers accused Versalles of taking advantage of the aging Mantle with his daring base running. The Yankees won the next day behind Mel Stottlemyre, a fluid, sinkerball-throwing master. He opposed Mudcat Grant in the game, a marquee matchup for the disillusioned Yankee fans because Stottlemyre was battling Grant for the league lead in wins. There were more than 30,000 fans in the stands.

Stottlemyre seemed more suitable for the Twins' cast of characters. As with Joe Cambria's discoveries, Stottlemyre had signed for no bonus. Scout Eddie Taylor – a short, bespectacled man similar to Cambria – found Stottlemyre at a junior college among the apple valleys of the Pacific Northwest – the same region of the country where Killebrew was born. Like Killebrew, Stottlemyre was a quiet, unassuming sort who could be counted on to work hard and get the job done. Grant had one more win on the season the Stottlemyre, but New York drove him from the game in the fifth inning. Stottlemyre's win tied Grant for the league lead with his 14th win. The pair battled to season's end, with Grant winning 21 games, one more than Stottlemyre.

Merritt closed the three-game series that drew more than 82,000 customers. Yankee fans streamed into the stands at an average of 31,000 a game to see the 1965 Twins, and about 20 percent of the Yankees' home attendance that season came with Minnesota in town. Some of them saw Merritt, a former Los Angeles Dodger clubhouse boy, make his first start in Yankee Stadium. He had beaten Baltimore back in Minnesota for his first win, when observers thought he should start against the weaker Senators the next day.

It was Merritt's third big-league start, but Mele thought the youngster was so poised that not only could he handle a pennant race in Yankee Stadium, the notion was already forming in Mele's mind that Merritt could probably handle a World Series start if Pascual didn't return from surgery. Merritt was known for his good fastball and sharp curveball, and until the ninth inning the Yankees hit nothing on the ground against him as the Twins' outfield recorded 15 putouts and Merritt fanned eight. Mincher's two-run homer helped him to a 4-1 lead entering the bottom of the seventh, and Merritt got the win. He labored, throwing 155 pitches.

It wasn't as if Merritt was a "fresh arm" for the Twins' staff. He had thrown nearly 200 innings at Denver and would finish the season with 267 total innings pitched, more innings than subsequent Twins' pitchers such as Frank Viola and Brad Radke ever threw during a 162-game season. The rookie provided a legitimate boost, similar to Perry's impact earlier in the season, and he did it with a lot of hours on his arm.

Merritt had missed a complete-game win by a third of an inning during his first start, when Killebrew was injured. Mele had brought in Johnny Klippstein to get the final Baltimore batter – pitcher Jim Palmer – in the top of the ninth of Merritt's debut. In the bottom of the inning, Minnesota's Jimmie Hall, who had not started the game in center field because of a knee injury and a feeble batting history against Steve Barber, hit a pinch-hit home run. It was an opposite field shot off Palmer on a no-ball, two-strike count in the bottom of the inning to give Klippstein and the Twins the win. Reporters asked Hall if he had decided to go the opposite way on Palmer after two huge swings and misses. "You don't 'go' anywhere with this guy," Hall said. "He throws bullets."

The Orioles would ride Palmer to a long string of pennant races starting in 1966, when the Orioles won the American League title. Merritt and Palmer both would play in Baltimore's 1970 World Series win, Merritt with Cincinnati, where he became the first Reds' pitcher in four years to win 20 games, and the last Reds' pitcher to start a home opener at Crosley Field.

Merritt was just part of the August raid on the Denver farm club. The Twins demoted Siebler about a week after his start against the Senators and called up six-foot-three outfielder Andy Kosco to help balance the lineup with a right-handed bat. Kosco had been batting .327 with 27 home runs and 116 runs batted in at Denver. He didn't need to approach Killebrew's production, just place a notion in the minds of opponents that he might be able to do some offensive damage from the right side of the plate. Kosco smashed a home run off Cleveland's Sam McDowell for his first major league hit the day after he joined the team.

It was a curveball, not a fastball, and word would spread around the league that the rookie had not beaten the hard-throwing McDowell on his best pitch. Still, no one in the league had hit a home run off McDowell since Memorial Day. He had thrown 123 innings without watching someone trot around the bases while he was on the mound. McDowell struck out Kosco in his next three at-bats. "I think it upset him that some rookie had done that," Kosco decided.

Kosco knew the assignment in Minnesota would be temporary because Killebrew was originally expected to be out for just a couple weeks. Kosco was more excited about playing his first big-league game in Cleveland. He was born about 50 miles away in Youngstown, Ohio. "When I arrived, Sam told me I was going to be there while Harmon was mending and he would platoon me and play me against left-handed pitching. I was happy to be there, but I guess I was also a little disappointed I never got to the big leagues sooner."

He was 23 when the Twins promoted him. The Detroit Tigers had signed Kosco out of high school in 1959 for a figure reported to be $80,000. The bonus rules had changed, and he was not required to be on a major league roster. He spent the next five years playing in places such as Decatur, Illinois; Syracuse, New York; and Amarillo, Texas. He found himself with Duluth, Minnesota, of the Northern League in 1964. He was losing interest in the game and sometimes lamented the fact he had not pursued a football career. The Tigers released him early in 1964.

The Twins had a Northern League affiliate in North Dakota, and Bismarck-Mandan manager Vern Morgan read about Kosco's release. Morgan believed teams released "big, strong youngsters" for two reasons: injury or attitude. Morgan investigated and learned Kosco was not injured and had caused no trouble. Tiger officials did perceive Kosco's diminishing enthusiasm and decided he had grown stale in their farm system. Morgan knew a change of scenery often helps these situations and asked Kosco if he would consider coming over to the Twins' system. Morgan immediately began to work on Kosco's game, first suggesting he abandon switch-hitting.

"He made the difference for me," Kosco recalled years later. "Vern thought I had more power from the right side, so he started working with me on going the other way with the ball against right-handers. I went up to him shortly after we started and said, 'Vern, this right-handed thing just isn't working.' But he told me to keep with it. His persistence paid off."

Kosco had by far his best minor-league season to that point in his career under Morgan. He won the 1964 Northern League Triple Crown with a .346 batting average, 28 home runs and 97 runs batted in. Kosco had a six-point lead in the batting race entering the season's final game, and Morgan invited his outfielder to watch the finale from the bench. Kosco declined. Winnipeg had a power-hitter named Felix DeLeon, who never made it to the big leagues, but he was chasing Kosco for the league home run and RBI titles. DeLeon hit home runs in his first two at-bats of the season finale, one of which Kosco almost caught as it sailed over the fence. Entering his final at-bat, Kosco found himself tied with DeLeon for the league lead in home runs and runs batted in. Even a tie in those categories would still give Kosco the triple crown, but he wanted to win it outright. Kosco homered in his final swing of the season to capture the Northern League lead in batting average, home runs and runs batted in.

It's rare for a player to put up impressive minor league numbers, as Kosco did at Bismarck and then Denver, and have those statistics translate into something as good or better in the major leagues. The Twins had six players on the team who could be said to have done that: Killebrew, Oliva, Battey, Mincher, Versalles, and Allison. When a team has an offensive nucleus of players who advanced, level by level, and carried similar numbers with them, that team needs only to fill the roster with competitors such as Kosco: intelligent men who strain to play and who understand they mostly might not play but are industrious enough to be ready when the chances come.

Kosco was a good enough player that by 1969, when he was with the Dodgers, he led the team in home runs and runs batted in, but as a rookie in '65 he needed to make contributions that might not glare from a box score. A few days after he homered against McDowell, Kosco's sacrifice fly brought in the go-ahead run in a game against the Angels, the second-division club the Twins struggled to beat all season. A day later, he contributed a pinch-hit single.

It was a great time of the season for Minnesota Twins' fans, who were proud and excited. The team continued to win without Killebrew, The Beatles had played a concert at Metropolitan Stadium on Sunday, August 22, and then the Yankees came to town. New York was more than 16 games behind the Twins, who had a six-and-half game lead over second-place Chicago. This four-game series with New York was the Yankees' last trip to Met Stadium for the season, and fans packed the stands.

In the opening game of the series, Kindall's broken-bat, bloop single off the leg of Yankee center fielder Roger Repoz drove in the winning run in the 10th inning of a 4-3 win. The Yankees had led that game 3-2 behind Whitey Ford, but in the ninth inning Versalles scooted from first to second on a bounding ball back to the pitcher's mound. It was a likely double-play ball with most runners on first, but Versalles got such a jump toward second base that the Yankees opted to take the sure out at first. Oliva then doubled home Versalles to tie the score, which sent the game into extra innings and set up Kindall's game-winning hit. The hit raised Kindall's batting average to .200. He welcomed having a good week, since the team was to honor the Saint Paul native with Jerry Kindall Night that upcoming Friday.

That 10th-inning win over the Yankees helped douse the second-place White Sox, who were on a ten-game winning streak and hoping to get within striking distance of the Twins. Baltimore beat the White Sox the same night Kindall dumped that hit off the leg of Repoz. The White Sox would have been five-and-half games behind Minnesota if they and the Yankees had both won. Instead, Chicago was seven-and-a-half games back.

Minnesota continued to do little things to win, and in the third game of the Yankees' series Kosco's defense helped save Merritt and preserve a win. Merritt was pursuing his fourth win of the month, and led 1-0 in the top of the fifth when New York third baseman Clete Boyer slammed a pitch into the right-center field gap with no one out and Yankee runners on first and second. Kosco was in right field and playing Boyer a little too shallow. It appeared the ball would sail past him, then carom off the fence for a certain double, maybe a triple. Kosco sped after the ball, left his feet, reached his left hand across his body toward center field and caught the ball as he flew through the air. Mickey Mantle was impressed.

"You see some guys who leave their feet but come down before backhanding a ball on a play like that" Mantle said, "but Kosco caught the ball while he was suspended in the air."

Rather then relish the catch, Kosco scrambled upright from his headfirst slide over the grass. He knew the runner on second base, Elston Howard, was not fast, and certainly Howard would be well off the base, because when Boyer hit the ball it appeared to be a sure hit. Howard was closer to third base than second as Kosco fired the ball to Kindall, who wheeled and threw to Versalles covering second for a double play in the Twins' 5-4 win.

Rollins got the big hit, a two-run triple in the bottom of the seventh. He crushed the ball, and even managed some half-hearted praise for himself, telling reporters, "I waited four months to get a hit like that." The glory was again diffuse: Joe Nossek doubled after he replaced Oliva, and Allison contributed a home run, his first in 19 games. Worthington got the save.

"It seemed like the kind of team," Frank Kostro recalled, "where almost every day, even if you weren't a star, even if you didn't have great numbers, you contributed. Someone was always making the play, getting something done, even if it was just a matter of moving a runner over from second to third, doing what you need to do to win ball games."

They had the athleticism to get the job done. Even though they were baseball players, these men would have excelled in almost any pick-up sport. Pascual and Allison were among the team's accomplished golfers; Garry Roggenburk had captained his college basketball team; Sevcik, Kosco, Killebrew, and Allen were among those who had played football; Siebler, Allen, Rollins and Versalles were fine bowlers; and Pascual and Oliva inveterate swimmers. What pushed them over the top was they did not reluctantly shuffle into pressure situations.

Outfielder Sandy Valdespino was a rookie with 245 major-league at-bats, yet Mele asked him to start the opening game of the World Series, the first in Minnesota history. "I was a little nervous before the game," Valdespino recalled. "I think you'd always be nervous in a situation like that, but I was positive I belonged. I was a major league ball player and I was not afraid to go out there between the white lines. I did it in Venezuela, Cuba, Puerto Rico. I could do it here." He batted .261 with a .322 slugging average in '65, but with men on base he hit .317 with a .385 slugging average. That included a couple key pinch hits in Killebrew's absence, including a game-winner in the second game of a doubleheader in Detroit the third week of August.

The Twins did need more than just a few key pinch hits to keep winning in Killebrew's absence, and Battey, Mincher, and Jimmie Hall joined Oliva's surge to keep the offense humming. Battey drove in 25 runs and went 51-for-176 the final two months of the season. Mincher homered nine times and drove in 26 runs while replacing Killebrew and drew 15 intentional bases on balls. During a mid-August game in Detroit, Mincher slammed a three-run homer and drove in four runs as Grant got his first complete game in two months and his first win over Detroit in three years. Mincher was averaging a home run every 12 trips to the plate and batting a productive .327 since Killebrew's injury.

Hall drove in 25 runs, went only 40-for-163, but drew 19 walks. He was in a home run slump, however, and had not hit one since his pinch-hit shot off Palmer. The Twins' home run production was obviously affected without Killebrew. They had managed at least 30 home runs in May, June, and July, but hit only 25 in August and September combined. They still scored more runs in August than all but one month that season.

The trio of Merritt, Kaat and Grant stepped up to the challenge to lead the pitching staff, which pitched well in August and even better in September. Merritt kept pace with the veterans. He started seven times in August and won four of those, matching Kaat in wins and trailing Grant by one. The trio went 13-4, and Kaat's wins were particularly welcome. He was only 9-8 entering August, although he had pitched better than his record. It seemed ironic that Kaat remarked after the season-opener – when Tovar dropped that cotton-candy pop fly – that he would probably get a win later in the season that he didn't deserve. He had probably lost far more than he deserved. His teammates gave him excellent run support in about half his wins, but in well over half of his 11 losses he never got more than two runs.

By season's end, opponents had scored 27 unearned runs against Kaat. The Twins' infield defense had not really improved; it was just that the errors were typically not leading to a river of runs – except when Kaat was pitching.

Unearned runs are a bane to pitchers. To give a team four or more outs an inning not only means a pitcher has to throw more pitches, it means he has to pitch from the stretch rather than with a windup, and it means the infield usually has a big hole in it. The first baseman typically will hold the runner, which creates a larger space between first and second base for a hitter to drive a ball through. Despite pitching from the stretch far too often, Kaat finished the season 18-11. He allowed no more than three earned runs in 36 of his 42 starts.

Kaat was at his best after Killebrew's injury. Despite tendonitis in his left arm, he went 9-2 with a save after Killebrew went down, allowing 103 hits in 102 innings those final two months of play. Grant was 9-4 in that span. Grant was on his way to a throwing a career-high 270 innings, but he finished in a sprint, allowing 28 hits and 13 bases on balls in 50 September innings.

When Pascual returned, Merritt had one more start, the second game of the Twins' final scheduled doubleheader in early September. After that, Grant, Kaat, Perry, and Pascual handled all the starts, with Merritt and Boswell strengthening the bullpen. Boswell had rejoined the team during the second half of August but started just once after that and struggled with his control. He was a welcome addition to the clubhouse anyway.

Boswell, 20, was poised beyond his years on the mound and considered to have a rustic brashness, which fell somewhere short of being called "cocky." After pitching well in relief early in the season, he approached Mele and told him, "If you do put me in the starting rotation on this road trip, I'd like to pitch against Chance in Los Angeles." Dean Chance was considered to be one of the better pitchers in the league.

Boswell threw fastballs and allowed base hits to the first two batters he faced during his 1964 big-league debut, which brought Battey to the mound to settle him down. Boswell spoke first. "So, is this next guy a fastball hitter?" Boswell kept life interesting, and the players welcomed that. It had been six long months together, half a year that included all the mundane aspects of baseball life: packing and unpacking bags, cab and bus rides, restaurant food, repeated viewings of matinees, waiting out rain delays, and the pause after awakening to recall what city they were in. Most of them were tired and beat up. Boswell could make them laugh.

Perry arrived at the park one day and mentioned he had purchased a new stereo. "Does it have a pinion gear on the seventh cycle?" Boswell blurted. Others joined in as the clubhouse conversation proceeded down an absurd path. Pascual and Boswell shared the same birthday and roomed together in 1965. They wore uniform numbers 23 and 17, and on one road trip were assigned to hotel room 2317. Boswell kept the key as a souvenir. "After all," he explained, "that's a real odyssey." There was a late night in the clubhouse when Zimmerman examined one of his fingers that had been damaged by a foul ball. Boswell expressed concern. "I hope it hasn't affected the rigitation." He had boasted of his vocabulary since grade school.

As August ended, the Twins were laughing at more than Boswell. Seemingly, the season should have imploded on them, but as September dawned the Twins had emerged like a dog in a war zone. Killebrew and Pascual were still sidelined, Allison wasn't hitting and Oliva finished the month missing a week of play, including three crucial games with the Indians. The team hit only one home run in seven games at one point during August, and went without a home run in 11 games during one 17-game stretch. They had no home runs in an important three-game series with Cleveland at the end of August, and Cleveland won two of them.

In the Twins' sole win in that series, Mele moved Battey to third in the order, the highest slot he had occupied all season. Battey walked twice and drove in a run, as he did on almost a daily basis as August moved into September. Indians' manager Birdie Tebbetts found no reason for optimism after winning the series. He could already guess how it was going to end. Tebbetts conceded it was easier, but not easy, to beat the Twins without Killebrew and Oliva – but he knew both would soon return.

Despite all the injuries, the Twins completed the month going 19-13. They had a six-game lead when Killebrew injured his elbow, expanded that to nine games at one point in August and still had a seven-and-half game lead with a month to play. The team even finished August repeatedly outdrawing The Beatles.

The hottest rock group in history played to about 30,000 screaming teens at Met Stadium on Sunday, August 22. That same night, about 2,000 Twins fans, led by Saint Paul mayor George Vavoulis, welcomed the Twins back from their 7-7 road trip at the Twin Cities airport. The Twins began a home stand the next day, and in six of their seven games drew more than 31,000 fans. They finished the week playing before 203,213 patrons. If fan interest was any gauge, the Twins were going to win the pennant.

Mel Nelson, Jim Perry and Jimmie Hall

ELEVEN

"My stuff was kind of sleepy on the mound." – Jim Grant

Harmon Killebrew received a letter of encouragement from United States Vice President Hubert H. Humphrey as the calendar turned to September. Recovery from the dislocated elbow was going slower than expected. Humphrey could have served as mascot for the constantly hobbled Twins: he had once been a pharmacist.

At least Killebrew was healing and could sense productive days were near. Allison's August slump was lapping into another month, and he was growing more confused with each at-bat. His September began badly as the Twins completed a split of a four-game series at home against Detroit. Minnesota stranded 46 base runners during the series, and Allison contributed to the futility when he struck out five times in one game to tie the major league record for a nine-inning game.

He stared at the floor in the Twins' clubhouse after enduring the indignities of the night, quietly answered reporters' questions and dressed slowly. He was batting .238 for the season and .185 in the past two weeks. Fans had booed him loudly when his name was announced with the tying run on second base in the eighth inning. Abruptly, they cheered as he stepped to the plate, hoping they could will him to drive in the run and end the misery. He struck out swinging to tie the record, and then faced another round of boos as he carried his bat back to the dug-out. When he trotted onto the field to start the top of the next inning, there were pockets of applause from the fans near his spot in left field, but it was far too little and late in the season.

"Those fans are out for blood now," Detroit manager Charlie Dressen said after the game. "They all get that way when they smell that pennant."

As John Sain had said to Whitey Ford long ago, the sun will come up tomorrow, and figuratively it was about to become a fireball. The minor league season at Denver had ended and the major league rosters could be expanded, so the vacancy left by Killebrew could be filled. Ted Uhlaender, a 24-year-old left-handed hitting outfielder, made his major league debut. Minnesota also recalled Cesar Tovar, who gave Mele a right-handed bat off the bench and insurance in the infield and outfield.

There was little cavalry support for Versalles, who had lost more than 15 pounds since spring training and weighed a butcher's thumb above 150 pounds. Martin chose the right days to coax, "Zoilo, you have to go today. I know you feel a little down and have to push yourself, but this game means a lot to the club." Tovar could play shortstop in a pinch, but he was better suited for the outfield or third base.

Versalles handled it well. Maria Josefa had observed, "Zoilo's a good man. Like so many, it took him a while to mature. It seems as though he's grown up a lot in the last two years." He was openly complimentary of Mele, who allowed him to skip infield practice whenever he felt tired, although skipping infield practice was hardly blasphemy. Many veterans disliked the tradition of taking infield practice after fielding dozens of ground balls during batting practice. Braves' manager Bobby Bragan went so far as to announce during spring training his team had little intention of taking infield practice during the season, particularly after the midway point of the season, when players start to wear down.

The two Twins who were expected to carry the team, and thus should have been fatigued – Pascual and Killebrew – were the freshest. Pascual had recovered from surgery, had thrown on the sidelines, and Mele expected him to start early in September. Pascual always pitched well after returning from injuries, retaining his perfect form and throwing his curve with that straight overhand motion, rather than compensating and dropping his arm angle down to the side. In '63, he returned after an injury to win 12 of his last 16 starts to finish with 21 wins. In his third game back in '65, he fanned 13 batters.

Killebrew had tired of his routine, running to keep his legs strong and lifting weights to strengthen his elbow, but at least he was with the team and felt like he was a small part of it. Often during long recovery periods, as Bernie Allen noted after his knee injury in 1964, players begin to feel emotionally separated from their teammates. But Killebrew would sit on the trainer's table for treatment on his elbow and absorb the clubhouse noises, card games and jokes. Boswell sometimes sat on the trainer's table with Killebrew, back-to-back, to give him support. Boswell would talk or sing a tune, then provide disc jockey commentary such as, "I made that one up in the bathtub in Fenandina Beach. I caught a cold when I got out." The clubhouse mood was electric, anxious and upbeat.

Killebrew was still in pain when he swung a bat, but Mele knew if the Twins' lead began to dwindle he could insert Killebrew into the lineup and give the team a mental boost.

Minnesota had a five-game lead over the White Sox when the pennant race turned petty. Killebrew traveled with the team to Chicago, where the Twins' requested use of the field so he could take early batting practice. He needed the work to regain his timing but more importantly to loosen the elbow and get accustomed to the daily workload of playing again. The White Sox devised an excuse to prevent Killebrew from using the batting cage. The Twins took it out on the Sox: Grant beat Chicago 3-2 for his 18th win, and Kaat won the next day for his 15th victory.

Jimmie Hall's two-run home run – his first since that pinch-hit home run off Jim Palmer way back at the beginning of August – was the decisive blow in Grant's win. Mele thought it was one of the bigger home runs in a season of great rallies, because Minnesota's lead would have been down to four games with a loss.

In that game, the Sox jumped to a 2-0 lead off Grant because of an error by Kindall, but Kindall's single in the third inning helped the Twins' get one run back. Grant allowed just three hits after the first inning and waited. The Twins had won 87 games, rallying from behind 28 times, and it was about to happen again. Battey singled with one out in the seventh before Hall slammed a breaking ball for his two-run home run. He had been batting about .200 during the previous two weeks and his production had declined in the second half of the season, but the home run seemed to ignite him.

Hall stole a base and homered again with Kaat on the mound the next day, and the Twins also got help from Valdespino, who was in left field in place of Allison. Valdespino went 3-for-4, Kaat was 2-for-3, and with the help of Worthington's 20th save the Twins left Chicago with a seven-game lead. The majority of their remaining schedule comprised games with Boston, Kansas City and Washington. Those three teams had a combined winning percentage under .400, so suddenly September had a warm glow.

"That should be it," Versalles said as the Twins packed up in Comiskey Park and prepared to fly to Boston. "It should be easy now, I think."

It was. Relatively. The Twins swept both Boston and Kansas City, increasing their lead to 10 games with a half month to play. The team was devastating in Boston as Oliva returned to the lineup to chase Yastrzemski for the batting title. The Boston star had a seemingly comfortable .326-.316 lead when the series began. In 10 days, Oliva would be in front, .317-.315.

The post-mortem focus was on Merritt in the opener against Boston. The rookie relieved Perry with one out in the sixth inning and fanned eight Red Sox in three and two-thirds innings, helping Perry to his 10th win of the season. The Twins belted six doubles and stole four bases. Pascual was the beneficiary of the next day's barrage, which included five stolen bases and three more doubles. The Twins hadn't hit a home run in two days at Fenway but had scored 16 runs and helped Pascual to his first win since July 8. He allowed five hits in nearly eight innings.

Grant polished off the decisive sweep on a getaway Sunday, when the Twins stole three more bases. He picked a good time to throw a four-hitter, shutting out Boston 2-0. Shutouts were not necessary in his four previous wins against the Red Sox because his teammates had provided him with 46 runs.

Mele saw more good news in Hall's resurgence. He had raised his batting average nearly 10 points to .298 by batting .409 against Chicago and Boston. Hall had helped carry the team early in the season, when Killebrew was without a home run and Oliva's hits wouldn't fall. The 27-year-old center fielder was weak with a virus at the time, but he stayed in the lineup. Even players of Killebrew's stature were afraid to miss too much playing time. Hall had won his starting job during the 1963 season when Lenny Green left the lineup briefly, and he knew the same thing could happen to him. So he kept playing.

With the Twins a game-and-a-half out of first in early May, Hall helped his mates launch a five-game winning streak with a 420-foot home run and a volley of runs batted in. He complained of not being able to catch his breath when he ran hard, but told Mele he preferred to keep playing. Hall was batting .325 with 16 home runs and 50 runs batted in at the All-Star break, but he hit only four homers the rest of the season.

A slim, swift, left-handed batter with power against right-handed pitching, it was almost as if Hall were a light-hitting middle infielder against left-handed pitching. Hall batted .240 against lefties in '65, rarely drew a walk, and struck out about once every three at-bats. He was raised in rural North Carolina and said he saw right-handed pitching almost exclusively as a kid. It didn't help that he suffered a beaning by Angels' left-hander Bo Belinsky in 1964. Hall missed a week of play, donned a batting helmet with an earflap and suffered questions about his ability to hit lefties.

He did stand further back in the batters' box against lefties after the beaning, which became evident after he studied photographs in 1965. His position in the batter's box against lefties made it almost impossible for him to reach an outside pitch. He had adjusted and gone 9-for-14 in one stretch, which seemed to dash the notion he was jittery against left-handed pitchers. Still, he did not display much power against them, which was a concern for Mele going back to spring training.

With Allison struggling against right-handers and Hall limping against lefties, Mele had to start giving consideration to platooning during the World Series. It would be a tough call because both Hall and Allison had the potential to put the ball into the seats, and unlike many power hitters, each was a fine base runner. Hall beat out 20 infield hits in '65 and stole 14 bases in 21 attempts, which was not bad, but not in Allison's league. Allison was a tremendous base-stealer and welcomed Mele's running offense at the start of the season. Although he was not asked to steal bases often, Allison had 10 steals in 12 attempts in '65. Spanning a four-year period in the middle of his career, he was thrown out just four times in 36 attempts, or an average of once a season.

It would be a gamble if Mele decided to platoon Hall and Allison with Valdespino and Joe Nossek. Platooning was a strategy Casey Stengel employed when he managed the Yankees to a string of successful seasons, but Stengel was more eager to platoon in the regular season than during the World Series, when he preferred to slot his best hitters. Neither Valdespino nor Nossek was a better overall career hitter than Hall and Allison.

Nossek had batted just .238 with 8 home runs and only 29 RBI in Atlanta in '64, not good production for a AAA outfielder with more than 400 at-bats, even one who missed some games with a broken thumb. He batted just .218 during the '65 season, although had a .250 average as a pinch-hitter. He was a fine defensive outfielder, thanks in part to help from Lenny Green. Nossek could also play third base and even stood in for Versalles at shortstop in an exhibition game.

The Twins had scouted the Ohio native in high school but let him marinate for nearly four years at Ohio University before signing him in '61 for $48,000 the day after they gave Allen a bonus somewhere between $20,000 and $40,000. The signings were a signal the Griffith family's financial fortunes had shifted with the move to Minnesota. That improved fiscal picture was one reason the team was a contender by 1965.

September wore thin on Mele quickly, but not because of lineup choices. He was barraged with interview requests from domestic and foreign reporters, claimed he didn't get any sleep and couldn't get in a round of golf. "I wasn't like a Dick Williams, a guy who let things roll off his back," Mele later said of a man who managed in three decades. "I took it all too damn seriously." Dealing with reporters was something he accepted but rarely relished, even though Mele had once been a sports writer. Reporters wanted him to start talking about the World Series before the pennant was clinched. That was fine for Versalles, who was a player, and everyone knew his moods still often shadowed his performance. It was bad form for a manager to count World Series money before the season was over. "One game at a time," Mele would tell reporters. "You've written that before? Write it again."

Back in Quincy, Massachusetts, construction was concluding on Mele's new home, and talk there was a little bolder. When the Twins responded with the two-game sweep over Chicago after the White Sox refused to let Killebrew take morning batting practice, Connie Mele said, "The Twins are in." She was in the late stage of her fifth pregnancy. "You better reserve me a bed in a Minnesota hospital, because I'm not going to miss the Series for anything."

A computer at the Franklin Institute reassured there would be a World Series in Minneapolis. After the Twins' commanding sweep of Boston, the computer indicated there was one chance in a thousand the Twins would falter.

Fans certainly seemed to think the race was over. They didn't even stick around for the credits to roll. With students back in school, the thermometer working overtime to hit 60 degrees and a computer telling fans a trip to the World Series was assured, families stayed home and wondered if the purchase of World Series tickets was in the budget.

The club had already announced it would accept World Series ticket requests postmarked as of September 15. Thousands lined up outside the Minneapolis post office in cold, rainy weather, waiting to drop their letters in the mail after the clock struck midnight. Saint Paul officials had a better plan and established a special box for ticket applications. Anything dropped in the box would automatically be postmarked September 15. There were 32,000 requests at the Twins' offices the next day, but a little more than World Series fever was in the air. It snowed that night in Whitefish, Montana, with flurries sighted in the Dakotas and northern Minnesota.

The weather worked its way east to the Twin Cities, and although it didn't snow September 20, it was 52 degrees and drizzling when 537 fans appeared to watch Grant lose a Monday game to Catfish Hunter and Kansas City. The team had about 4,500 season ticket holders, but the leagues recorded the turnstile count at the time, so it remains the franchise's record low in attendance.

In the fans' defense, the weather lashed at them, and it was an unattractive part of the schedule. Minnesota had just beaten struggling Washington twice during the weekend. Kansas City was at the bottom of the league with the Senators, and a two-game series with Baltimore would begin Tuesday. The Orioles were 10 games out of first, but not mathematically eliminated from the pennant race. The Twins didn't average 8,000 fans a game during their final five games before departing for the last road trip of the season.

Although Griffith's franchise drew far better – and played far better – in Minnesota than Washington, attendance was becoming a problem in the American League. It is easy now to see why the league's owners adopted the designated hitter in 1973 and hoped it would generate more fan interest. When the 1965 season was complete, the National League had won eight of the past twelve World Series and seven of the past eight All-Star Games. Since 1954, the only time the American League had outdrawn the National League was 1961, when Roger Maris and Mickey Mantle were chasing Babe Ruth's record of 60 home runs in a season and the American League added two teams. The feeling in baseball was New York's dominance was beginning to keep fans away. By '65, the National League averaged 6,000 more fans a game than the American League.

The contrast between the leagues was vivid in mid-September of '65, when the big news in the National League was that Willie Mays had hit his 500th career home run while his San Francisco Giants were in the middle of a fourteen-game winning streak that helped them take a two-and-half game lead over Los Angeles. Sandy Koufax broke Bob

Feller's single-season strikeout record that day, and Koufax had recently pitched a perfect game for his fourth career no-hitter. In the American League, Minnesota had a 10-game lead, the pennant race was seemingly over, and the big news was Kansas City's showman owner Charlie Finley had signed pitcher Satchel Paige for the rest of the season as a public relations stunt. Paige, like Finley, was one of baseball's great characters and reportedly 59 at the time of the signing.

The signing did focus some attention on African-American pitchers. Paige was a brilliant pitcher who had played most of his career in the Negro Leagues, so he never had a legitimate chance to win 20 games in a single major league season. Mudcat Grant, however, was on the verge of history. He was about to become the first black man to win 20 games in the American League. The media and fans focused on Grant's race, a focus he found to be misplaced.

"I'm shooting to win 20, not as the first Negro necessarily, but as Jim Grant. When Joe DiMaggio led the American League in hitting, they didn't say he was the first Italian to do it."

There was ample time for fans and the media to discuss it. In the middle of September, Grant started just three times in a two-week period and went 12 days between his 19th and 20th wins.

Meanwhile, the temperature squeaked out of the '50s, so Mele decided to get Killebrew into the lineup for Tuesday and Wednesday mid-September games against Baltimore. Mele hoped the temperature was warm enough to let Killebrew's elbow feel loose, and if the Twins clinched at home, Killebrew could be in the lineup when it happened. He went hitless his first game and 2-for-4 the second, the Twins lost both games, and the magic number was still three as they flew to Washington.

There had been debate between the Minneapolis and Saint Paul mayors about which city would hold a pennant-clinching celebration if the title was won during the home stand. That became a moot point. Mele and the players were disappointed with their three-game losing streak and their inability to clinch the pennant at home. As they landed in Washington, everyone connected with the team was eager to see it end.

Rain, rather than the typical Washington heat and humidity, greeted the Twins in D.C., and their Friday opener against the Senators was postponed. The Twins had played only twice in four days and their lead had fallen from nine to seven-and-a-half games. Mele wanted to get back at it soon. The 1964 Phillies' collapse down the stretch was too recent a nightmare for any manager. After the Friday game was called because of bad weather, Hubert Humphrey entered the Senators' visiting clubhouse. "Sam, Sam. The suspense is driving me crazy. When are we going to clinch the pennant?"

Mele stood when he saw Humphrey. "I wish I knew, sir. I know one thing: we're going to win three in a row. That's all it takes. I'm not going to depend on anyone else."

In the first game of Saturday's doubleheader, Grant won his 20th game – a one hitter – scoring the only run he needed with no score in the top of the fifth. Versalles drove him home with his 18th home run of the season. Versalles had four hits and later tripled to light the torch on a three-run seventh inning. Valdespino, pinch-hitting for Allison, delivered a two-run single.

Grant had not slept well the night before. He was kept awake by a cough and tickle in his throat rather than by the customary snoring of his roommate, Battey. "My stuff was kind of sleepy on the mound, too," Grant said, so he quickened his delivery to fool the Senators. Battey said Grant lacked the good curve that helped push him to 20 wins, but he had a hopping fastball. Only one Senator reached third base as Grant fanned seven, walked two, and changed his mind.

He admitted there was no way to predict how he would feel when he became the first black pitcher to win 20 games in the A.L. He talked about the numerous black fans who had written or approached him as he neared this coveted circle. They expressed pride that Grant would be the first black man to accomplish the feat, and he decided this moment in baseball history was a great and important honor.

Pascual had a little something extra to pitch for as well in the second game of the doubleheader, although nothing as historic as Grant's milestone. With Humphrey so prominent in the Twins' clubhouse in

Washington and so eager for a win, Pascual was happy to bring a smile to the vice president's face. Humphrey had been instrumental in getting Pascual's parents out of Cuba.

Pascual pitched six innings of the nightcap against Washington. He allowed one earned run and left trailing 3-1. Merritt entered and allowed one hit over three innings, and the Twins scored three runs in the eighth with Valdespino, Nossek, Quilici, and Mincher playing the key offensive roles in a 5-3 win that clinched a tie for the pennant. In 18 doubleheaders, Minnesota had swept a league-high seven.

Baltimore was playing a doubleheader at home, and had won the first game when the Twins completed their sweep. If the Orioles lost later, the Twins would be the American League champions.

Twins' traveling secretary Howard Fox asked Allison to group the players away from the media so the team could discuss whether to wait in the clubhouse for the outcome of the Orioles' game or dress and return to the team hotel. Battey suggested they bring on the champagne and fake a celebration for the television and news photographers. He said it could be broadcast whenever the pennant was clinched. The players voted to wait. Killebrew and Zimmerman hovered near a radio while others talked, played cards and drank beer, prompting Killebrew to observe that clinching a tie was to beer what winning the championship was to champagne.

Baltimore won again. The Twins peeled off their uniforms, padded to the showers, and left the champagne on ice.

Kaat took the ball for Minnesota on the last Sunday in September, Minnesota's 157th game of the season. The Senators countered with left-hander Pete Richert. Gil Hodges decided to start two left-handers in the three-game series to thwart Oliva, who started the series with a seven-point lead over Yastrzemski in the batting race. Oliva got one of the Twins' three hits – enough for Kaat.

The left-hander's error on a throw led to Washington's only run in the third, but Versalles sparked the Twins for the second straight day. He tripled in the sixth and scored when Don Zimmer, who was catching, was charged with a passed ball. The score remained 1-1 until the eighth, when Quilici doubled and advanced on an error, then scored on Versalles' sacrifice fly. Kaat allowed eight hits and fanned 10, the last being Zimmer for the game's final out. It was Kaat's first complete game in eight starts.

When the umpire's arm went up for the final strike on Zimmer, Kaat pushed into the air, toes dangling downward, and smacked his fist into his glove. Players in the dugout erupted with hollers and hugs and charged onto the field. Kaat was swarmed as he walked off the pitcher's mound.

TV cameras and lights were stationed in the clubhouse. Oliva popped a cork on the first bottle of champagne. Battey shook a bottle, tugged on the cork and shot a stream of champagne across the clubhouse. Equipment manager Ray Crump kept cautioning the players that they had to take care of the uniforms, which were supposed to last through the end of the regular season before new garments were distributed for the World Series. Mincher and Killebrew were draped on each side of Zimmerman, whose uniform number was 22. As Crump continued to scold, Killebrew looked at Mincher. Each smiled and grabbed a sleeve of Zimmerman's jersey, ripping it off the catcher's back, perfectly splitting the material between the 2s on the uniform top. After that, if a player slipped on the floor, slick with champagne, other players would pull him up by the shirt, ripping it off his back.

Valdespino drenched Mele's gray thatch of hair with an entire bottle of champagne. "We're in," Mele shouted. "And we went right in through the front door, winning three straight." Mele hugged Versalles, who wore a new-haircut smile that teammates rarely saw during his early playing days. Soon, everyone was squeezing the wiry shortstop. Killebrew moved to the side and told reporters that because he had missed seven weeks, "I'm looking forward to another seven games." He then took a drink of champagne and remarked it was hard to get used to the taste.

The phone began to ring in the manager's office. First, Calvin Griffith called from Minnesota. Washington reporters, who remembered Griffith's pauper days running the Senators, asked if the call was collect. No, Mele said, but Griffith was speechless. "For a full minute. Honest." Connie Mele phoned. Telegrams arrived. A horseshoe of flowers was brought in and Battey, Perry and Grant – Grant's head covered with a pile of shaving cream – grouped together and wrapped the horseshoe around them.

Most of them had never won anything. Zimmerman and Klippstein were the active players to have seen World Series play, along with coaches Naragon, Sain, and Martin. Mele had started his big-league career 18 years ago. Jim Lemon had 15 years in, playing mostly with Washington and Minnesota. He had retired as a player in '63 at the age of 35. If he had been a couple years younger he might have been playing on this team. All the players from the Washington days had never tasted anything like this. "I knocked around in the minors for four years and never won anything," Hall said. "I love it. We're better than Cassius Clay. We are the greatest."

Naragon endured the crossfire of champagne for a while, congratulated everyone in the room, then dressed and went outside to reflect on the season. "I'm not much of a celebrator," he recalled, "and I have to admit when you're supposed to be an athlete and an example, and then this appears on television, it looks pretty silly. People wonder, 'Why would they do that?' I don't think any pennant is won easily. When players do that, they're just letting off steam and pressure."

"The air was out," Frank Quilici recalled. "That celebration was unbelievable. Hubert Humphrey came in with the Secret Service men, and I remember calling him over and asking him, 'Mr. Vice President, do you think this social system you started is working?'"

When the Twins later saw a tape of the celebration, some said they knew it was a "wild, wild deal," but did not realize it had become so seemingly juvenile. Some of the players hoped the fans would understand and pleaded that when a player has been in the big leagues for years and has never won anything, it's difficult to keep the lid on.

Soon, letters arrived at Twin Cities' newspapers from people who thought splashing champagne on each other's heads – particularly on a Sunday – was a bad example for children. Some thought it was a "terrible thing" to see on TV, which was held in high esteem by the letter writers. Forty years later, players celebrated in a similar manner, and the criticism was much the same.

When the mops came out to swab the floor, the Twins had done a remarkable job of celebrating. One of the Senators' clubhouse attendants had been a clubhouse boy for the Yankees during their years of pennant-winning celebrations. "I never saw one like this," he said.

With the old Senators' franchise dislodging the Yankees as American League champion, it was impossible to avoid the notion life was imitating art.

The musical "Damn Yankees" was based on a sports writer's Faustian book, "The Year the Yankees Lost the Pennant." A Washington Senators' fan sells his soul to assure the Senators win the American League pennant. Calvin Griffith had not won the pennant for Washington fans, and the title didn't cost his soul, but the price was high. He was suffering the anguish of a lawsuit from one of the team's shareholders, Washington fans and legislators were still angry over the team's departure, and he had spent millions of dollars developing a farm system good enough to keep feeding the 1965 Twins during all their injuries.

Former Washington Senators' manager Charlie Dressen noted the difference between the '65 Twins and the old Senators was that Griffith never had any money back in Washington. The team might draw 500,000, with the Griffith family doing all the work in the front office. When the season was over and everyone was paid, the club might realize about $50,000 in profit, Dressen said. It had been a long, difficult road to an American League pennant for the Griffiths.

Calvin, the serious one, succeeded Clark Griffith as Senators' president in 1955. Calvin inherited that position more than 30 years after Clark and Addie Griffith adopted him. He was 10-year-old Calvin Robertson then, and his family was living in poverty in Montreal. After the Griffiths adopted Calvin and his sister, the two youngsters took Griffith's surname.

When Clark died in 1955, Calvin and Thelma inherited majority interest in the Senators. They also inherited about $100,000 of debt. The entire family became involved in the baseball operation. Calvin's brother, Sherry Robertson, was the best ballplayer among the boys and played in the major leagues. He was the farm director. Thrifty Billy Robertson was director of stadium operations, and twin brother Jimmy, the fun-loving big spender in the family, directed concessions. Thelma was team vice president.

The Senators didn't have the money to sign players, and since Ossie Bluege managed the team to second-place finishes in two of three seasons ending in 1945, a Griffith team had never finished higher than fifth place. Not only was the Washington club not drawing enough fans, the American League's attendance had fallen from more than 10 million fans per year in post-war 1948 to just more than seven million in 1958. By that time, Griffith was openly shopping for a new city for his baseball team.

The Twin Cities had built Metropolitan Stadium in '56 with the intent of luring a major league team. It had seating for barely 18,000 fans but was engineered for expansion. In 1957, Minneapolis officials had made an offer to Griffith of low stadium rental and a guarantee of a million fans per season.

Senators' shareholder H. Gabriel Murphy didn't want the team to leave Washington and began to battle Griffith for control of the franchise in 1958. The insurance man owned 40 percent of the team stock and wanted controlling interest. Addie Griffith had died, and her 12 percent of the team stock was being held in a trust. Murphy offered to purchase the stock, but Calvin Griffith said he would never sell. Murphy also wanted the team to hire a general manager. Griffith handled all those duties as team president, but Murphy argued, "Successful management of the club is beyond the capabilities of the present management." With the Griffiths controlling majority interest, it was simple to defeat any resolution Murphy put up for adoption.

To quiet the fans' concern about any move, and to improve attendance before the 1958 season, Griffith stated, "Never in my lifetime will the Washington team be moved." Those who came to know him in Minnesota would be inclined to say Griffith truly believed this at the time. "Calvin couldn't lie," recalled Glenn Redman, who was a Twin

Cities sports writer during the 1960s. "He'd hem and haw if you asked him something he didn't want to answer, but he couldn't lie."

It was just impossible for Griffith to stop listening, however. He moved the franchise as the American League was voting to expand to another two cities. The Senators' annual attendance actually increased from less than 500,000 in '58 to nearly 750,000 by '60, so Griffith was perceived as a villain, and it was suggested he was a racist because he wanted to leave D.C., with its high population of African-Americans. It seems the true motivation was simpler and more common: money. Since 1901, the Senators had drawn a million fans once, and even though attendance was nearly 750,000 during the franchise's last season in D.C., that was lower than attendance in the latter half of the 1940s. As Dressen said, the Griffith family was always just scraping by.

When it rained, vendors had to leave their hot dog and beverage trays and rush out to help cover the field with a tarp. To owners of contending teams, the Senators were commonly a carcass with a little meat on it, the direction to look when they needed a player. In the winter of 1959, the Cincinnati Reds' Gabe Paul reportedly offered Griffith $500,000 apiece for Killebrew and Pascual. The offer was said to be legitimate by some, a mere publicity stunt by others. Griffith reportedly had no interest because, as he long maintained, "you can't play money." Without Killebrew and Pascual, the Senators' gate certainly would be worse than it was.

Griffith eventually viewed the offer from Minneapolis in terms of cash flow. Because he supported anything within reason that could help his family turn a profit, it's likely he would have stayed in Washington if drawing African-American fans could have helped his finances. He certainly defended the minorities on his team. In 1958, a Wisconsin senator called Griffith's players "wetbacks" during debate about a Washington stadium bill, saying the bill would be an 8.5 million "memorial to Calvin Griffith and the wetbacks he passes off as ballplayers." Griffith considered the comment to be a terrible insult to his players and demanded an apology.

Minnesota had too much appeal for Griffith in the midst of such screeds. In addition to leaving the league's smallest city for a fresh start in the Midwest, there was the guarantee of a million fans a year, and the television and radio rights paid to him would double.

The state greeted Griffith as a hero. There was news coverage of his home on the shores of Lake Minnetonka, one of Minnesota's larger lakes, situated among wooded, affluent suburbs minutes from downtown Minneapolis. He was named honorary chair of the state's Christmas Seals campaign. Attendance topped the million mark for 10 straight seasons after the move, and the Twins led the league in attendance in two of their first five seasons. Griffith had gone from using vendors as grounds crews to having his team fly chartered airlines. As the host of the '65 All-Star Game, the 53-year-old Griffith had a pool at the league's official hotel stocked with freshwater fish, and poles were provided for the game's dignitaries. For the All-Star Game, he had the foul line at Met Stadium chalked in red, white and blue, rather than white. When the Twins clinched the pennant, $18-a-bottle champagne flowed.

The Twins' 1965 American League pennant was such a confluence of terrific stories, coincidence and good fortune that there would be believers if someone suggested Griffith had sold his soul for it. The addition of Worthington and Klippstein was the result of the collapse of the bullpen in 1964. Hiring Martin sparked speculation about the security of Mele's job, but resulted in Versalles playing the best ball of his career. And although Griffith endured the withering criticism of fans and media when he had made just one trade during the previous off-season, it was indeed that trade that fell through that was the best trade of all.

Griffith tried hard to make a trade before the 1965 season, and he was talking with the New York Mets during baseball's 1964 winter meetings. The Twins would send Hall, Battey, and Perry, plus either Allen or Rollins, to New York. In return, the Twins would get their long-coveted, dependable, second baseman in Ron Hunt. They would also receive catcher Chris Cannizzaro and pitcher Al Jackson.

Jackson went 8-20 in 1965, Cannizzaro drove in seven runs, and Hunt broke his shoulder. Fortunately for the Twins, New York Mets' general manager George Weiss called off the deal.

Of course, the trade would not have mattered if the Twins had lost Oliva to Houston years earlier, when Oliva seemed so unpolished. The Twins also nearly let Oliva's minor league teammate, Jimmie Hall, get away in previous years, and only because of John Sain's advice did the team retain Jim Perry in spring training. Hal Naragon was right: no pennant is easily won.

It was a bittersweet season for Griffith and eventually a bittersweet life in Minnesota. Griffith was ill with phlebitis and pneumonia during the spring, so he had missed the 1965 home opener. He could not be with the team in Washington when it clinched the pennant because a subpoena awaited him as a result of a lawsuit brought by Murphy. Being back in Minnesota when the team clinched the pennant was odd for Griffith and his siblings, who had roots in Washington, roots deeper than any of the players, who were gracious enough to acknowledge their former fans.

"I wish we could have done this while we were in Washington," Battey said as the Twins celebrated in the clubhouse. "A lot of us who played in Washington wish the town could get some kind of credit. Those Washington fans had to put up with us when we finished fifth in 1960."

The 1965 season was the pinnacle of Griffith's tenure in Minnesota. When the World Series opened, Griffith brought in two helicopters to hover over the damp Metropolitan Stadium outfield to dry wet spots on the grass. When the team was set to head to Los Angeles for the third game of the World Series, Griffith invited so many minor league directors, friends, and relatives that he had to rent a second chartered airplane. When the Twins began to struggle in the 1970s, however, he became the object of scorn, almost as though this was the punishment for the successes during the Twins' first decade in Minnesota. It was during the '70s that billionaire banker Carl Pohlad began to make overtures for the club.

In 1984, the last of the grass-roots owners in baseball sold his team to Pohlad in an emotional pre-game ceremony in the Minneapolis Metrodome. There was a sliver of satisfaction for Murphy, the club shareholder who didn't want the team to move to Minnesota. He outlasted

Griffith as a stakeholder in the team. After Pohlad bought Griffith's controlling interest in the Twins, Pohlad still needed Murphy's shares – without 80 percent of a team's stock, a franchise owner could not fully depreciate player salaries.

And in '65, it was Murphy who was able to stand freely in the Senators' visiting clubhouse and watch the players celebrate. Murphy was well attired and stood off to the side, avoiding champagne spray. "It's a great day, isn't it?" he said.

By the time Griffith and the Twins' fans could have a great day with the team, the excitement of the moment was long gone. The Twins had a day off, then played a three-game series in Baltimore. They won there the last day of September, with Versalles hitting the first grand slam of his career. Kaat also homered and won his 18th game of the season. The team then flew back to Minneapolis.

It was the last Thursday night in September, and it would probably be Friday before the plane landed at Wold-Chamberlain Field. It had rained all day in Minneapolis. The early evening temperature was 45 degrees and falling as fans began to assemble along runway fences at 8:30. Lazaro Versalles was among the early arrivals. Fans emptied the vending machines of coffee and hot chocolate, and some stayed inside to play pinball. When the team's arrival was at least three hours away, one couple arrived at the airport, saw no plane, walked into the airport security office and asked, "Well, where are they?"

Some fans wore buttons that had been produced as a promotion by a local nightspot. The buttons read, "Sam Mele for President" and "Harmon Killebrew for Governor." One fan held a sign, "Doc Lentz for Surgeon General." A souvenir manufacturer from Winona, Minnesota, had a salesgirl on hand to sell championship pennants that carried the Twins' logo. She sold 100 within an hour. In the continuing display of one-upmanship, Saint Paul managed to sneak two bands into the celebration, even though it had been agreed there would be one from Minneapolis and one from Saint Paul.

The players' wives arrived and were allowed to park cars on the airport runway so police could easily escort them and their husbands away after the celebration. By the time the twin-engine charter was spotted in the sky, 4,000 people had assembled and began to cheer. It was another welcome chance for people to get lost in the team.

Earlier in the day, it was announced that Minnesota's 47th Infantry Division was among the units picked by defense secretary Robert McNamara to form a select force of National Guardsmen and Army Reservists to be trained for combat in Vietnam. The sun had failed to make an appearance on 23 of September's 30 days, and most people were hard pressed to call the sunny days anything beyond partly cloudy. Rain fell during half the days in September, raising the year's precipitation total to more than 35 inches, nearly 15 above normal.

The plane taxied to a floodlit stand mounted on a trailer truck at the end of a runway. Fans pushed closer; others streamed out of the warmth of the airport, and cars continued to arrive. Cheerleaders struggled through the crowd to reach the area where the plane would stop. The players emerged in sports coats and raincoats. One of the louder cheers went up when Zoilo Versalles emerged.

The Vietnam War was continuing. The weather was still awful. And the Minnesota Twins had warmed the summer of 1965.

Bob Allison

TWELVE

"Many people thought we would lose in four." – Tony Oliva

The cool of the evening had arrived. With more than a week between clinching the pennant and the start of the World Series, there was ample time for Twins' players and fans to sit back and revel in the festivities and atmosphere of October baseball in Minnesota. Mele had traveled to Massachusetts to visit his children and pregnant wife and left Naragon to manage the team in Baltimore. Mele ensured Versalles got some rest and conferred with Sain on how to distribute the season's remaining innings among the pitchers, so each man could get in some work and stay ready for the World Series. Pascual was concerned about a long layoff. He felt he needed work because he had pitched so little in the second-half of the season. Worthington was healthy again, and he also needed innings.

Battey welcomed some days off. He had injured his right knee during the winter of 1962, when he fell off a hassock at his home while doing some home improvements. He had knee surgery before the 1964 season, but his leg was always taking abuse. The knee bothered him so much in spring training that Naragon suggested that he do his daily catching in camp while kneeling on his left knee, which would take pressure off the right leg. In early August, Battey had suffered a mild injury to his problem knee sliding into a base. He was barely 32 when he retired after the '67 season, his skills chiseled away by a stream of injuries.

He was the only man on the 1959 White Sox roster who did not play in that World Series, and he would have missed the 1965 Series if events had fallen differently. Griffith had tried to trade him before the '65 season, and he told Battey during a meeting there were no takers. They agreed during the meeting that Battey would earn an extra $1,000 if he arrived at camp weighing less than 230 pounds.

After meeting with Griffith, Battey, 29, defiantly said, "Maybe a lot of people think I'm through, but I have to disagree. I know what I can do, and I'm still a major league catcher. I've caught more games over the last five years than any catcher in baseball, and hit as well as the next catcher. I'm going to initiate an exercise program designed to bring me close to 220 pounds. I'll be ready to play, and am confident I'll have a good year, even if others have their doubts."

During the season, his hands ached and there were times he was wrapped like a mummy, so he cut down his stroke and hit just six home runs but batted nearly .300 by taking the ball to the opposite field. He drove in as many runs as he had in all but one of his previous six seasons.

After a hard winter of conditioning and the grinding 1965 season, Battey knew the days off before the World Series would rejuvenate him. Sevcik was in the opposite frame of mind and strained to play after spending a summer warming pitchers in the bullpen. He started twice in five days after not batting for about three months. He doubled in his first at-bat for his only major league hit.

Oliva took treatments on his sore knee and for a pulled muscle. He did not play the final games of the season, which made him unhappy. The rest after clinching the pennant reminded him of that first winter when he didn't play ball and grew lonely and bored. The World Series would not be a festive affair for him. Friends and relatives of most players had begun to arrive in the Twin Cities, but unlike countryman Versalles – who now had many of his relatives residing with him in Bloomington – all of Oliva's family members remained in Cuba.

"It was a great feeling for all the ballplayers to win it, especially for Minnesota," Oliva recalled. "In New York, this type of thing was different. They were used to winning, but it was new to our fans. You went to these places like New York from Minnesota, and I remember things like the Yankees telling us the only people in Minnesota were cowboys. I think anytime you have success like that, it's fun, but this was different for our fans, because it had never happened.

"And it was different from some ball clubs I played on. There was no jealousy on this team. If you failed, there was always someone there to pick you up. I was happy for everybody. It was such a dream to be in the World Series. But I missed that I was not able to share this with my family."

Quilici lived a dream of stark contrast. His family and friends were ready to watch him play in the World Series after his mere half season in the major leagues. "I don't think my feet were ever touching the ground," he recalled. "You felt so fortunate. How many great ballplayers never had the experience of playing in a World Series? Here I was, a rookie."

He resided in a Bloomington apartment complex, where many employees of a burgeoning corporation lived. Some of Quilici's neighbors had tickets to the Series, and others were entertaining friends who had traveled to the Twin Cities hoping to scratch for some tickets, which were in such short supply that Minnesota Viking season ticket holders were paying for newspaper ads that offered to swap prime football seats for Series tickets. The foragers at Quilici's apartment complex were in a party mood, and they knocked on the ground-level security door at all hours to gain access to their friends' apartments. One group asked if they could sleep on the floor of Quilici's apartment.

While the interlopers at Quilici's residence were improvising ticket and sleeping arrangements, community leaders and team officials were busy with various plans associated with the Series. Jimmy Robertson, the Twins' fun-loving concessionaire, saw to it that local high schools identified responsible students who could serve as additional vendors at Met Stadium during the Series. City buses were driven from storage to accommodate the flood of charter requests to the games, and Bloomington city officials decided all traffic around Metropolitan Stadium during the World Series would be directed by hand. Bloomington barely had 50,000 residents. Met Stadium could hold them.

Law enforcement officials prepared for small-time crooks and hustlers. The police focused their energy on uncovering illegal card and dice games and on prostitution. The Minneapolis police chief shrugged off any serious concerns. He thought back to the late-night antics at The Beatles' hotel when the rock group was in town, after which city officials invited the group never to return. "If we can survive The Beatles, we can handle a World Series," the police chief said.

The baseball commissioner's office was concerned about the weather in Minnesota and designated a former baseball official to monitor field conditions. The Minnesota Vikings were scheduled to play a football game against the New York Giants at Met Stadium after the Series shifted to Los Angeles. If the official decided the combination of bad weather and a football game could render the field unplayable for the potential final two Series games, the football game would be moved to, of all places, Atlanta.

Merchants worked overtime selling World Series memorabilia. Souvenir mugs with the Twins' logo were available at a local department store for $4, which in 2004 would translate into a pricey $24. Ashtrays were two bucks each. A local bank offered a transistor radio bearing a Twins' logo as a premium for opening an account. If fans had enough money in the bank, they could own a car driven by a genuine Twins' player. A Ford dealership had provided cars to some players during the year. With the cars about to be returned, the dealer advertised their availability.

The National League pennant race was not over, but either the Dodgers or Giants would arrive for the opener. Both teams had fans in the Twin Cities: the Dodgers once had an American Association affiliate in Saint Paul, and the Giants fielded a club in Minneapolis. Calvin Griffith paid the American Association $540,000 to surrender its territorial rights to the Twin Cities before he moved his franchise to Minnesota. The Dodgers received $150,000 of that money.

A smattering of Dodger fans remained, particularly in Saint Paul, but most fans in the Twin Cities seemed to want Minnesota to meet

San Francisco. The Dodgers had Sandy Koufax, but the Giants had Willie Mays. When the Giants promoted Mays in 1951, his departure from the Minneapolis Millers created such an uproar and negative fan reaction that Giants' owner Horace Stoneham made the unprecedented decision to purchase a four-column ad in a Sunday edition of the *Minneapolis Tribune*. Stoneham pleaded with fans to consider the fact Mays was entitled to the promotion, and ensured the Giants would continue to field a first-rate Millers team.

Some Twins players assumed they would play against Mays, and even shouted "Bring on the Giants" during the clubhouse celebration in D.C. The reason San Francisco seemed to be the likely opponent was that they led the National League by a game the moment Kaat struck out Don Zimmer in the pennant-clincher. The Dodgers' pitchers were supposedly tired. They weren't as tired as people suggested. The Dodgers had tied the Giants for first place before the champagne had been mopped from the clubhouse floor following the Twins' pennant celebration. Los Angeles never trailed the Giants after that.

The Giants were a preferable opponent for the Twins, and not just because Los Angeles had better pitching than San Francisco. Minnesota was not eager to play at vast Dodger Stadium with its rock-hard infield. The American League's Angels played home games there during the 1965 season, so the Twins were familiar with the nooks and crannies of the outfield walls, how to play the caroms, and the fashion in which pitches twirled in against the hitting backdrop.

Candlestick Park in San Francisco would be a foreign environment, and there were the unpredictable, swirling winds to contend with, but Dodger Stadium was a big park, and the Twins' batted just .201 there during the season. Mincher was the only Minnesota player to hit a home run in nine games at the park that overlooked downtown Los Angeles from a hill in Chavez Ravine. The Dodgers played 81 games there and hit just 24 home runs. It was a difficult place to score runs against any pitching staff, let alone the Dodger pitchers.

Milwaukee Braves' manager Bobby Bragan predicted a Dodger victory. He noted the Braves and Twins were similar teams because both could hit the ball out of the park and score runs. Minnesota had scored more runs in 1965 than all but one other team in the majors, but that team, Cincinnati, finished eight games behind the Dodgers. Bragan firmly believed good offensive teams could not beat Los Angeles.

"With the kind of pitching this club has, those Twins' hitters have no chance," Bragan predicted. "The Dodger pitching stops us, and if they can stop our power, they can stop anybody." The Dodgers had beaten New York in the 1963 Series, and Bragan noted Dodger pitching "went through the indomitable Yankees like water through a dike." Bragan backed the Dodgers even though "everyone knows their top batter is a pitcher."

That was Don Drysdale, and he had no qualms about making light of the Dodgers' lack of offense. He was away from the team when he learned by telephone that Koufax had thrown one of his no-hitters.

"Did he win?" Drysdale asked.

The Dodgers had to assemble rallies with duct tape. Los Angeles was near the bottom of the National League in scoring in '64 and '65, but was favored to win the Series because of great pitching and World Series experience. As with most champions, the Dodgers were regarded to be a team with character, and they had sprinted through the last half of September to finish two games ahead of San Francisco. It had been exhausting.

When the Dodgers clinched the pennant, a television reporter asked the normally understated Koufax if the team had backed into the championship. The Milwaukee Braves had not played particularly well against them. Koufax stormed away from the reporter and then stopped, turned and said, "We've won 14 of our last 15 games. How can anyone say we backed in?"

He was right. The Dodgers had been two games behind the Giants with 10 games to play on September 22 and were losing a game 6-1 to Milwaukee. They rallied to win 7-6 in 11 innings. After weeks of grueling September games such as that, the Dodgers had little chance to unwind. The season ended on a Sunday; then the team flew to Minnesota for a Wednesday World Series start.

Hotel space was a problem because two of the larger hotels in the Twin Cities had scheduled conventions before the baseball season began. A World Series team would have no difficulty with lodging, of course, but the Saint Paul Hotel put the Dodgers into its rooms for free. The former general manager of the Saint Paul Saints when the Dodgers supplied players to them had become the coordinator for the Saint Paul Area Chamber of Commerce. Luring the Dodgers to the state capitol was another mark for the city in an endless effort to divert attention from larger Minneapolis.

Dodger manager Walter Alston was comfortable in Saint Paul. He managed the Saints in the American Association for two seasons starting in 1949, his first stop as a non-playing manager. A former schoolteacher, Alston had a career almost as modest as Archie "Moonlight" Graham of "Field of Dreams" film fame. Graham played in one major league game and never batted. Alston played in one game, batted once, and struck out. After he arrived with the team on owner Walter O'Malley's private plane, Alston drove around the Twin Cities to reacquaint himself with the area and expressed disappointment that Lexington Park in Saint Paul and Nicollet Park in Minneapolis had been demolished.

Alston's counterpart, Mele, was able to entertain family as the Series neared. Connie Mele, very close to giving birth to another child, flew in, and Mele's 70-year-old mother made her first airplane trip. Even with his family near, it was difficult for Mele to relax.

He had decided to platoon Hall and Allison in the World Series. This meant Allison – the veteran who had helped the Senators and Twins so much – would be on the bench for the opener. Allison was struggling too badly against right-handers and Hall not doing well enough against lefties to keep Joe Nossek and Sandy Valdespino out of the lineup. Mele knew it would be difficult to score runs off the Dodgers' pitching with most any hitter in the lineup. Defense and putting the ball in play, he thought, would be crucial against the Series' favored team.

Oliva recalled there wasn't much second-guessing of the decision. "Sam Mele, he thought a lot about this, and he put the best players we had at the time on the field."

Earlier in the season, Hall had quieted Mele's thoughts of platooning him by launching into a confident hot streak. In one game, Mele sent Oliva to the plate to sacrifice bunt base runners to second and third. As Oliva walked to the plate and Hall grabbed his bat to head to the on-deck circle, Hall assured Mele, "I'll get the runs in." He promptly lined a single to left field to score both.

Hall neither lived with the attention Allison received as a young athlete nor suffered the poverty of teammates such as Grant or Versalles. His childhood fell in between. When Hall's family moved from the farm to Mount Holly, North Carolina, when he was a youngster, he recalled there was always a "fancy family" in town. Hall's family lived on the street with the fancy family's chauffer, whose kids were his playmates.

He debuted with the Twins at age 25 in '63, hitting 33 home runs to break Ted Williams' rookie record of 31. From the age of 18, Hall drifted around the minor leagues. He had been eligible in the draft of players when the leagues expanded in 1961, but he was a difficult player to assess because injuries and a military hitch all but took away his '61 and '62 seasons. The Twins sent him to the Florida Instructional League in the winter of 1962 to gain some playing time. He was old for the league.

Cigar-smoking scouts in straw hats, toting clipboards and stopwatches, filled the bleachers daily. Hall out-hit players such as Oliva and Pete Rose and finished at .351. But the Twins didn't want to showcase Hall to scouts. They just wanted him to get some at-bats, so he was inserted at third base. Hall couldn't play third base. Scouts dismissed him after they watched his struggling infield play and learned of his long tenure in the minor leagues. Teams would review scouting reports and attribute Hall's instructional league batting average to the fact he was a 24-year-old facing plenty of teen-aged pitchers.

Twins' farm director Sherry Robertson later said Hall played third base in the league because the club was experimenting with a place to play him, but that seems contrived. Killebrew could play third base, and Rollins drove in nearly 100 runs in his first full season in the American League in '62. The team was well stocked at third base.

In a uniform, Hall was a seemingly slight, six-foot 175-pounder. His broad shoulders stood out in the clubhouse. Teammates called him

"Wedge" because he wore a size 44 sport coat but had a 34-inch waist. He said his strength came from field work as a kid, and while he had an aversion to farming, he enjoyed outdoor life and thought he might like to raise cattle when he retired from baseball.

Hall had an adequate arm, but it was accurate, and he knew how to hit the cut-off man on throws from the outfield. He threw over the top with excellent spin on his release, which made the ball carry a little further and made his arm seem stronger than it was. He could run, which was perfect for Mele's relentless offense. But Hall tended to uppercut on his swing, and he had struggled against lefthanders since Bo Belinski's pitch struck him on the right cheek in the middle of the '64 season. That record against lefties made him a poor choice to start against Sandy Koufax, the poster boy for left-handed pitchers.

Allison and Hall were Minnesota's starting left and center fielders during the '65 season, and they combined for more than 1,000 plate appearances. Nossek and Valdespino started so infrequently that the pair led the team in pinch-hitting appearances. Either Allison or Hall alone played in more career games than Nossek and Valdespino combined, yet Valdespino started the first game of the '65 Series in left field, and Nossek started five games in center field – all three against Koufax – as Mele played the percentages and tried to gain an edge with a platoon approach against the Dodgers' stingy starting pitching.

Mele badly wanted to play the veteran Allison in the World Series, and he saw that Allison got plenty of at-bats against right-handed pitchers as the season wound down. Allison did not respond as Mele had hoped. Mele was concerned that hard-throwing, right-handed Drysdale would eat up Allison with fastballs and sliders. "Sandy Valdespino could run and he was a good fielder," Mele explained years later. "Bob was a good runner, too, but not as good as Sandy, and Sandy could make contact."

People said the smile of Hilario "Sandy" Valdespino, was as wide as he was tall. A rookie at age 26, he was a chunk of energy who could run and field. In his fifth year of Class AAA ball in 1964, he had led the International League in batting at .337, with 16 home runs and 73 runs batted in. Just five-foot-six, but 170 pounds, Valdespino wore a size 42 coat and, like Hall, attributed his broad shoulders to his early labors.

Valdespino came from poverty in Cuba. After his father had died, Valdespino went to work in a pipe factory at age 9, but he lived for baseball. He kept himself going by dreaming of a better life. "When I was eight, nine years old, I knew I wanted to play ball in Yankee Stadium," he recalled.

Valdespino's mother was by nature a happy woman, and he inherited her disposition. He could not control his family's poverty as a youngster, "but to be happy is something you can control," he said. He insisted he did not get a poor draw in life despite going to school in the morning, holding down a man's job in the afternoon, and playing ball at night.

Joe Cambria signed Valdespino, who languished in the minor leagues while teammates such as Oliva, Versalles, and Kaat moved on. Valdespino insisted he would follow them if he kept working and improving the weaker parts of his game, and in 1964 he learned to spray rather than pull the ball, which led to his league-leading average.

"He made a big contribution with his attitude," Naragon recalled of Valdespino's rookie year in 1965. "Players responded to him when he would go in and pinch hit, steal a base, go out and play some defense for us. He's a fellow people forget about, but he was a big part of the team."

Mele later agreed he probably would have caught plenty of heat for his decision to platoon Valdespino and Nossek in the outfield if he had managed in the era of ESPN and Internet chat-board scrutiny. On paper, Mele's move seemed odd to the average fan. Nossek hit just 14 home runs spanning the 1963-1965 seasons, and only two of those came in the major leagues. Hall hit 78 home runs in that span, all in the majors, and he was an All-Star in '64 and '65. In addition, left-handed Hall hit a tolerable .240 average against left-handed pitchers. Nossek hit only .228. Yet Mele used a straight platoon with two of his outfielders in a seven-game World Series.

Nossek and Valdespino did put the bat on the ball, however, and that was a benefit against the Dodgers – where base runners were precious. The pair lived up to Mele's expectations in that category, whiffing just twice in 31 plate appearances, while Allison and Hall struck out 14 times in 24 at-bats. Nossek and Valdespino out-hit the more vaunted duo of Allison and Hall during the seven-game Series, and Valdespino's .273 World Series average trailed only those of Versalles and Killebrew on the Twins.

With Versalles, Valdespino, Pascual, and Oliva in the Series, there were thoughts of Cambria among the Cuban players, Griffith and his family. Cambria would have been a little surprised to see Versalles, rather than Oliva, featured on a two-page, pull-out cover of Sports Illustrated as the Series was about to begin. Oliva was always the gem among Cambria's many fine finds, but the national media were following the lead of those in baseball who were championing Versalles as Most Valuable Player. Versalles was, in truth, the man who had the greatest impact on that Twins' team by playing 160 games and leading the league in total bases.

Cambria would have been more surprised to see Versalles handling the reporters and TV crews, who approached him 20 or 30 at a time. The formerly reclusive shortstop fielded all the questions happily. He credited Martin for understanding him, and when the reporters went to Martin for his point of view he told them, "They used to call Versalles all kinds of names, but he's human, just like everyone else. All he needed was a little patience, handling, understanding and consideration."

Because Dodger shortstop Maury Wills was the game's best base stealer, he received more fan and media attention than Versalles, but Versalles actually scored a higher percentage of his team's runs, despite Wills' 94 stolen bases in 1965. Offensively, the Twins had it all over the Dodgers. At second base, rookie Jim Lefebvre – who had once worked as a Dodger clubhouse boy with Jim Merritt – was the only offensive player who had easily out-homered a Twin counterpart. Quilici would start the Series at second base, and he had not homered during the season. Lefebvre hit 12, which tied him for the Dodger team lead. Los Angeles hit just 78 home runs all season, about half the Twins' total.

The Dodgers' game was pitching and speed. They led the National League in earned run average and stolen bases. The Twins were considered by scouts to have an "N.L. look," because they stole bases, bunted and used the hit-and-run, but the Dodgers' 172 steals were nearly double the Twins' total.

The Dodgers had an odd advantage in their infield: it comprised an unprecedented four switch-hitters. This meant Alston did not have to pinch-hit or platoon for first baseman Wes Parker, third baseman Jim Gilliam, Lefebvre or Wills. Wills had a modest arm and was a capable but unspectacular fielder. Gilliam was nearly 37 and trying to retire, but the Dodgers kept requesting his services on the field. The left side of the Dodger infield was not remarkable defensively, but Alston was never eager to replace them because the Dodgers' infield reserves provided little offense.

Good pitching doesn't always beat good hitting, but great pitching usually does, and the finesse of the Dodgers staff prevailed in the 1965 Series. It went seven games, and the winning team's pitcher threw nine innings in each. Fans got their money's worth, regardless of how much they paid to see the games.

Tickets were so scarce the evening of the opener that entrepreneurs with an $8 ticket could easily find someone to pay $50. There were 4,000 standing-room-only tickets for sale for $4 each on game day – a World Series practice that dated back decades, but to land these tickets required fans to camp out at Met Stadium the night before. First in line was a man named Ralph Belcore of Melrose Park, Illinois. Today, he would have attained modest celebrity for his claim to fame.

Belcore was a 50-year-old carnival worker who had been first or second in line at every World Series played since 1940. He had a curious habit of counting the number of pitches each starting pitcher threw in each Series game, which was usually slightly above 100. He was photographed before most every World Series, lounging with a suitcase and a bag of sandwiches outside the stadium where the opener would be played. He wore a fur hat with earflaps in the sun and the chill as his back rested against the wall under the ticket window of Met Stadium a day before Hubert Humphrey tossed out the first ball to launch the '65 Series.

Only about 1,000 people had settled into their seats under overcast skies when the Twins finished batting practice before the afternoon opener. The sun broke through just before game time, and the thermometer passed 60 despite a strong wind. Alston had complained that it was impractical that all Series games were played during the day when most games during the regular season were played at night, but the weather would have been challenging if the games had started after dark, when the temperature deflated into the 40s.

A record 47,797 fans saw Grant open for Minnesota against Drysdale. Both pitchers had the distinction of being accused of throwing illegal spitballs in the Series. By all accounts, they probably did. Mele's attitude was, "If they can get away with it, good for them."

Koufax, the best pitcher in baseball, did not start the opener because he was Jewish. He was back at the Saint Paul Hotel, observing Yom Kippur. The Dodgers were still favored, and plenty thought it would be a sweep. Los Angeles had 11 players, including Koufax, Drysdale, and star reliever Ron Perranoski, with World Series experience.

"Many people thought we would lose in four," Oliva recalled. "How could a team beat Sandy Koufax and Don Drysdale? You can play a bad team and not win. They were good. But we were all in a high mood. We thought we could win."

Grant allowed a home run in the second inning, to right fielder Ron Fairly, a fine fielding first baseman who moved to the outfield in 1964 to make room for Wes Parker. It was Fairly's first home run in three World Series appearances. He was batting fourth in the lineup yet had not driven in a single run during the final month of the National League season after being struck on the wrist by a pitch. He probably should have sat down for part of September, but Fairly, 27 and a veteran of seven seasons with Los Angeles, thought it was important to set an example for younger teammates.

In the bottom of the second inning, Mincher hit a solo home run over Fairly's head in right field, and then in the third the Twins bruised the 1.50 earned run average Drysdale had accumulated in three previous World Series. Quilici tied a Series record with two hits in an inning. The hits were bookends to a six-run rally that included Versalles' three-run home run off an inside fastball from Drysdale. Valdespino doubled and Killebrew singled during the rally, but the Dodgers deflated when Battey's little flair single drove them both home.

The Twins led 7-1 after three innings and won 8-2. Versalles drove in four runs, Oliva set a Series record with nine putouts in right field, and Grant became the first black man to get a Series win.

Drysdale did not have World Series outings like that, so the Twins and their fans had reason for confidence, even if Koufax was starting the second game. He was 26-8 for the season with a 2.04 earned run average, but after nearly 336 innings pitched– more than anyone in either league – he was tired. He had gone nine innings on two days' rest to beat Milwaukee to assure the National League pennant, but his legs were heavy in that game from the fifth inning on.

The Twins won, which isn't to say they beat Koufax.

It had begun to rain shortly after the opening game ended and continued through the night, so the outfield was soggy for the second game. Griffith ordered two helicopters brought in to hover low over the grass so the whirling blades would dry wet spots. Grounds crew worked to dry the wet foul territory by pushing flamethrowers that resembled tiny Civil War cannons. After the automatic tarpaulin machine rolled back the infield covering, the field was deemed playable. Neither team took batting practice. It was 56 degrees with a 17-mile-an-hour wind – what Minnesotans call "breezy." A record 48,700 fans sat under low clouds.

Koufax said the drizzle that fell in the first couple innings didn't bother him. His fastball missed high, and he was harmed by third baseman Gilliam's fielding. Playing in his 32nd World Series game, Gilliam called this game the worst of them. He made two errors.

Koufax held the Twins hitless for three innings, and the game was scoreless in the sixth before Versalles slammed a ball down the third base line that Gilliam could not backhand. It became a two-base error with the cricket-like Versalles running. Nossek sacrificed him to third, and Oliva doubled in the run. Killebrew then singled for a 2-0 lead in Kaat's 5-1 win. The score was deceptive, as the game was very close, but Allison had made it seem less so.

It is ironic there had been so much concern about Allison's shift to left field at the start of the season because Allison's catch in the 1965 World Series is still recalled as one of the great defensive gems in Series play. "Let's see, 1965," Allison mulled years later. "I was 31. Yes, I'd say I was a damn good outfielder then."

He had struck out twice before running out to his spot in left field to start the fifth inning. The drizzle had stopped, the game was scoreless, and he stood on the damp turf as Fairly skipped a single toward Oliva to start the inning. Lefebvre stepped in and sent Kaat's fastball into a line drive.

The ball seemed destined to sail between Allison and the left-field foul line as the ball curved away from Allison, whose long strides splashed him across the field. From home plate, the 344-foot sign fastened to the left-field fence served as a backdrop about 10 yards behind him. Allison stretched toward the curving baseball, reached out with his left hand, and made Kaat ecstatic. Allison caught the ball a foot off the ground and 10 feet inside the foul line. He slid on his right hip over slick grass into the wet dirt in foul territory.

His momentum ended about 20 feet from where he gloved the ball. Allison hopped up, flashed a glimpse of the ball to the umpire, who was racing toward the play, then rifled a throw back to the infield. He nearly doubled up Fairly, who had rounded second base and was heading for third.

The importance of the catch was magnified when Parker followed with a single over second base. Had Lefebvre's ball streaked past Allison, the Dodger second baseman would have scored when Parker singled. If the Dodgers had tied the game with Koufax pitching, everything would have changed.

Alston took some heat after the game for a move he made late in the game. He had Parker, the seventh batter in the Dodger lineup, bunt in the top of the seventh with no outs and runners on first and second. Fairly and Lefebvre had both singled to left field before the bunt. With the eighth and ninth hitters due up, why give away an out with a respectable hitter like Parker at the plate? Alston responded that the light-hitting Dodgers were successful all season by playing for a tie first, then for the lead.

Roseboro, batting eighth, singled, which scored Fairly and moved Lefebvre to third. Roseboro alertly advanced to second on the throw to the plate. Alston then sent Drysdale in to pinch hit for Koufax. Drysdale hit seven home runs in 1965 in just 130 at-bats, five short of the team lead, and his .508 slugging average easily led the team. Kaat struck him out and then got Wills to fly out for the last out of the inning. Kaat breezed through the eighth inning and then worked his way out of a one-out situation with two runners on in the ninth. He caught a line drive for the final out, which gave him a World Series record five putouts. Meanwhile, Versalles could have watched the game from the dugout: he had no fielding chances in the entire game.

Kaat said he "kind of enjoyed going against an unbeatable guy." No one expected him to win, so the pressure was off. He matched Koufax in the early going, pitching four perfect innings before Allison helped him in the fifth. So Kaat had his first World Series win, and he drove in two runs after the Dodgers elected to walk Quilici late in the game to get to the pitcher's spot.

Koufax had certainly pitched well enough to win. He struck out nine, walked one in six innings, and allowed one earned run. After watching Koufax, the Twins wondered how many games he would have won in 1965 if he pitched for a team that hit as well as Minnesota.

Despite the loss, the Dodgers were headed back home for three games and didn't seem to lack confidence. They had allowed barely 2.5 runs per game in Dodger Stadium during the regular season against teams that had players such as Willie Mays, Frank Robinson, and Hank Aaron. Los Angeles had scored only three runs in two Series games but had 17 hits, and the Dodgers certainly could have won the second game if Allison had not made that catch. The mood was not sour in the Dodgers' clubhouse, and when reporters asked players to identify the game's turning point, relief pitcher Ron Perranoski said, "When it stopped raining."

Although the Twins led two games to none in the Series, Mele faced a decision. Camilo Pascual had pitched acceptably since returning from his injury, but he had a high leg kick and was right-handed. Jim Merritt was left-handed, so he faced first base when pitching with runners on, and he had that terrific pickoff move. It would certainly be more difficult for Wills and the Dodgers to run on Merritt. Merritt was a rookie, but he seemed unaffected by pressure, and the 21-year-old would be pitching in his home state.

Mele went with Pascual. He said it was the only decision he made during the World Series that he ever wondered about.

"Camilo had plenty of rest, but I kind of went with my heart and not my head on that one," Mele said 40 years later. "Camilo had that big, high leg kick, and I knew if guys like Wills got on base they were going to steal. It's the only thing I regret. It's all hindsight, and maybe I shouldn't think about it. Camilo had been a big part of our ball club and this was his chance to pitch in a World Series."

Pascual recalled that when he came back from surgery his arm felt healthy, but "I didn't throw the ball like I used to. I couldn't throw my breaking pitch, and when you don't have your best pitch, it's very difficult. But you try to do things, work the batters on your control and move the ball around."

Pascual would not have to pitch in the cool, damp, windy environment that Grant and Kaat worked in during the first two games. Warm Los Angeles sunshine gnawed through the smog and overcast and eventually bathed a record 55,934 patrons, who were briefly in danger of owning tickets to the Dodgers' first rainout since moving from Brooklyn.

Pascual's curve ball had no bite, his fastball was high, and the Dodgers, who could see Pascual's breaking pitch had abandoned him, were waiting for the fastball. They hit the ball well off him. The last of the record crowd – trapped in a mammoth traffic jam – arrived at their seats to see the Dodgers break a scoreless tie in the bottom of the fourth with a pair of runs. The Dodgers stole three bases off Pascual in five innings, but none of the stolen bases resulted in a run – and the Dodgers needed only one.

The Dodgers left-handed starter, Claude Osteen, stood only five-foot-ten and appeared frail at 160 pounds. He allowed five hits and shut out the Twins. Osteen possessed a decent fastball and a good curve but didn't become an effective pitcher until he developed a change-up. He was a 17-year-old high school pitching sensation when he rejected offers from 10 other major league teams and three colleges to sign with the Cincinnati Reds in 1957. He had pitched against the Twins in the American League before being traded to the Dodgers in the 1964 off-season for towering power-hitter Frank Howard. Osteen's career record against the Twins was 5-0 before his Series start.

He received far less attention than Koufax and Drysdale, but Osteen was a capable and successful pitcher who notched double-digit wins in 10 straight seasons – nine with Los Angeles – and he twice won 20 games. As with Drysdale and Koufax, he lost games during the season despite brilliant pitching performances, which accounted for his 15-15 record. On the first day of the summer of '65, Osteen carried a no-hitter into the seventh inning. He eventually lost the game 1-0 after allowing a solo home run.

The Twins' best threat against him came on the game's first pitch. Versalles cracked a double down the left-field line, and Nossek's ground out to the right side of the infield moved Versalles to third. Oliva grounded out to second, but the Dodgers had played their infield in and Versalles could not score on the play. After Killebrew walked, Battey had a two-ball, no-strike count, and Mele decided to employ the running game that helped get the Twins to the World Series. He signaled for a hit-and-run, but Battey missed the sign. Killebrew was running on the pitch and was caught between first and second. Versalles knew Killebrew would eventually be tagged out in a rundown and tried to rescue him by racing home. Wills threw the ball home; Versalles was trapped between third and home and was eventually tagged for the last out of the inning.

It was a bad game for Battey. It was in the seventh inning of that loss when he chased a foul pop fly while looking skyward and his windpipe crashed into a metal railing. He left the game hitless, and the Dodgers had stolen three bases against him.

Merritt did pitch that day. He relieved Pascual in the sixth and picked Wills off second base after the shortstop had doubled in a run.

Merritt gave Quilici the pickoff sign, whirled, and Quilici went to the third-base side of the bag to take the throw. Wills dived head first back to the bag, but Quilici's leg blocked his path. Wills was angry and stuck his arm between Quilici's legs to flip him off the bag, but Quilici rose when he realized what Wills intended and pushed off the bag, a smile on his face.

The next day around the batting cage, Wills told players he would be flashing his spikes if the rookie tried to get in his way again. Quilici had a bit of Billy Martin in him, so when he heard about Wills' remark, he waited until the game was about to start, walked past Wills, grinned and said, "Hey. Maury. We'll see you at second base, pal."

Drysdale was back on the mound against Grant in the fourth game, and he shelved his fastball and threw plenty of breaking pitches. Some were said to be spitballs.

The Dodgers had urged fans to carpool or take buses, which trimmed the pre-game traffic jam and allowed the 55,920 fans to see more of the game. It was a satisfying afternoon for them. The Dodgers won 7-2, getting their first two runs without pushing the ball out of the infield.

Los Angeles got what Minnesota players thought was a favorable call in the first inning when Valdespino was called out at second base while trying to stretch a single into a double. It was the second out of the inning and a break for Drysdale. He admitted to some anxiety before the game, rightfully so after the manner in which the Twins smacked his pitches in the opener. This time around, he finished with 10 strikeouts, his best in World Series play.

The Dodgers' speed was on display. In the Dodger half of the first, Grant – a man with bad knees – was late covering the bag on Wills' bunt. Quilici alertly raced to the bag on the play but couldn't handle the throw from Mincher. Quilici and Wills collided behind first base on the play. After Wills stole second, Grant was again late to the bag on a ball hit to Mincher. Wills moved to third and eventually scored on a ground out.

Grant's bad day in the field continued when he fell while trying to field Parker's lead-off bunt in the bottom of the second. Parker then stole second, advanced to third on a wild pitch, and scored on an error by Quilici.

Killebrew homered in the fourth to make it 2-1, the Dodgers got the run back, and it was 3-1 when Oliva hit a solo home run. Wills had robbed Versalles of a base hit before Oliva's home run, and that out proved to be crucial because Oliva's home run would have tied the score if Versalles has been on base. A three-run sixth inning for Los Angeles sealed it, although the Twins continued to battle, and Versalles continued to sting the ball. As Oliva had long maintained, hitting was all luck. Versalles was driving the ball hard during the entire Series, but just one of Versalles' line shots that day fell for a hit.

After Nossek managed a pinch-hit single in the eighth with one out, Versalles followed with a smash down the third base line that seemed destined for at least a run-scoring double. Alston had inserted John Kennedy, an excellent fielder, at third for defensive purposes, and Kennedy made a diving stop on the ball and was able to force Nossek at second base.

Now the Series was tied at two games each, and Koufax was due to pitch. He had thrown well enough to win the first time out, and he would now have three days' rest. The sun was shining and the temperature reached the 70s. It was, Koufax said, the kind of weather he liked to pitch in. The first dozen Twins went hitless before Killebrew was awarded a single on a batted ball that Willie Davis misjudged in left field. Koufax faced the minimum three batters in seven of his nine innings and allowed four hits in the 7-0 win. Two of the hits were so feeble it was embarrassing to call them hits. In three games in Los Angeles, the Twins had been outscored 18-2.

"We've looked bad before and always come out of it," Mele told reporters, "and we better come out of it, or it will be too late." Mele knew even with a win in the sixth game the Twins would have to play another game against Koufax. Mele had already decided Koufax was "without a doubt" the best pitcher he had ever seen.

As the teams headed back to Minnesota, Martin commented the Met was a real baseball field and criticized Dodger Stadium, with its concrete infield designed to help the light-hitting Dodgers skim baseballs past infielders. "This is a baseball field, like Doubleday ordered," Martin said of the Met. "We can play baseball here and win."

Griffith was unhappy with the playing field in Dodger Stadium, too, and also irritated over the fact Dodger owner Walter O'Malley had provided the Twins with only 25 good seats in Dodger Stadium after Griffith had been generous with 1,000 prime seating assignments for O'Malley's entourage in Minnesota. The wives of the Dodgers' players, for example, had excellent seats at the Met. The Twins' wives were assigned outfield seats in Dodger Stadium.

So when the Dodgers – who had stolen eight bases in Los Angeles – returned to the Met they noticed the dirt around home plate and near the bases at Met Stadium had been liberally mixed with sand. It was an effort to make it more difficult for players such as Wills to get a good first step. The Twins almost comically pleaded ignorance. Twins' public relations director Tom Mee was quoted that the field was covered with "pure Minnesota dirt. Minnesota and Georgia are the two best places in the country for infield dirt," Mee informed the media. He even pointed out, honestly, that the Twins had shipped two boxcars of dirt to Tinker Field before the season so the infield at their spring training complex would be similar to the one at Met Stadium.

The Vikings had played a football game at the Met days before the sixth World Series game, the Twins further explained, and the field might have seemed different because it had to be tended to get it back into shape for baseball. The umpires ordered the quagmire raked and modified before the sixth game began.

Grant got his third start against the Dodgers with Osteen going for Los Angeles. Grant pitched on two days' rest and had fought a cold for weeks. He said he felt old and alluded to the notion he was older than people thought. "Thirty is only my baseball age," he said. "Where I come from, they write your birth certificate on the bark of a tree."

It was 54 degrees at game time, and Grant wore a heavy, gray sweatshirt under his jersey. On the front was a brightly-colored pussycat, a nod to his off-season nightclub act, "Mudcat and the Kittens."

Grant never was close to walking a batter and retired the first dozen Dodgers. His mates attacked Osteen, getting the leadoff man on in each of the first four innings. Twice it was Versalles, and twice it was Battey. The heavy-legged Battey tripled to lead off the second and later beat out an infield ground ball that second baseman Dick Tracewski could not handle. Allison homered to left field after Battey had reached for a 2-0 lead.

The Series had become a microcosm of the season for Allison, who made the brilliant defensive play in the second game and had homered for all the runs Grant needed in his 5-1 win. Statistically, Allison's Series looked bad, and he had struck out seven times in his 10 at-bats before the home run. He batted .125 in the Series with nine strikeouts in 16 at-bats. But Allison's catch and home run were both vital contributions to two of Minnesota's three wins.

Grant helped himself with a three-run home run in the bottom of the sixth. For the second time in the Series, a Twins' pitcher had thwarted Alston's move to get at the last spot in the batting order by walking the Twins' eighth hitter. Kaat had driven in two runs after Alston walked Quilici in the second game, but what were the chances of the lightning bolt striking twice? So after Allison led off the sixth inning of the sixth game with a one-out walk, and then stole second base on Mincher's strikeout, first base was open. Quilici had done enough damage in the opener. Walking him to set up a force out at any base seemed logical. Grant hit relief pitcher Howie Reed's first pitch, a curveball, on a sharp line 392 feet into the right-center field stands for a home run. He was only the second pitcher to hit a World Series home run.

So it came down to Kaat and Koufax in the seventh game. Both would pitch on two days' rest, but Kaat had not pitched even three innings in his last start against Koufax in Los Angeles. Koufax had gone nine, and he admitted he was tired.

John Sevcik recalled warming Kaat in the bullpen before the game. A screen separated the bullpens in Met Stadium, and Sevcik heard the loud pop of the ball hitting the catcher's mitt, Kaat took the mound first, so he finished his routine before Koufax and headed toward the field. Sevcik went over to watch Koufax.

The muscular shoulder and back muscles of Koufax were tightly wound, and the temperature was about 20 degrees below what he preferred to pitch in. At one point, Koufax turned and stretched his arms above his head. He saw Sevcik.

"I can't get loose," he complained. Sevcik wanted to laugh.

"Holy mackerel," Sevcik said years later. "I thought 'What do you throw like when you're loose?' My gosh, what stuff. Who could touch that guy?"

Kaat and Koufax each pitched scoreless ball for three innings, although Alston had Drysdale warming in the bullpen after Koufax issued two-out walks to Killebrew and Oliva in the bottom of the first. Battey struck out to end the threat. In the top of the fourth, Lou Johnson hit a solo home run. The Dodgers had promoted Johnson in early May after outfielder Tommy Davis broke his right ankle. Johnson had largely been a career minor leaguer and seemed to be a dime-store answer to Davis, who won National League batting titles in 1962 and 1963. But Johnson hit two home runs in the Series, more than any Twins player, and he drove in four, which was matched by only Versalles on the Minnesota team.

Koufax would not need another run, but the Dodgers scored a second time in the fourth inning on a little chopper over Mincher's head at first base with the infield drawn in. Kaat was not pitching badly, but Mele replaced him with Worthington.

Al Lopez long ago had told Mele that even if a pitcher seems to be doing all right – and Kaat was not pitching poorly – once little things begin to go against you, make a change. "Al told me it might keep on going for five, six more batters. You've got to put a stop to it right then," Mele said.

With Koufax on the mound, it did not matter. The Twins managed three hits and very little luck. Quilici slammed a double to left with one out in the top of the fifth. Koufax was laboring. Rollins then pinch hit for Worthington and walked. If Koufax's control would fail, the Twins could win. His pitches were coming in too high.

With runners on first and third, Versalles smashed a one-hop grounder down the third-base line. Gilliam smothered the ball and scrambled toward third base for a force out on Quilici. Koufax wriggled out of the inning and from that point allowed only a ninth-inning, ground-ball single to Killebrew.

When Koufax fanned Allison to end the seventh game and clinch the championship, Koufax had shut out Minnesota twice. The Twins were shut out three times all season, but Dodger pitching had shut them out three times in seven games. Koufax had allowed a combined 18 hits and walks, struck out 29, and allowed an earned run in 24 innings. The Dodgers were a cohesive, competitive team, just like the Twins, but the Dodgers had Koufax. One teammate said of him, "Most people get on top and try to keep other people down. Sandy Koufax got on top and tried to pull others up there with him."

The Dodgers' celebration carried the excitement of a Tuesday morning mall opening. No one piled onto Koufax atop the mound. The 29-year-old left-hander hadn't stayed near the mound long enough for that to happen. When the umpire called the final strike, Koufax strode off the mound in almost a continuation of his pitching motion. The smiles, handshakes and claps on the back as the players walked off the field were similar to any other game in the Series.

Wes Parker rushed from his spot at first base, but he slowed when he was a few feet from Koufax, almost as if dampened by a force field. Parker was about to slap Koufax on the back, but instead he gently touched him with a light pat. After pitching nearly 360 innings, a challenging physical feat, Sandy Koufax was almost too fragile to touch.

He pitched the Dodgers to the World Series once more, in 1966, and never pitched again.

EPILOGUE

It was a hot summer day in Ohio, and Rich Rollins had just finished mowing his lawn. He stood in the garage and looked over an old promotional item from the Theo Hamm Brewing Company, a poster of the 1965 Twins. Forty years later, he still spoke with some of those men weekly. He surveyed the photo to see who was gone.

Zoilo Versalles died in 1995. He had suffered two previous heart attacks, and the cause of death was arteriosclerotic heart disease, or hardening of the arteries. He was 55. He had played his last season of baseball in Japan in 1972.

Versalles found it difficult to find decent employment after his baseball career, partly because of his problem with the English language. He worked in a series of undistinguished jobs, and to make ends meet he eventually sold many of his rings and trophies, including his Most Valuable Player award. He was separated from Maria Josefa at the time of his death.

As early as 1963, Versalles had all but prophesized part of his future. "No matter how good I be, the day she come and they kick me out. You are no person with feelings, just a player with hits and errors. No matter how good I be, gonna come someone to take my place, someone to say to me, 'Now you get out.' Where to? Havana? I don't know."

In late November of 1967, Versalles was preparing to make a speech in Iowa as part his public relations job for the Twins. Twins official Don Cassidy pulled him aside. Versalles and Mudcat Grant had been traded to the Dodgers for John Roseboro, Ron Perranoski and another player.

Versalles was hurt by the news, never recovered from it, and as the rest of his baseball career played out he publicly wished to be traded back to Minnesota. It never happened.

Earl Battey died in late 2003 from complications of cancer. He was 68. He was a four-time All-Star, won three Gold Gloves and on three occasions finished among the top 10 vote-getters in the Most Valuable Player balloting.

Bob Allison had trouble catching and throwing one day at an old-timers' baseball game. John Sevcik's wife, Glenda, first wondered about Allison's health when she visited with him one day on the phone. She thought, "I never remember Bob being much of a drinker. He's slurring his words."

He had ataxia, a disease more prevalent than amyotrophic lateral sclerosis, or Lou Gehrig's Disease. Ataxia is not always fatal, but the form Allison had affects nerve cells in the brain, robs a person of coordination and impairs other functions, such as speaking and swallowing. Patients eventually lose the ability to feed themselves. Allison, with his matinee idol looks and a natural physique that would impress those baseball players who later found physical stature in steroids, spent his last year in a wheelchair. He stopped breathing while watching television in his Arizona home early in April of 1995.

"His condition was not known to be hereditary," said Dr. Christopher Gomez of the Bob Allison Ataxia Research Center at the University of Minnesota. Gomez was Allison's physician at the center that now bears his name.

Allison would complain of stiffness during his playing days if he stood around in the outfield too much. Gomez is unsure if that could have been a very early sign of the disease.

Allison's offensive production usually tumbled in the second half of a baseball season, but that pattern is hardly unique among baseball players.

"Bob would come in and we would try to determine when it began," Gomez recalled. "He would say, 'I felt this or that all my life.' He claimed he would always get cold sores in spring training, and then one year he stopped getting them." Whether any of Allison's recollections is a clue to the disease remains a mystery.

The under-publicized disease had nipped at Allison for more than five years, and he knew he could not be saved. But he would visit Gomez, and the first words to the doctor were always, "How's the research going?"

"He knew what was going to happen," Gomez said, "and at that point he just wanted to know if we were making progress, so someone else might not have to go through this."

Teammates knew what Allison was enduring because they stayed in touch. Years after the new millennium dawned, many would contact each other at the start of each year, their calendar of celebrity golf tournaments in front of them. They would discuss their personal schedules – Killebrew's was always the fullest, as he was one of the busier and more generous members of the baseball Hall of Fame. They would select events that dovetailed with each other's schedules so they could all get together.

"I go to these tournaments and people find out I played for the 1965 Minnesota Twins," Kostro said. "Then they ask me, 'Did you play with Harmon Killebrew?' One day I had to ask Harmon if people ever approached him and asked, 'Did you play with Frank Kostro?' "

Kostro sat in his Colorado insurance office in the summer of 2004. He had just received a letter from Jerry Zimmerman's widow with the news she was moving back to Oregon. Jerry Zimmerman died in 1998, and Kostro had not been Zimmerman's teammate for 30 years, yet Zimmerman's family was still in touch.

"You just can not believe how these friendships were such a genuine part of the deal," Kostro said.

They looked after each other until the end.

Floyd Baker was 88 years old as autumn arrived in 2004. He had scouted and signed men such as Rollins and Bernie Allen, players who came from the Ohio-Pennsylvania region of the country. The players called him "Gabby" because he never said anything.

Andy Kosco ran his insurance business near Baker's residence of Youngstown, Ohio, and spoke with Baker often. Baker's wife had died, and Baker was left with his two dogs. Eventually, he had to put down each aging animal. Kosco chatted frequently with his former 1965 Twins teammates, and as conversations would end Kosco reminded, "Hey. Don't forget to give 'Bakes' a call. He's all by himself now."

Baker died before Thanksgiving in 2004.

Johnny Sain had suffered a series of strokes and required constant medical attention as his 87th birthday passed in 2004. Naragon called Illinois frequently to speak with him, including on his birthday. Sain's health didn't allow him to speak that day, so Naragon spoke with relatives instead. Kaat, Sain's disciple, was a radio commentator for the New York Yankees by then. "Whenever we travel through Chicago," Kaat said, "I always stop to see John Sain."

Frank Quilici said sometimes people wonder why the Twins didn't have a dynasty. The club advanced to the post-season two times in the five seasons that followed '65, but that is hardly a dynasty.

Earl Battey's career ended early. That was part of it. Mudcat Grant never had another season as a starting pitcher that equaled his 1965 performance. Quilici was sent back to the minors for all of 1966. Jerry Kindall, Bill Pleis, and Johnny Klippstein, who died in 2003, were released.

"I think some of the moves seemed inconsequential to the public," Quilici said. "But they did deteriorate the chemistry on the team. Guys who truly liked each other and had some talent weren't together anymore."

Quilici eventually managed the Twins for four seasons. He was Martin's friend. He was a baseball insider with a wealth of knowledge about the game. Years later, he looked back on the '65 Twins and said, "You get that kind of talent put together and you usually get some explosions. But that was as fine a major league team as you'll ever find from a standpoint of camaraderie."

ACKNOWLEDGEMENTS

The gate dropped on this horse race when Twin Cities public relations executive and broadcaster Dave Mona, who was a Minneapolis journalist in 1965, assured me this premise had some merit. Thanks for preventing me from driving into the ditch, Dave. On the other end of the project, former Minnesota Twins' beat writer Glenn Redmann was of similar help

Tom Mee, the Twins' public relations director in 1965, is a book himself. He sat in on every spring training personnel meeting Calvin Griffith held regarding Minnesota Twins' players. Thanks for your help here, and during my years covering the Twins. You set the standard for professional sports' public relations directors.

Thanks as well to Dolores Pieper, a high schoolmate of late Twins' promotions executive Don Cassidy. She put me in touch with another classmate, Glenn Gostick, student and teacher of baseball, domestically and internationally. Glenn's statistical records of the Twins and Major League Baseball would fill a computer hard drive, except Glenn does it all with paper and pen in tiny, detailed penmanship.

Dave Campbell of WCCO Radio got back to me with the right answers. Bryan Donaldson, of the Twins' Community Relations department, kept returning my phone calls, and Molly Gallatin let me flick through all those metal file cabinets in a corner of the Metrodome basement. Pam Ganley of the Red Sox put me in touch with Sam Mele, whose charming honesty was as welcome as his sharp memory and sense of humor.

Bernie Allen helped me begin piecing together the 1965 Twins. Jim Kaat kept calling back when the cell phones burped, and Tony Oliva graciously worked to dovetail our schedules. Hal Naragon could make a week fly past with his baseball stories. Andy Kosco, Frank Kostro, Frank Quilici, John and Glenda Sevcik, Dick Stigman, and Camilo Pascual provided a panorama of perspective, anecdotes and humor.

Jerry Kindall has forgotten more baseball than even Glenn Gostick will ever know, which speaks volumes about Jerry. Harmon Killebrew's schedule seemed too busy for him to help with someone else's book, but he took the time anyway. Garry Roggenburk's eloquent anecdotes were invaluable. Rich Rollins wondered if he would have much to say, then made wonderful contributions. Sandy Valdespino's smile beamed through the telephone lines. Al Worthington's relaxed, deliberate insight showed how he handled all those late-inning, pressure situations.

Unfortunately, I caught Floyd Baker during his final days. I hope he, Bob Allison, Zoilo Versalles, Jerry Zimmerman, Earl Battey, John Klippstein and the rest of the Twins who have passed on are sipping a tasty beverage and basking in glory days.

Also, thanks to Chris Gomez of the Bob Allison Ataxia Research Center at the University of Minnesota for his prompt, helpful responses.

The work of Rena Hall and Jane Harred accounts for the readable portions of this manuscript. Thanks to Claudia Daniels for her knowledge of Minneapolis, further edits, suggestions, love and inspiration. George Brust and Bill Brady contributed editing comments, but even better, fine observations. Tim Cain, Todd Glasenapp, Mike Dougherty, Kent Hensley and my mom, Ruth Thielman, aided the process with edits, remarks, compliments and insults.

On the dull, detailed, publishing end of it, thanks to Dave Wood for his guidance; Tony Mommsen for making his artistic and philosophical skills available between sculling sessions; Lance Lewey for his production knowledge and advice; and Leonard Flachman for his publishing expertise.

I appreciate my aunt, Georgia Nelson, for all she did for me, including listening to the beginning of this. I don't take it as a critique that she decided to leave the planet before it was over.

And thanks to my father, Al Thielman, for taking me to that first baseball game in 1965 – although he preferred golf, even during weather like we had that summer. I hope he was allowed to take his eight-handicap to eternity's golf course.

INDEX

On the cover: Zoilo Versalles

On the back: Earl Battey, Jim Grant and Jim Perry

STATISTICS – 1965 MINNESOTA TWINS

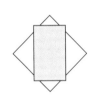

Player	G	AB	R	H	2b	3b	HR	RBI	BB	K	SB	CS	AVG	OBP	SA
Allen, Bernie	19	39	2	9	2	0	0	6	6	8	0	0	.231	.326	.282
Allison, Bob	135	438	71	102	14	5	23	78	73	114	10	2	.233	.342	.445
Battey, Earl	131	394	36	117	22	2	6	60	51	23	0	0	.297	.376	.409
Boswell, Dave	36	38	7	12	0	1	0	1	1	6	0	0	.316	.333	.368
Cimino, Pete	1	0	0	0	0	0	0	0	0	0	0	0	–	–	–
Fosnow, Pete	29	5	0	0	0	0	0	0	0	0	0	0	.000	.000	.000
Grant, Mudcat	50	97	13	15	3	2	0	8	7	27	0	0	.155	.212	.227
Hall, Jimmie	148	522	81	149	25	4	20	86	50	79	14	7	.285	.345	.464
Kaat, Jim	56	93	6	23	4	0	1	9	4	29	2	0	.247	.273	.323
Killebrew, Harmon	113	401	78	108	16	1	25	75	72	69	0	0	.269	.384	.501
Kindall, Jerry	125	342	40	67	12	1	6	36	36	97	2	2	.196	.274	.289
Klippstein, John	56	8	0	0	0	0	0	0	0	3	0	0	.000	.000	.000
Kosco, Andy	23	55	3	13	4	0	1	6	1	15	0	0	.236	.241	.364
Kostro, Frank	20	31	2	5	2	0	0	1	4	5	0	0	.161	.250	.226
Merritt, Jim	16	22	1	3	0	0	0	3	2	4	0	0	.136	.240	.136

STATISTICS – 1965 MINNESOTA TWINS (continued)

Player	G	AB	R	H	2b	3b	HR	RBI	BB	K	SB	CS	AVG	OBP	SA
Mincher, Don	128	346	43	87	17	3	22	65	49	73	1	3	.251	.344	.509
Nelson, Mel	28	9	0	1	0	0	0	0	0	5	0	0	.111	.111	.111
Nossek, Joe	87	170	19	37	9	0	2	16	7	22	2	0	.218	.250	.306
Oliva, Tony	149	576	108	185	40	5	16	98	55	64	19	9	.321	.378	.491
Pascual, Camilo	27	60	7	12	1	0	2	8	2	8	0	0	.200	.226	.317
Perry, Jim	36	53	3	9	1	1	0	3	1	16	0	0	.170	.200	.226
Pleis, Bill	41	7	0	0	0	0	0	0	0	3	0	0	.000	.000	.000
Quilici, Frank	56	149	16	31	5	1	0	7	15	33	1	1	.208	.280	.255
Reese, Rich	14	7	0	2	1	0	0	0	2	2	0	0	.286	.444	.429
Roggenburk, Garry	12	3	1	0	0	0	0	0	1	2	0	0	.000	.250	.000
Rollins, Rich	140	469	59	117	22	1	5	32	37	54	4	0	.249	.309	.333
Sevcik, John	12	16	1	1	1	0	0	0	1	5	0	0	.063	.118	.125
Siebler, Dwight	7	1	0	0	0	0	0	0	0	0	0	0	.000	.000	.000
Stigman, Dick	33	15	0	2	1	0	0	0	0	7	0	0	.133	.133	.200
Tovar, Cesar	18	25	3	5	1	0	0	2	2	3	2	0	.200	.259	.240
Uhlaendar, Ted	13	22	1	4	0	0	0	1	0	2	1	0	.82	.182	.182
Valdespino, Sandy	108	245	38	64	8	2	1	22	20	28	7	4	.261	.319	.322
Versalles, Zoilo	160	666	126	182	45	12	19	77	41	122	26	5	.273	.319	.462
Worthington, Al	62	10	1	1	0	0	0	0	2	5	0	0	.00	.250	.100
Zimmerman, Jerry	83	154	8	33	1	1	1	11	12	23	0	0	.214	.275	.253

STATISTICS – 1965 MINNESOTA TWINS (pitching)

Player	G	GS	CG	SHO	SV	IP	H	HR	R	ER	BB	SO	W	L	ERA
Boswell, Dave	27	12	1	0	0	106	77	20	43	40	46	85	6	5	3.40
Cimino, Pete	1	0	0	0	0	1	0	0	0	0	0	0	0	0	0.00
Fosnow, Jerry	29	0	0	0	2	46.2	33	7	29	23	25	35	3	3	4.44
Grant, Mudcat	41	39	4	6	0	270.1	252	34	107	99	61	142	21	7	3.30
Kaat, Jim	45	42	7	2	2	264.1	267	25	121	83	63	154	18	11	2.83
Klippstein, John	56	0	0	0	5	76.2	59	8	22	19	31	59	9	3	2.24
Merritt, Jim	16	9	1	0	2	76.2	68	11	29	27	20	61	5	4	3.17
Nelson, Mel	28	3	0	0	3	54.2	57	7	29	25	23	31	0	4	4.12
Pascual, Camilo	27	27	5	1	0	156	126	12	67	58	63	96	9	3	3.35
Perry, Jim	39	19	4	2	0	167.2	142	18	57	49	47	88	12	7	2.63
Pleis, Bill	41	2	0	0	4	51.1	49	3	20	17	27	33	4	4	2.98
Roggenburk, Garry	12	0	0	0	2	21	21	1	10	8	12	6	1	0	3.43
Siebler, Dwight	7	1	0	0	0	15	11	2	7	7	11	15	0	0	4.20
Stigman, Dick	33	8	0	0	4	70	59	14	34	34	33	70	4	2	4.37
Worthington, Al	62	0	0	0	21	80.1	57	4	25	19	41	59	10	7	2.13

1965 World Series player shares:

Los Angeles Dodgers, $10,297.43 – Minnesota Twins, $6,634.36